Graeco-Egyptian Magick: Everyday Empowerment

Graeco-Egyptian Magick: Everyday Empowerment

By Tony Mierzwicki

Preface by Donald Michael Kraig

Graeco-Egyptian Magick: Everyday Empowerment
By Tony Mierzwicki

Cover by Vincent Chong
Typesetting: Storm Constantine/Kid Charlemaine
Editor: Taylor Ellwood
Photo by Jo-Ann Byers

First edition by Megalithica Books, 2006

A Megalithica Books edition
An imprint of Immanion Press
http://www.immanion-press.com
info@immanion-press.com

ISBN 1905713037
(From Jan 2007 9781905713037)

Immanion Press
8 Rowley Grove
Stafford ST17 9BJ
UK

Acknowledgements

I would like to give special thanks to the many people who have participated in my rituals and shared their valuable insights in the USA and Australia workshops. Without their encouragement, this project would have been far more arduous.

I would like to thank Elena Raskov for her tireless efforts in proof-reading and preliminary editing to cull and mould three and a half years of writing into an ordered coherent whole; and Jeannette Durick of Web Genie Design, who set up and updated my website during the crucial 2003–04 period during which my Magick of Alexandria workshops took their final form.

I would like to express my appreciation to Immanion Press for their faith in this book, Taylor Ellwood for his encouragement and editing, Lupa for her copy editing, Storm Constantine and Kid Charlemaine for their typesetting, and Vinny Chong for his cover art.

I would like to thank Donald Michael Kraig for prefacing this book. While I had read other books on magick, it was his "*Modern Magick*" that got me out of my armchair and actually practising magick. Having Don involved is not only a great honour, but gives me a sense of coming full circle.

The PGM and PDM selections from "*The Greek Magical Papyri in Translation*" edited by Hans Dieter Betz © 1986, 1992 by The University of Chicago appear with the permission of the University of Chicago Press. The selections used were translated by D E Aune, John Dillon, W C Grese, J P Hershbell, R F Hock, Janet H Johnson, Roy Kotansky, Hubert Martin Jr, M W Meyer, E N O'Neil and Morton Smith.

The Homeric Hymns appearing in this book are reprinted by permission of the publishers and the Trustees of the Loeb Classical Library from "*Hesiod, Homeric Hymns, Epic Cycle, Homerica,*" translated by Hugh G Evelyn-White, Cambridge, Mass.: Harvard University Press, 1914. The Loeb Classical Library ® is a registered trademark of the President and Fellows of Harvard College.

The extracts from the Tetrabiblos appearing in this book are reprinted by permission of the publishers and the Trustees of the Loeb Classical Library from "*Ptolemy: Tetrabiblos*," translated by F E Robbins, Cambridge, Mass.: Harvard University Press, 1940. The Loeb Classical Library ® is a registered trademark of the President and Fellows of Harvard College.

"*The Thunder, Perfect Mind*" appears with the permission of Professor Anne McGuire and "*Diotima*."

I would like to thank Aaron Atsma for allowing me to quote from "*Theoi Project: Guide to Greek Mythology*."

I would like to extend my heartfelt appreciation to Jo for contributing the photo on the back cover, assisting with formatting, as well as for her love and support during the lengthy polishing process of preparing this book for publishing.

Lastly, I would to like to state the blatantly obvious. Had it not been for the heroic efforts of the Graeco-Egyptian magickians in recording their art, this book would never have come into being. It is to their memory, and to their deities (especially Aiôn), that I dedicate this book...

Table of Contents

List of Tables

Abbreviations

CE	Common Era
BCE	Before Common Era
PGM	Greek Magickal Papyri
PDM	Demotic Magickal Papyri
*Tr.:	Translated by

Preface

by

Donald Michael Kraig

One of the most common questions among occultists is "Where did all of the magickal rituals and techniques come from?" Some point to the medieval texts of magick, the grimoires, but those clearly come from earlier sources. In looking for the original sources some point to ancient Sumer or Egypt. Others point to the early Hebrews, the Greeks, or the Romans. Curiously, with the exclusion of dry, academic tomes, rarely do we actually find mystical or occult books that clearly identify the earliest sources for their rituals or spells.

One of the richest actual sources of such material comes from the Graeco-Egyptian period. This consisted of the period from about 200 B.C.E. to 400 C.E.. Many of the magickal techniques of today were derived from the work and experimentation of that time and place, especially as seen in such texts as the Greek Magickal Papyri and the Demotic Magickal Papyri.

In this book, Tony Mierzwicki has done both magickians and researchers an invaluable service by deeply researching this ancient magickal system and recreating it for modern use. The results reproduce the actual language and its pronunciation, along with actual ritual techniques.

As the popularity of Spiritualism as a major force in occultism began to wane, it was replaced with something known as "New Thought." Many of the books from this movement, similar to some books of the "New Age" movement today, are just some of the older concepts with a more modern veneer. But that veneer that gives popularity often removes the essence of the original. This is not meant as a condemnation of either New Thought or New Age beliefs, it's just an acknowledgement that the originality of them lies in their simplification and presentation. I remember one New Age book that was published in 1995. Its incredible popularity has resulted in a veritable cottage industry leading to a major motion picture. And yet, when I read the entire book one morning my feelings were, "There's nothing here that isn't found in a basic psychic development class."

Unfortunately, some practical occult books that claim to be based on ancient works simply reverse this practice. They follow a modern paradigm of magick, theology, and philosophy, and by using a few words or names of deities from an older pantheon try to give it a veneer of antiquity. If sales are an indication of success, some of these books are quite successful. But that doesn't make them historically accurate and makes one wonder about their ethical integrity.

This book, then, is something new—because it really does present the ancient methods and beliefs. For example, the author points out that the ancient Graeco-Egyptian magicians did not use a protective magickal circle for their rituals as do most magicians today. Nor does he introduce this as part of the system. If that sounds odd or foreign, it is. It comes from more than 1,500 year ago when people had different belief systems. So if you're looking for something that is genuinely original because it *is original,* this book will fill your needs.

But while the magick presented here is the "real deal," one of the first modern revelations of this system, it is not entirely foreign to the modern paradigm. After all, much of what is here is the source material for modern magickal (both ceremonial and Pagan) systems. One of the important aspects of it is a concept that I have stressed in my own work: Magick isn't something you do; Magick is something you are. Although it is filled with exercises and rituals to do, there are also things to do every day so that you end up living a magickal life. The focus of the book is on the ancient planetary magick system, and it suggests methods as simple as wearing clothes of the color of a particular planet so you become attuned to the energies of that planet not just in ritual, but every hour of every day. You can also wear jewelry of the metal or gemstone associated with the planet, as well as the scent of it. Magick fills your day and becomes part of your life, as opposed to simply being "that thing you do on the full moon."

This leads to another problem. When should you be living in tune with a particular planetary energy? Initiation is an important part of this system, but it requires a different attitude than most people have today concerning the experience of being initiated. The current interpretation of initiation is that it is a ritual that establishes a new level of spirituality in your life. That is, when you've assimilated one set of spiritual experiences, the initiation ritual permits you to have a new set of experiences. However, as the book points out, "Initiation does not occur within a ritual, but is a transformation that occurs within everyday life." The ritual of initiation may indicate that the inner initiation has taken place. It may even be that a person is ready for that initiation to occur and the ritual may trigger it. But until that inner initiation results in a transformation that results in a change in everyday life, the true initiation has not occurred.

This book is not intended for the neophyte or poseur. As the author writes, "This book is primarily an intermediate level text aimed at those people who are serious about their spiritual development and already have a grounding in basic spirituality..." However, I would not let this deter a beginner who is willing to become dedicated to this complete spiritual and magickal system. If something is unclear, you can investigate and practice techniques from other sources to bring your basic abilities up to the level required to do magick. While there are many books that are completely basic, the magickal tradition has always been to spend time in training, whether it is the year-and-a-day of some Pagan traditions, or the "Outer Order" of some ceremonial magick groups.

The evidence of success for this book will go beyond simply measuring sales. It will be determined by the number of individuals and groups who begin to practice this system. This is a beginning of something very new, and simultaneously very ancient. It's amazing to observe the miracle of birth.

—Donald Michael Kraig
Venice Beach, California

Foreword

So many people in modern society feel that their lives lack meaning and a sense of purpose. Many feel disempowered and somehow incomplete. In our consumer culture we are expected to find fulfilment in our possessions, yet there is often a sense that something is lacking.

We live in a fast paced world where everything is required to be streamlined, rapid and efficient. There is a clear need for an effective system of spiritual development that requires as little time as possible, yet yields real results.

The ancients encouraged us to discover who we really are, what our own individual life path is, and then harmonise with it. It is this that true spiritual development encompasses. Harmonising with your life path leads to spiritual growth, empowerment, wholeness, healing, as well as discovering purpose and meaning in life.

The ancients developed a systematic way for all of us to achieve perfect harmony and attunement with our life path. They saw the body as consisting of seven subtle energies, at the core of which is a "divine spark," variously referred to as the spirit, essence, higher self, genius, pneuma, Augoeides, Maggid, and Holy Guardian Angel. The energies that compose the body are the same energies that permeate the entire universe. The divine spark is that which we truly are.

Each of seven energies is experienced sequentially through a series of initiations. Once experienced and embraced individually, these energies are then brought into balance. We are then in a position to experience the divinity we have within. With access to our divinity, we become privy to true knowledge of who were are, and are in a position to reclaim our birthright of being fully empowered, whole and complete.

Does this sound difficult? Believe me, it's not. It's a simple step-by-step process.

It makes sense that in order to follow such an ancient spiritual path, authentic ancient spiritual techniques should be used. All the spiritual techniques in this book are a reconstruction of the spiritual practises of the first five centuries CE in Egypt, based exclusively on writings of the time. These spiritual techniques are referred to as Graeco-Egyptian Magick.

This book is primarily an intermediate level text aimed at those people who are serious about their spiritual development and already have a grounding in basic spirituality, but beginners who carefully follow the instructions sequentially should not be deterred. This book is an important tool for those who are searching for that elusive something to make them feel complete, whole, fulfilled, at peace within themselves, and seeking to balance their spirituality within their everyday lives.

Introduction to Graeco-Egyptian Magick

The most hauntingly beautiful writings produced by humanity are inspired by profound spiritual experiences. Within the writings of the Hermeticists and Gnostics of the first few centuries of the Common Era (CE) are numerous shining examples. While the specific techniques used to achieve these experiences are largely lost, there are sufficient clues in the writings of the time to construct a complete self-initiatory system.

Although there are many forms of spiritual development, none offer the flexibility, potency and rapid results of an authentic magickal path. The self-initiatory system in this book consists of totally authentic Graeco-Egyptian Magick techniques, practised in Egypt during the first five centuries CE, and ultimately gives access to profound spiritual experiences, self-knowledge and empowerment. The system presented in this book is a simple step-by-step process that can be readily applied on a daily basis for the enrichment of life.

Comprehending the divinity within leads to true empowerment. Empowerment goes beyond the material world and means attaining self-realisation and standing fast both physically and spiritually. A truly empowered individual fears no one and welcomes empowerment in others. Such an individual stands in their own power and allows all others to stand in their own power as well.

Authority figures suppress empowerment, as empowered individuals are difficult to control. Disempowered individuals fear empowered individuals out of ignorance. This is the reason that magickal systems and their practitioners have been suppressed over the ages.

Ancient magick, suppressed by the powers that be, was the product of thousands of years of experimentation by dedicated individuals. It was, and is, an incredibly powerful technique for spiritual transformation and empowerment. Studies of Sumerian, Babylonian and Egyptian magickal writings indicate continuous traditions of magickal practice that show a remarkable degree of consistency. In broad terms this indicates that these people arrived at magickal systems that were effective and not subject to constant improvement. To the unbelievers I would say that, whilst a hoax can be maintained over a short period of time, to suggest that it could be maintained for thousands of years beggars belief. [Unless of course, those imposing the hoax have political clout.]

Magick in ancient times was powerful and empowering. While magick may not hold all of the answers for all of mankind, it is very capable of enhancing life if used responsibly. In a modern world where individuals feel powerless against multinational corporations and war mongering governments, magick provides an effective bulwark. Perhaps the practice of ancient magick is the key to a Utopian world where all men and women are truly equal and truly empowered, fearing no one and respecting everyone.

The aim of true spirituality is a re-union with the all-pervading God force, which in the Western world, has come to be referred to as the Great Work. Many people who develop an interest in this path devour books and accumulate vast amounts of theoretical knowledge. This is certainly commendable. Often, however, the more they read the more obstacles manifest to stop them actually putting their knowledge into practice. There are numerous accounts of the pitfalls of practising magick. How many of these accounts are real, and how many are written by hysterical armchair occultists?

Our aim is to complete the Great Work, not the Great Study. The Great Work requires a balance between head and heart, or between theory and practice. Each is of limited use without the other.

Why practice Graeco-Egyptian Magick?

This book, through the recreation of a system of planetary initiation using authentic Graeco-Egyptian Magick, provides a practical guide to one method of completing the Great Work. It is a system which aims to empower and enrich the life of the individual by working with the philosophies of a number of diverse Egyptian spiritual cultures using the Graeco-Egyptian Magick that was practiced in their midst. (See Appendix 1: Background to Graeco-Egyptian Magick – for a brief history.)

Inscriptions in ancient temples exhorted those individuals who entered to "Know thyself." The Oxford Dictionary definition of knowledge is "familiarity gained by experience." Our complexity makes truly "knowing" ourselves difficult no matter how much we experience. A complex concept is best comprehended by contemplating each of its components.

A number of these ancient spiritual cultures used systems of self-development based, at least in part, upon working with planetary energies. They divided the entire spectrum of spirituality, intellect and emotion into seven segments and attributed a segment to each of the planets. Each such segment corresponded to a portion of the self. The divine spark was seen as enveloped by these seven segments.

Each of the seven segments can be targeted and experienced individually, through the corresponding planetary sphere, by means of an initiation rite. The portions of the self corresponding to these segments can thus be comprehended and implemented into daily life. The system of the seven planetary spheres provides the individual with a roadmap of sorts to ensure that the ultimate journey – the journey within to true self-knowledge – proceeds optimally. Through the practical application of this process the entire range of divine archetypes can be experienced, effectively constituting a complete initiatic process. Once each of the spheres is experienced, they can then be understood in relation to each other, and brought into balance.

The early Christian church zealously destroyed the records of the planetary magick of these spiritual cultures. However, with the discovery of the Graeco-Egyptian magical papyri in the early nineteenth century CE, the first stirrings of the phoenix of Graeco-Egyptian Magick were felt amongst the smouldering ashes. These writings are collectively referred to as the Greek Magickal Papyri (PGM) and the Demotic Magickal Papyri (PDM).

The PGM and PDM writings are the primary source texts for "Graeco-Egyptian Magick: Everyday Empowerment." These were mainly from the second century Before Common Era (BCE) to the fifth century CE in Egypt. The secondary source texts are the Curse Tablets. The Curse Tablets were written during the period from the fifth century BCE to the fifth century CE in an area spanning northern Africa and Europe. The Curse Tablets were typically binding spells written on strips of lead. There are numerous similarities between the spells of the Curse Tablets and the PGM and

PDM writings. Also used are the Orphic and Homeric Hymns. The Orphic Hymns appear to have been written between 100 BCE and 150 CE, and the Homeric Hymns between the sixth and seventh centuries BCE.

At the time of printing, each of the rituals contained herein had been publicly "road tested" on numerous separate occasions over six years, with different groups in various locations on two continents. All of the rituals have proved very effective for most participants. Meanwhile, the "road testing" continues.

Whilst scholars bicker over the finer points of Graeco-Egyptian Magick, many of these arguments can be resolved by actually practising the magick, because after all, magick was never meant to be purely theoretical. After experiencing the rituals in this book, ancient mythologies come to life, taking on a richness and beauty that eludes the scholars who use a purely intellectual approach.

The rituals contained in this book are not carved in stone. New source documents may be discovered and translated which may necessitate a revision. Notwithstanding, by the time the reader has finished the magickal odyssey in this book, any such changes will not pose too much of a problem.

A perusal of ancient manuscripts detailing the wide-ranging legendary powers of the ancient magickians amply explains the uneasiness of the Christians 1600 years ago. The Graeco-Egyptian Magickians were truly empowered individuals. So, just what did these magickians claim?

> *"... the sun will stand still; and should I order the moon, it will come down; and should I wish to delay the day, the night will remain for me; and should we in turn ask for day, the light will not depart; and should I wish to sail the sea, I do not need a ship; and should I wish to go through the air, I will be lifted up..."*
> *PGM* XXXIV. 1–10 [*Tr.: E N O'Neil]

Without any further ado, it is time to examine Graeco-Egyptian Magick in detail and how it may be applied to effective spiritual advancement.

Ritual Preparation

The aim of this chapter is prepare mentally, physically, emotionally, and spiritually for the Graeco-Egyptian Magick invocations which follow.

Assumed knowledge

It is assumed at this point that you have an understanding or experience of the following:

- ξ focus and concentration on intent without extraneous thoughts intruding
- ξ chanting
- ξ active visualisation
- ξ passive visualisation or meditation
- ξ basic knowledge of astrology and mythology

A basic text or course on meditation would provide the necessary training for most of these skills. I personally like Ernest Wood's "*Concentration: An Approach to Meditation*." Practice will improve your skills in these areas, so do not stress about being somewhat less than perfect initially.

Focus and concentration

The most important ability required to successfully work a ritual is will power. Will power requires focus and concentration on the intent of the ritual without extraneous thoughts intruding.

Chanting

The vowels in the rituals which follow should be articulated either by singing or harmonically chanting. Experience has shown that harmonic chanting is particularly effective. Harmonic chanting is used by many indigenous shamans world wide, and involves altering the shape of the mouth, jaw and tongue to create bell-like overtones. This is something which can be practised (perhaps in the shower or while driving with the windows wound up)! It is a skill which comes readily to some and not so readily to others. It should however be remembered that just singing the vowels is perfectly adequate. The pronunciation of the vowels is given in Appendix 2: Pronunciation.

Visualisation

It is important to be able to perform active controlled visualisation as per the instructions in the rites that follow this chapter. Once the invocation has been completed, you should be able to relinquish control and passively experience any influences which come through. This should happen naturally and not be forced. Ability to rapidly alternate between passive and active visualisation during invocations optimises results, and is easily achieved with practice. If you cannot visualise, try to experience with one of your other senses or at least "know" that things are happening. Vivid visualisation will come with time.

Intuition

Intuition is a key skill to develop on any spiritual path. It is important to be able to intuit whether a particular practice is beneficial.

Basic knowledge of mythology and astrology

A familiarity with mythology and knowledge of the properties associated with the planets in astrology is advantageous to understanding the finer points of the rites.

Working with the Planetary Spheres

The procedure in this book is to access the energy corresponding to the seven planetary Spheres, one at a time. Each of these triggers an initiation.

> NOTE: It is VERY IMPORTANT to work with the Spheres IN SEQUENCE and the process should not be rushed. Some of the participants in my workshops have had unpleasant experiences when they have performed rituals out of sequence. This has been a result of attempting to force an experience before they were ready for it. For those participants who work with the Spheres in sequence and do not rush matters, the whole process flows naturally.

The planetary Spheres comprise the totality of spiritual, intellectual, emotional and physical existence. Each Sphere should be repeatedly worked with until your intuition determines that its effects have run their transformative course.

While a number of deities could be used to experience each of the planetary Spheres, the Greek pantheon is familiar to most people. [The other deities I use for the planetary Spheres will be detailed in the sequel to this book, and are listed on my website, www.hermeticmagick.com.] The PGM and the Orphic Hymns contain invocations to all seven of the Greek deities ruling the planets, and there are Homeric Hymns for six of them.

The series of initiations involves systematically targeting and experiencing each planetary Sphere in Ptolemaic order; and so, working outwards from the Earth, we have the Moon, Mercury, Venus, Sun, Mars, Jupiter and Saturn. This geocentric system represents the macrocosm. Each of us is a microcosm of the macrocosm, where the Earth represents our physical body and the planetary Spheres correspond to progressively deeper levels of the psyche. It is perhaps paradoxical that the further away from the Earth we move in a macrocosmic sense, the deeper within we move in a microcosmic sense.

We live in a sea of energy where all the planetary energies are present, but we will target only one at a time. The experience of these energies is basically a passive meditation. Some people are more skilled at meditation than others, which is the reason why a ritual to experience the targeted energy is so important.

A useful analogy is that of a radio, selecting a desired frequency out of a myriad of frequencies being simultaneously transmitted. A person skilled at meditation is like a high quality radio pinpointing only the targeted planetary energy, while the less skilled person is like a poor quality radio which picks up interference from neighbouring frequencies.

Now, imagine an experiment where a radio transmitter and a radio receiver are placed at opposite ends of a large hall which filters out all external radio waves. Because there is one frequency only, the radio receiver will receive a good signal regardless of its quality. In a ritual to invoke a particular planetary energy, that energy is powerfully brought in to the exclusion of all others. Hence, as in the analogy of the radio experiment in the large hall, all ritual participants should be able to tune into the targeted planetary energy regardless of their skill in meditation.

Once each of these initiations have been performed, they can be understood in relation to each other, brought into balance, and integrated into everyday life resulting in empowerment, wholeness and completeness. The procedure for this will be outlined in the Integrating Graeco-Egyptian Magick into Daily Life chapter.

Procedure for initiation

Initiation does not occur within a ritual, but is a transformation that occurs within everyday life.

Each ritual opens a doorway for the energy of the corresponding planetary Sphere to enter into your life resulting in initiation. Alignment with planetary energies through contemplation is effective, but is a slow laborious process. The rituals in this book force planetary energies into alignment, accelerating the process of spiritual development. Even though the techniques used are 1600 years old, their effectiveness and speed are very much in keeping with the time management demands of the modern world.

Each initiation causes changes to a lesser or greater extent depending on the needs of the individual. Change can be difficult and challenging, and the natural reaction for many is to fight against it. However, when it is accepted and embraced, your life begins to flow and naturally attune to the energy that caused it on a cosmic level, as the energies which compose the body are the same energies which permeate the entire universe.

The continuation, in everyday life, of the process of initiation into a Sphere is ensured by on-going study undertaken simultaneously while obtaining as many of the correspondences of the Sphere as possible. The relevant information is detailed in the Planetary Properties and Planetary Correspondences chapters as well as the various chapters specific to the Spheres.

It should be noted that all the suggestions regarding jewellery, robes, clothing, essential oils and incenses in the following do not mean that you should race out and purchase them immediately. These things can be obtained inexpensively over a period of time by being aware of bargains as they present themselves. These bargains can be seen as symptomatic of your intuition becoming specifically attuned, helping you manifest initiatory change. You should not delay your spiritual progress purely because something appears to be temporarily unattainable. Be guided by your intuition.

Study and Meditate on the Planetary Sphere

The first step is to undergo the theoretical process of studying the properties associated with the Sphere being worked. These are detailed in the Planetary Properties chapter. The mythology of the deity aspected to the planetary Sphere should be studied, along with the Homeric and Orphic Hymns. These are all detailed in the chapter specific to the Sphere being worked with.

I believe that it is important to recreate the mindset of the Graeco-Egyptian magickians by using only that with which they would have been familiar for study. This includes studying images and texts pertaining to the deities that would have been available in, and prior to, the first few centuries CE.

Select some items of clothing of the aspected colour

Each Sphere has a colour aspected to it (detailed in the Planetary Correspondences chapter). Even a little amount of the aspected colour serves as a potent reminder of the Sphere being worked with.

Ties and scarves are a discrete way of remaining mindful of the planetary Sphere being worked with. Black work socks and white sports socks with a small splash of the aspected colour are another discrete option. People who wear uniforms in the workplace can opt for coloured underwear.

Tasteful wardrobe expansion with the aspected colours for each planetary Sphere is out of the scope of this book and will be left to your discretion.

Burn the aspected incense or essential oil

Each Sphere is also associated with a fragrance (again, detailed in the Planetary Correspondences chapter). Burning the aspected incense or essential oil first thing in the morning or in the evening is an easy way to focus on the planetary Sphere.

With the burgeoning growth in esoteric matters, oil burners, and incense censers are readily available and easily obtained.

However, while a number of the incenses and essential oils are readily available, some are far more difficult to source. I have sourced all these essential oils and incenses for my personal use and have a complete range of the oils and incenses available through my website (www.hermeticmagick.com).

Dab on a small quantity of the aspected essential oil (take care with these)

A tiny dab of the aspected essential oil on the hair, the skin, or clothing ensures that the focus can be maintained on a subconscious level. Take care, as one of the essential oils will burn the skin, while the others may stain clothing (see Planetary Correspondences chapter). Avoid getting any oil near your eyes, mouth and other sensitive areas. Aftershave or perfume can be applied over an essential oil to mask it from recognition, should this be deemed necessary.

Wear the aspected gemstone or metal as a ring or other piece of jewellery

You should acquire a collection of seven pieces of jewellery (such as rings, pendants and bracelets) with the aspected gemstone or metal for each planetary Sphere. Apollonius of Tyana (discussed in Appendix 1: Background to Graeco-Egyptian Magick) was reputed to have had seven such rings according to Philostratus.

> "... *Iarchas gave seven rings to Apollonius named after the seven stars, and that Apollonius wore each of these in turn on the day of the week which bore its name.*"
> The Life of Apollonius – Book III Chapter XLI
> "... *he accepted the seven rings named after the stars, and held it needful to wear these all through the rest of his life upon the days severally named after them, and that although, as you say yourself, they had a secret power in them.*"
> The Treatise of Eusebius – Chapter XXII
> [Selections from "*Philostratus: The Life of Apollonius of Tyana*" F C Conybeare, trans.]

Only one item of gold and one item of silver are required, the other items may be of a metal of your choice (see Planetary Correspondences chapter). Silver jewellery is quite inexpensive and it is fun hunting for items which feel just right.

Recite the Orphic Hymn and the Homeric Hymn

The Orphic Hymns and Homeric Hymns were once considered magickal and are a potent means of calling upon a number of Greek deities. The appropriate Orphic and Homeric Hymns have been included in each of the various planetary Sphere chapters. (For background on them, see Appendix 1: Background to Graeco-Egyptian Magick.)

The translation of the Orphic Hymns used in this book was produced in 1792. I have modernised the translation and have restored the Latinised deity names to the original Greek.

Preparation for the Graeco-Egyptian Magick rituals

Indoors or outdoors?

The rituals are just as effective indoors as outdoors. It is best to use the same area as the energy released builds up after a few rituals giving a particularly sacred feel to the area chosen.

Quite often the Graeco-Egyptian magickians performed their rituals in tombs, caves and various indoor settings. An indoor setting amplifies the acoustics to the extent that the chants in the rituals become far more intense. However, private outdoor settings, particularly in places of power, tap into the ambient energy of the surroundings, leading to powerful experiences. In outdoor rituals, set in nature, far from city lights and sounds, the night sky effectively becomes the roof of the ritual temple, and it is a roof stretching out to infinity...

Ritual circle not required

There is no evidence of the Graeco-Egyptian magickians working within a circle. They confronted spiritual energies directly, much as many shamans still do. The Graeco-Egyptian magickians were only interested in facing each of the four cardinal directions and not tracing a 360° circle. This is discussed in the Opening Rite and Closing Rite chapters, as well as Appendix 3: Rotation and Counter-Rotation.

Most people with a background in modern Western magick feel safe working within circles. As a historical precedent, Babylonian sorcerers worked within a circle traced out with flour. A circle in a group working, if insisted upon by the group, may be traced out for purely psychological reasons. Each ritual begins with a short invocation to Aiôn, the ultimate god, whose protection is sought. With his protection, no harm will befall the ritual participant.

Altar set up

An altar of sorts should be placed in the middle of the ritual area. While some magickians procure very ornate altars, this is not necessary. As a bare minimum, the altar should have an oil lamp or candle as a light source, a censer burning incense, and a bottle of essential oil appropriate to the deity being invoked.

Additional altar set up ideas include other correspondences to the planetary energy such as items of the aspected gemstone or metal, objects of the aspected colour and even pictures or statuettes of the deity being invoked. This may help to further pinpoint the energy being targeted. These are fully outlined in the Planetary Correspondences chapter, and summarised in the various chapters for each of the planetary Spheres. There is no need for any elemental tools, wand, rod or staff.

Ultimately, even an altar is discretionary. I have performed rituals in nature where the ground at my feet and rocky outcrops have served as altars.

Eucharist

If you choose to have eucharistic sacraments, select ones which feel appropriate well in advance of the ritual. Cakes and a beverage, such as de-alcoholised wine, are excellent as sacraments. They will be placed on the altar, so they can absorb the energies invoked and impart it when consumed.

Ritual attire

While ritual robes are not essential, they are a nice touch. A robe or a special outfit has a powerful psychological effect as it becomes associated with the requisite mindset for ritual workings.

The ritual robe should be made of a natural fabric. My preference is for linen, which was worn by the Egyptian magickians. Modern magickians may also opt for cotton, wool, silk, ramie and hemp. It should be noted however, that Egyptian magickians never used wool for their robes.

I normally use a plain black hooded robe for all my workings, but plain white robes appear to have been traditional in Graeco-Egyptian magickal operations. The advantage of a hood is that it can be pulled over the head as an aid to improving focus on the planetary energies experienced within rituals.

Black and white are neutral colours which are suitable for all workings. Some well-heeled magickians have numerous robes in different colours – one for each planetary working.

Journalise

Obtain a journal so as to record all your experiences and chart your progress. Record your experiences in as much detail as possible – include date, time and any observations that seem relevant and out of the ordinary such as changes in weather conditions, or moods at each working.

Also record any general observations of the day-to-day experiences in your life. This enables you to establish and follow any patterns that are occurring in your life. Also important are dreams and unusual day-to-day occurrences that appear to be linked to the initiation process.

All of your experiences will impact and form a pattern that can be more easily understood when observed over a period of time. The journal is very important in this process as it enables you to put the pieces together, somewhat like a picture emerging as all the pieces of the jigsaw puzzle come together.

Ritual purity

Always bathe before a ritual whenever possible to ensure that the body is pure. This is also being considerate towards others when engaging in a group ritual.

The Egyptian magickians bathed in pools and cleaned their mouths with natron prior to rituals. Natron was traditionally used in many purification operations in Egyptian magick and as part of the mummification process. It is unfortunately difficult to obtain in most parts of the world outside Egypt.

Sodium bicarbonate or baking soda, which is a major constituent of natron, is a good cost effective substitute. It has a salty but not too unpleasant taste. It also has a nice side benefit of whitening teeth and promoting strong gums.

Some rituals call for specific diets or fasting, and some magickians will fast before their rituals as a matter of course to purify the body.

Timing

The solitary practitioner has the luxury of experimenting with the timing of rituals. While occasionally a certain time is nominated in the source texts, mostly the timing of rituals is left up to your discretion. An ephemeris (an astronomical almanac) can be consulted to select relevant astronomical phenomena with which rituals could be timed to coincide. Thus, solar and lunar eclipses, solstices, equinoxes, close approaches of planets to the earth, and even meteor showers, are all possibilities.

Each day of the week is ruled by a planet. In practical terms this means that each day has a different predominant planetary energy. This theme comes up repeatedly in ceremonial magick throughout the centuries.

Many modern magickians work with "planetary hours," where each hour of the day is believed to be ruled by a planet. I have not found any evidence for the Graeco-Egyptian magickians working with planetary hours, as most of their spells did not stipulate a time apart from sunrise, sunset or when the relevant planet was visible.

The planetary days are as follows:

Table 1: Planetary Days

Day	*Planet*	*Deity*
Sunday	Sun	Hêlios
Monday	Moon	Selênê (Mênê)
Tuesday	Mars	Arês
Wednesday	Mercury	Hermês
Thursday	Jupiter	Zeus
Friday	Venus	Aphroditê
Saturday	Saturn	Kronos

When the planetary energy is invoked, either the deity can be viewed with the third eye, or the planet itself can be viewed with the physical eyes. So, while not essential, it would not be amiss, to time a ritual to coincide with the visibility of a planet.

It should always be remembered that the planetary deities rule the planets and not vice versa. Fortunately the rituals can all be made to work at any time, whether or not the planet is visible. The various commitments of the participants in my group workings have meant that often Saturday evenings, just after sunset, have been the most convenient time.

Additional research

While not compulsory, additional research may enhance the experiences of the initiations.

If you choose to further investigate the deities aspected to each of the planetary Spheres, you will develop an increased theoretical understanding. As a rough rule of thumb, the more ancient a mythological text is, the more accurate it is likely to be in portraying the true nature of the deities discussed. More recent texts appear to have undergone a degree of homogenisation whereby the distinct attributes of various gods became somewhat blurred.

Health considerations

To progress spiritually, all areas of lifestyle should be considered. Health is of vital importance. Less than optimal physical health results in less than optimal spiritual health.

> NOTE: A check-up from a health professional is recommended before embarking on the rituals in this book. Ritual participants have experienced powerful physical and emotional responses; reporting rapid fluctuations in body temperature and accelerated heart rates. Participants have also reported the resurfacing of long-suppressed memories.

Very little is known about the health of the Graeco-Egyptian magickians. We do know however, that many of the magickians and philosophers of the ancient world were vegetarians.

I have decided to include some of my own thoughts about health.

The physical body requires food, liquid and air. I strongly believe that only that which is natural is conducive to health. Foods and liquids consumed should be unprocessed (and preferably not genetically modified) wherever possible, and with no synthetic additives such as colourings, flavourings and preservatives. Organic is best, if available. Raw food is preferable to cooked wherever possible, as cooking destroys nutrients and enzymes. A vegan diet does away with animal suffering and is hence karma-free. (I use the word karma in the colloquial sense.) The inclusion of eggs and dairy products is discretionary – always choose cruelty free options such as free-range eggs and animal rennet-free products.

Ensure that all the following food groups are represented, and choose organic products where possible as they are much more nutritious:

- Protein – pulses and legumes (eggs and dairy products if vegetarian).
- Complex carbohydrates – grain products and other starches such as potatoes and corn.
- Fibrous carbohydrates – low calorie vegetables such as greens and mushrooms.
- Simple carbohydrates – fruits.
- Fats – cold pressed oils where possible.

One of the spiritual arguments levelled against vegetarianism is that it overly sensitises individuals and hence makes them less suited to life in the cities. Is not sensitivity a valuable asset for someone wishing to rend the veil obscuring subtle dimensions?

When in doubt, it is prudent to seek professional advice. If a carnivorous individual decides to try a vegetarian diet, nutritional advice should be sought. If a sedentary individual decides to try an exercise programme, medical advice should be sought. In the case of illness which does not rapidly respond to natural remedies, medical advice should be sought.

Every living thing is surrounded by an aura, or energy field. When food is ingested, the physical component of the food nourishes the physical body, whilst the energy field of the food nourishes the energy field of the body. When food is processed, its energy field is destroyed. Here again, raw unprocessed wholesome food is the diet of choice. When eating and drinking be conscious of the energy being ingested rather than just the nutrients.

Air contains an energy called “chi” or “prana” which can be taken in by the body with various breathing exercises. The basic principle behind these is that breathing should be slow and deep, while you are conscious of the energy being breathed in. Fresh unpolluted air from the coastline or the country-side is preferable to polluted city air.

Two other important requirements for the physical body are exercise and recuperation. Some sort of exercise a number of times a week is essential for optimal fitness. Requirements for recuperation vary between individuals, but here, quality of rest is much more important than quantity – a short deep sleep is superior to many hours of tossing and turning.

If, despite practising the above, sickness prevails, I opt for natural remedies. I choose herbs over pharmaceutical products, and non-invasive therapeutic techniques in preference to surgery if they are available. As with all things, I recommend people apply discretion, and to remember that orthodox medicine also has its place.

Avoid that which interferes with the body’s energy systems. Avoid prolonged exposure to electro-magnetic radiation (televisions, computer screens, concentrations of electrical wiring, transformers, microwave transmission towers, microchips, and so on). Wear clothing made of natural fibres. Avoid quartz watches, opt instead for an automatic self-winding mechanism.

The subtle bodies in man are non-physical and hence do not require physical nutrition for their sustenance, but thrive on sensory impressions. For this reason it is important to experience beauty on a regular basis. This can take the form of contemplating landscapes and works of art, listening to music, smelling alluring aromas, savouring fresh food and drink, and feeling different textures against the skin. While such sensory exploration can make an enjoyable exercise, it can easily be incorporated into everyday life by experiencing each moment to its fullest.

Learning from past mistakes and planning the future both have their place, but it is important to set aside time to live consciously in the present moment. Focus on the "now" rather than dwelling on the past or the future.

Many occultists speak of balancing head and heart, while a neurobiologist would refer to it as balancing the left and right hemispheres of the brain. Left-brained activity is more analytical and logical, while right-brain activity is more artistic and emotional. To achieve a balance those who are by nature analytical should take up an artistic pursuit (for example singing, playing an instrument, painting or sculpting), while those who are artistic should take up an analytical past time (for example sacred geometry, book keeping or programming their computer rather than just surfing the net). Taking up new and challenging activities regularly keeps the mind far more active than if the same routine is followed.

The divine spark within can be experienced through contemplation of inspirational writings and music. Beautiful compositions often cause the soul to provoke feelings of longing for the fulfilment of spiritual destiny.

The bottom line for optimal health is simple. Consciously eat and drink raw unprocessed wholesome foods and liquids. Consciously breathe fresh air. Develop focus through mindfulness in everyday life. Take up some form of inspirational pursuit. Challenge your mind by taking up new activities. Spend time away from the city whenever possible and get in contact with nature.

Ritual Performance

By this stage you would have followed the Procedure for initiation in the Ritual Preparation chapter for a number of days, so as to form an association with the planetary Sphere. You have now prepared extensively for the ritual. Your intuition is telling you that the time is appropriate to perform the Graeco-Egyptian Magick invocation.

Structure of Graeco-Egyptian Magick rituals

Each ritual is composed of at least one spell where the deity of the planetary Sphere is invoked. For the less popular deities there is only one spell available. The greatest number of spells available, in the PGM, are for the solar gods, closely followed by the lunar goddesses. In the Curse Tablets, Hermês was called on more frequently than any other deity.

With the notable exception of the short low magick spells (discussed in Appendix 1: The Background to Graeco-Egyptian Magick), most spells employ a similar structure. The Graeco-Egyptian magickians would call upon one or more deities by using a knowledge of their mythology and various names of power.

They invoked deities to assist in spells by asking directly, persuading through flattery, or compelling through threats. At other times the magickian would identify with the deity. Sometimes deities were persuaded to compel other deities to do the magickian's bidding. Once the deities had been summoned through one or more of these techniques, they would manifest the desired effects of the spells. [Note that spells can also call on spirits or angels.]

It is interesting to note that when a deity is compelled to do a magickian's bidding in a spell the instructions sometimes advise that a protective amulet is required (see Third Planetary Sphere – Venus and Seventh Planetary Sphere – Saturn chapters for examples). My experience indicates that when the motivation behind a spell is pure, such protective amulets are not required.

For each deity, I have looked at all the available spells in the PGM, PDM and Curse Tablet texts and have put together the invocation components of the spells but have omitted the desired effects, or purposes, of the spells. This way, the energy of the deity comes into the ritual area in its pure form.

Calling upon the deities with no fixed purpose, enables them to effect transformation as they see fit. Over time you form a personal relationship with the deities called. It is not my place to interfere in any personal relationship and dictate how it should be conducted.

In the commentaries, I have included background on the original intention of the spells that make up the planetary invocations for information purposes only. The spells have proven to be effective without the occasionally elaborate preparations that are called upon.

Only the original spell in the Saturn Sphere incorporated a dismissal. I have produced a dismissal for all the other Spheres.

The original PGM source texts used are either hymns with occasional faulty lines or continuous blocks. The continuous blocks have been divided to facilitate comprehension, but the hymns have been left largely untouched.

Practical requirements for Graeco-Egyptian Magick rituals

The Graeco-Egyptian rituals in this book may appear daunting at first, but are really not difficult.

Performance instructions for Graeco-Egyptian invocations

The procedure to be followed for all Graeco-Egyptian Magick rituals is:

- Enter the ritual area and face East – the direction of the rising sun.
- Burn the aspected incense, and anoint your forehead, hair or robes, with the aspected essential oil while chanting the words of power. The technique utilised by Egyptian priests for anointing the statue of a deity was to hold a flacon of alabaster containing precious ointment in the left hand, plunge in the little finger of the right hand, touch the brow

with this finger while pronouncing the words of power. I merely substitute a bottle of essential oil for the flacon of alabaster containing precious ointment, and use this technique to anoint myself and any other participants.

- ξ Perform the Opening Rite. (This involves facing the other cardinal directions.)
- ξ Continue facing the East or turn to face the planet (if it is visible), unless otherwise instructed.
- ξ Perform the invocation. (See Notation in Rituals later in this chapter.) The instructions with some spells indicate that they should be repeated a number of times. I would recommend adhering to this the first few times. Eventually however, saying the spell once may be sufficient. Also, not all the spells in an invocation may be necessary, as the deity may manifest after just one. Each spell on its own should be sufficient, I have tried to cover all contingencies by linking all available spells to maximise the chances of success. Let your intuition guide you.
- ξ Focus on the deity being invoked. Sometimes other deities are mentioned in a ritual, do not attempt to bring these into the ritual area, as ideally only one deity at a time should be experienced.
- ξ Experience the planetary energy through meditation. You may close your eyes; look through the third eye and allow the planetary energies to wash over you; or study the planet through the physical eyes. The planetary energy meditation may be experienced for as long as is desired. The solitary practitioner may even choose to sleep with the energy all night. In a group ritual however, fifteen to thirty minutes is normally sufficient.
- ξ Consume the eucharist. As the sacraments have been on the altar throughout the ritual, they become infused with the planetary energy manifesting during the ritual, and so consuming them is another way of absorbing the energy.
- ξ Dismiss the planetary energy and offer thanks. Any leftover energy should either be channelled to a given purpose or grounded. I personally like to internalise it, as I do not see the point of raising energy only to let it go to waste.

- ξ At this point ensure you are facing the East and perform the Closing Rite to return the ritual area to its normal state.

Useful tips for Graeco-Egyptian invocations

Perhaps the following suggestions might prove helpful when performing Graeco-Egyptian rituals:

- ξ Do not get too comfortable in the meditation stage of the ritual as this may bring on sleep. Astral experiences are often triggered in response to discomfort such as cold.
- ξ The rituals open a doorway for the energy of the planetary deity to enter. The results obtained are not necessarily identical each time as they are influenced by your individual needs. I have found that the more a planetary energy is lacking in a participant in my group workings, the more powerful their experience.
- ξ When the planetary energy enters the ritual area, certain tangible things may happen. These will vary from person to person. It is important to not fear these but embrace them.
- ξ Do not attempt to force experiences, as they should flow naturally. A passive, receptive, fearless state is required for optimal results.
- ξ It is important to remember in these rituals to "go with the flow." If you feel compelled to move in any way during the ritual, or adopt a particular posture, you should do it so as to facilitate the experience as much as possible. Struggling against this will reduce the intensity of the experience.
- ξ None of my participants have ever felt an impulse to inflict harm during these rituals. Should such an impulse be felt, I would suggest that the mindset prior to the ritual was malevolent and that the ritual should be ended and resumed when a more appropriate mindset is adopted. The aim of each ritual is for spiritual development, which is incompatible with inflicting harm.
- ξ The planetary energy can be used according to your will, favours can be requested, and questions can be asked. When asking favours, it is customary to offer something in exchange, rather than just grovelling. However, for spiritual

development, making no demands, but rather just allowing the energy to work of its own accord is probably most effective.

Notation in Rituals

§ Headings (including the source text) are in bold italics and are not to be read out.
e.g. ***PGM XIII. 64–71 (First invocation of Aiôn)***

§ Performance instructions are in italics and are not to be read out.
e.g. *Face East – stretching out your right hand to the left and your left hand, likewise to the left.*

§ Text in normal typeface is to be stated in a commanding voice.
e.g. "I call on you, eternal and unbegotten, who are one..."

§ Text in bold typeface is to be sung or chanted (as a priest would). The pronunciation of these words of power can be found in Appendix 2: Pronunciation.
e.g. **ACHEBUKRÔM**

§ Combinations of vowels in bold typeface are to be sung, or chanted.
e.g. **A EE ÊÊÊ IIII OOOOO UUUUUU ÔÔÔÔÔÔÔ**

§ "NN" in a ritual is an opportunity to personalise it with either a name or a purpose.
e.g. "Accomplish for me NN thing, quickly."

§ Square brackets indicate that these are words not preserved in the original text but have been interpolated by the translator.
e.g. [Say **ACHEBUKRÔM**] 8 times; [it is] the name of Hêlios.

Calling the Sevenths

The Opening and Closing Rites show that Graeco-Egyptian magickians worked with a seven direction system. This ties in with the seven vowels of the Greek alphabet and the seven planets. Portals are opened to the seven directions by chanting the seven Greek vowels (see Appendix 2: Pronunciation).

One major difference between western type ceremonial magick and Graeco-Egyptian magick lies in the number of directions used. Virtually all modern western ceremonial magick and witchcraft work with the four cardinal points. The cardinal points are the four directions – North, South, East and West. Each one of these directions is aspected to one of the four elements. (Just which element is aspected to which direction is the subject of much controversy in magickal groups.) Portals are opened to the four cardinal points by "calling the quarters," whereupon spirit can enter through a fifth portal directly overhead. The portal to spirit opens automatically as a result of the portals opening to the cardinal points.

The Graeco-Egyptian magickians worked with a seven direction system, as there are seven vowels in the Greek alphabet, seven planets, seven days in the week, seven notes in the musical scale, seven strings in the lyre (the oldest stringed instrument of the Greeks, which developed into the *phorminx* and then the *kithara*) reputedely first played by Apollô, and seven colours in the rainbow. The first four of these seven directions are the four cardinal points. The fifth direction is straight down to the centre of the earth, grounding you. The sixth direction is the centre, the here and now, the present moment, the time at which you are truly powerful. It has been said that the past is a memory, the future uncertain, all you have to work with is the razor edge of the present. The seventh direction is straight up to the depths of the cosmos, connecting you to the outer reaches of the universe. I affectionately refer to this system as "Calling the Sevenths." After all, if modern witches and magickians working with a four direction system call the quarters, then I feel justified in Calling the Sevenths!

This seven direction system is not unique and has been used by various shamans in different parts of the world. It is particularly effective because it induces a state of four-dimensional balance. Directions five and seven take you from a two-dimensional system to a three-dimensional system, while the sixth direction delineates time, taking you into a four-dimensional magickal world.

Considerations for group rituals

Drug and alcohol use prior to and during rituals is to be avoided. It is a sign of disrespect to the divine forces invoked, and in the case of a group ritual, it is also a sign of disrespect to the other participants. The senses should be as sharp as possible – not dulled or distorted by intoxicating substances. Alcohol compromises the ability to be receptive to the energies invoked, while drugs detract from the objectivity of the experience.

Perfume, aftershave, or any fragrance other than the correct essential oil should not be worn. In group rituals, upon entry into the ritual area, all of the participants should be anointed with the appropriate essential oil in the region of the third eye whilst the appropriate words of power are intoned. At this point, I always remind participants that some of the oils may burn the skin.

Participants should be thoroughly briefed as to what is expected of them prior to the ritual. After the ritual, a debrief session is highly recommended. See Result section below for more information.

Bringing the planetary energies into everyday life

To effectively sustain the process of initiation, it is important to ensure that a link is formed between all of the planetary aspects. Perform as many of these activities as possible on a daily basis:

- dress in as much of the aspected colour as possible;
- wear jewellery with the aspected gemstone/metal;
- anoint with the aspected essential oil and burn the aspected incense;
- study the relevant mythology;
- recite the Homeric and Orphic Hymns; and
- perform the Graeco-Egyptian Magick invocation.

This creates links in terms of energy and forms subconscious associations ensuring that the process is synergistic and accomplishes a full initiation in the shortest possible time. Eventually any of the correspondences will be sufficient to trigger an alignment with the planetary energy being worked with, allowing the process to continue all day long.

The invocation is particularly potent and opens wide a door for the planetary energy to enter, leading to gifts as well as challenges in life. Repeated invocations of the planetary energy intensify the transformational effect. It is important to repeatedly invoke the planetary energy until no further directly attributable changes in life are intuited, and everything has been assimilated and understood.

Just how many of these activities you are prepared to do is discretionary, but as with life in general, results are in direct proportion to input and effort.

Reciting the Graeco-Egyptian Magick invocation or the Orphic and Homeric Hymns will certainly ensure that the energy of the planetary Sphere permeates your day. If however, time is short, meditating on the predominant planetary energies of the day, perhaps while commuting to work, is a reasonable substitute.

Theoretical study enhances the understanding of concepts in the initiations. The more the planetary energy is experienced through invoking, the more you begin to discern the reality underlying the myths. The theoretical and practical processes are thus synergistic.

The study of classical texts detailing the mythology of the deities being invoked as well as philosophical writings analysing aspects of spirituality enhances the understanding of concepts in the initiations. The more the planetary energy is experienced through invoking, the more you begin to discern the reality underlying the myths and the truth espoused by philosophers. The theoretical and practical processes are thus synergistic.

It is important to note that each of the planetary energies has a positive pole and a negative pole. Hermetic writings tend to stress the positive pole of the planetary energies while Gnostic writings tend to stress the negative (see the Planetary Properties chapter).

The positive poles are the source of the many gifts to be obtained by working with the planetary energies. The negative poles are the sources of the challenges to be faced. These challenges lead to growth in areas where you may be deficient. Remember that no-one is ever spiritually tested beyond their capacity to cope.

The length of time that each planetary energy initiation will run its course varies from person to person. Certain energies are easier to deal with and others more challenging. The time frame for results may vary from a few days to a year or more. I have found that one month usually yields good results. In the following chapter, I will be suggesting relative time periods for each of the planetary initiations. Intuition however, is perfectly adequate as a guide.

Experiencing successive Spheres may intensify the initiation received in the preceding Spheres as each new energy affects the progressively deeper levels of the psyche. Subsequent planetary Spheres enhance the gifts and challenges from each preceding planetary Sphere. The whole process forms a continuum.

Results

Each ritual chapter is written in a textbook format with the key elements being covered at the beginning. This is followed by a commentary on the ritual, explaining the finer points.

The results described are a distillation of six years of rituals on two continents with a large number of participants with various degrees of experience.

Novices have often asked me how magick manifests in a practical sense. A spell that has been cast manifests through normal channels. It is rare indeed for magick to manifest in the way Hollywood films portray it. The normal channels through which it occurs lead to "coincidences." These coincidences can invariably be explained away, but with repeated spell casting, the sheer number of them eventually necessitates a paradigm shift.

While this text is not about spell casting, a number of participants have reported that accessing planetary energies becomes much more effective after invocations. There is nothing wrong with requesting changes in life so long as the requests are needs rather than wants and no-one is disadvantaged by the results of the spell. Obviously the nature of the request needs to be in keeping with the nature of the planetary energy being worked. Thus, for example Arês would be the most appropriate deity to call on for matters connected to war. His aid could be requested by soldiers marching towards a fortified city which they intend to lay siege to. In the Fifth Planetary

Sphere – Mars chapter, in the Homeric Hymn to Arês, he is described as "Saviour of cities ... O defence of Olympus." While at the very end he is implored "O blessed one, give you me boldness to abide within the harmless laws of peace, avoiding strife and hatred and the violent fiends of death." Thus, Arês' aid could be requested by those cowering behind the ramparts, pleading for an end to hostilities. This indicates that in war, he could be called upon by those attacking as well as those defending. On an everyday level, Arês is called upon for drive, determination and will power.

In group rituals, I always conclude with a debrief, where each participant discusses their results. Whilst each participant has a personal experience, there are areas of commonality in these experiences. The debrief is of great benefit in discerning the objective components of individual experiences and not excluding that which may otherwise have been thought of as either fantasy or unimportant. Debriefing is also good for allaying any fears or concerns that the participants may have had.

In addition, there are certain experiences which are common to all the Spheres.

The intensity and nature of the results experienced and lessons learnt by participants are determined by their ability to attune to the energy and by their individual needs.

A solitary practitioner does not have the benefit of comparing their experience to that of a group, which is why it is so important to have a summary of group results for each of the planetary Spheres.

I recommend that you should NOT read the results of the ritual until it has been performed. The energies should not be experienced with any preconceived ideas, as this will undermine the objectivity of the personal experience.

It can be difficult to accurately determine the exact extent of the flow-on effect of the rituals in everyday life. It is a gradual and progressive voyage that is heavily influenced by the needs of the participants and is very personal. If you are deficient in a particular planetary energy, changes can be quite noticeable, as in the case of someone who has never known love. Encountering an Aphroditê energy can be a very profound experience that brings to this person an awareness of what s/he has been missing out on. If however, you are engaging in spiritual practices in addition to the ones in this text, it will be difficult to determine just which activity is responsible for the changes noticed in everyday life.

Planetary Properties

Each of the planetary energies has a different property or quality associated with it. It should be remembered that the planetary energies themselves are neutral, but can be adapted to numerous situations depending on your will. The qualities of the planetary energies as relevant to this book are listed below:

Table 2: Planetary Properties

Planet	General Properties	Positive Properties	Negative Properties
Moon	Beginning of the spiritual path. Sleep, dreams, cycles, change.	Generation, fertility, memory, growth and movement, capacity for change.	Energy of waning, inability to adapt to change, fear, lunacy.
Mercury	Development of intellect. Communication, commerce, magick.	Reason, intellect, invention, truth.	Fraud, greed for gain, using intellect for evil, light-minded.
Venus	Mastering emotions. Love, relationships, the arts.	Desire, harmony, bliss, physical and spiritual unions.	Concupiscence, depravity, guile of the desires.
Sun	The Ego. Achieving mastery over life.	Discipline, justice, success, honour, dignity, leadership, illumination.	Domineering arrogance, lack of success and refinement.
Mars	Development of the Will. Drive to overcome obstacles in life.	Courage, boldness, ardent vehemence, strength.	Wrathfulness, unholy daring, rashness of audacity, strife, struggle, belligerence, fiery, warfare.
Jupiter	Development of Power. Means to bring power about.	Creation, power of putting into practice, royalty, prudent ruling, practical intellect, fortune, hope, peace, benignity, salutory.	Lust for power, striving for wealth by evil means.
Saturn	End of one journey. Gateway to the next journey.	Philosophy, supreme intellect, powers of reason and theorizing, justice, necessity.	Gloom, tears, torpor, ensnaring falsehood.

To be diligent is to never take anything on faith, but investigate its origin. The remainder of this chapter is dedicated to showing where these properties are derived from.

Background of planetary properties

A number of the quotes below are taken from GRS Mead who noted the similarity in the approach of the Gnostics and the Hermetic philosophers to spiritual development. Both groups sought to ascend through the planetary spheres. However, the Gnostics generally saw the planetary spheres as being evil whilst the Hermetic philosophers often saw them as having very positive qualities.

It is important to remember that the Gnostics viewed themselves as "aliens" imprisoned on the earth, and that their spiritual salvation lay in penetrating through the planetary Spheres to return to their home beyond the stars. The planetary Spheres were hence evil as they barred their return home. Consequently the Gnostics focused on the negative properties of the planets.

The Gnostics taught that when the divine spark descended from beyond the stars to the earth, it took on planetary accretions. The differing percentages of these accretions account for differing personalities. This amounts to a primitive version of astrology. It should be noted that by invoking planetary energies, as described in later chapters, any deficiencies in a particular planetary energy can be rectified. This leads to an effective balancing of the personality.

To understand the verses quoted below it is important to bear in mind two ideas:

- Firstly, a very simple but profound concept is that to undo any process, it is merely a matter of reversing the steps in the process. (Think of a mechanic pulling apart an engine for maintenance.) It follows that for the divine spark to ascend back to its home beyond the stars, the process by which it descended must be reversed. Hence the divine spark must divest itself of its planetary accretions.
- Secondly, the concept of duality indicates that deities should be polarised into being either good or evil. This originated

with the Zoroastrians and was later incorporated into Christianity. A perusal of the myths of virtually all cultures however, shows that deities had their positive aspects as well as their failings. The Greek myths particularly portray deities with very "human" foibles. So it is with the planetary energies, they have both a positive pole and a negative pole. Both are important and just as valid as each other. Transcending duality is an important part of spiritual development. (See Appendix 4: Integration of the Divine Spark.)

For the sake of clarity, I have condensed every quote to a table. These tables are ultimately reduced to the master table above.

Positive planetary properties

In Corpus Hermeticum, Book XXIV: A Hymn of the Gods it is written:

"Seven Stars far varied in their course revolved around the wide Olympian plain; with them for ever will Aiôn spin fate: Mênê that shines by night, and gloomy Kronos, and sweet Hêlios, and Paphie [Aphroditê] who's carried in the shrine, courageous Arês, fair-winged Hermês, and Zeus the primal source from whom Nature doth come.

Now they themselves have had the race of men entrusted to their care; so that in us there is a Mênê, Zeus, an Arês, Paphie, a Kronos, Hêlios and Hermês.

Wherefore we are divided up so as to draw from the etherial spirit, tears, laughter, anger, birth, reason, sleep, desire.

Tears are Kronos, birth Zeus, reason is Hermês, courage Mars, and Mênê sleep, in sooth, and Cytherea [Aphroditê] desire, and Hêlios is laughter – for 'tis because of him that justly every mortal thinking doth laugh and the immortal world."

[Selection from "*Thrice Greatest Hermes: Studies in Hellenic Theosophy and Gnosis*" G R S Mead, trans.]

The important things to note in this hymn are that just as the planetary gods have an existence without, so do they have an existence within. The etherial spirit, represented by Aiôn, is the source from which our seven components come and will "spin fate." Each of these components is represented by a planetary deity. "Fair-winged" for Hermês refers to his function as a messenger and hence his association with communication and travel. "Carried in the shrine" for Aphroditê is a reference to the practice of carrying her image in a small shrine during processions. Zeus is referred to as the creator who gave birth to Nature.

Table 3: A Hymn of the Gods

Planet	Deity	Description	Property
Moon	Mênê	Shines by night	Sleep
Mercury	Hermês	Fair-winged	Reason
Venus	Aphroditê	Carried in the shrine	Desire
Sun	Hêlios	Sweet	Laughter
Mars	Arês	Courageous	Courage
Jupiter	Zeus	Primal source	Birth
Saturn	Kronos	Gloomy	Tears

The contribution of the planetary deities to the creation of mankind by God, the Master of the universe, is explained in The Virgin of the World verses 16–17 as follows:

> *"... And when He spake to them on human kind's behalf, they [all] agreed to furnish those who were to be, with whatsoever thing they each could best provide.*
> *Sun said: 'I'll shine unto my full.'*
> *Moon promised to pour light upon the after-the-sun course, and she had already given birth to Fear, and Silence, and also Sleep, and Memory – a thing that could be most useful for them*
> *Kronos announced himself already sire of Justice and Necessity.*
> *Zeus said: 'So that the race which is to be may not for ever fight, already for them have I made Fortune, and Hope, and Peace.'*
> *Arês declared he had become already sire of Struggle, Wrath, and Strife.*

Nor yet did Aphroditê hesitate; she also said: 'I'll join to them Desire, my Lord, and Bliss, and Laughter [too], so that our kindred souls, in working out their very grievous condemnation, may not exhaust their punishment unto the full.'
Full pleased were all, my son, at Aphroditê's words.
'And for my part,' said Hermês, 'I will make men's nature well endowed; I will devote to them Prudence and Wisdom, Persuasiveness and Truth, and never will I cease from congress with Invention, but ever will I benefit the mortal life of men born underneath my types of life.'"
[Selection from "*Thrice Greatest Hermes: Studies in Hellenic Theosophy and Gnosis*" G R S Mead, trans.]

Hermês' reference to men born underneath his "types of life" means the signs of the zodiac.

Table 4: The Virgin of the World

Planet	Property
Moon	Fear, silence, sleep, memory
Mercury	Well endowed nature, prudence, wisdom, persuasiveness, truth, invention
Venus	Desire, bliss, laughter
Sun	Illumination
Mars	Struggle, wrath, strife
Jupiter	Fortune, hope, peace
Saturn	Justice, necessity

Proclus, in his "Commentary on the Timaeus of Plato" wrote:

"Further still according to another division, the agricultural tribe of the city is analogous to the Moon, which comprehends the sacred laws of nature, the cause of generation. But the inspective guardian of the common marriages, is analogous to Venus, who is the cause of all harmony, and of the union of the

male with the female, and of form with matter. That which providentially attends to elegant allotments, is analogous to Hermês, on account of the lots of which the God is the guardian, and also on account of the fraud which they contain. But that which is disciplinative and judicial in the city, is analogous to the Sun, with whom, according to theologists, the mundane Justice, the elevator and the seven-fold reside. And that which is belligerent, is analogous to the order proceeding from Mars, which governs all the contrarieties of the world, and the diversity of the universe. That which is royal, is analogous to Jupiter, who is the supplier of ruling prudence, and of the practical and adorning intellect. But that which is philosophic, is analogous to Saturn, so far as he is an intellectual God, and ascends as far as to the first cause."
[Selection from "*The Commentaries of Proclus on the Timaeus of Plato*" Thomas Taylor, trans.]

The Lunar cycle's association with agriculture is recognised, insofar as the Moon is associated with the laws which govern seasonal planting. The Spheres of Mercury and Venus are interchanged in the text. The association of Mercury with fraud is the only negative planetary attribution on the list. Interestingly, Venus is normally associated with desire. Desire, however potentially leads to union of male and female, and hence, harmony. The driving force behind a union of form with matter could be seen as desire. The idea of the Sun being associated with the sevenfold planets is possibly a reference to the popular representation of Hêlios wearing a helmet with numerous rays. Jupiter is associated with the practical intellect required by a ruler. Saturn is associated with a wisdom transcending the mundane. Ascension to the first cause is a reference to Saturn being a gateway to the realm beyond the planets, the realm of Aiôn (see Graeco-Egyptian Magick Opening Rite chapter).

Table 5: Proclus' "Commentary on the Timaeus of Plato"

Planet	Property	Description
Moon	Generation	Agricultural, comprehends sacred laws of nature
Mercury	Allotments	Guardian of the lots, and the fraud therein
Venus	Harmony	Union of male with female, and form with matter
Sun	Justice	Discipline and justice
Mars	Belligerence	Governs contrarieties and diversity
Jupiter	Royalty	Supplier of ruling, prudence, practical adorning intellect
Saturn	Philosophy	Intellectual God, ascending to the first cause

In the first century BCE, Marcus Tullius Cicero in "On the Republic" Book VI (Dream of Scipio), section 17, wrote:

> "... *The universe is composed of nine circles, or rather spheres, one of which is the heavenly one, and is exterior to all the rest, which it embraces; being itself the Supreme God, and bounding and containing the whole. In it are fixed those stars which revolve with never-varying courses. Below this are seven other spheres, which revolve in a contrary direction to that of the heavens. One of these is occupied by the globe which on earth they call Saturn. Next to that is the star of Jupiter, so benign and salutary to mankind. The third in order, is that fiery and terrible planet called Mars. Below this again, almost in the middle region, is the Sun—the leader, governor, the prince of the other luminaries; the soul of the world, which it regulates and illumines, being of such vast size that it pervades and gives light to all places. Then follow Venus and Mercury, which attend, as it were, on the Sun. Lastly, the Moon, which shines only in the reflected beams of the Sun, moves in the lowest sphere of all. Below this, if we except that gift of the gods, the soul, which has been given by the liberality of the gods to the human race, every thing is mortal, and tends to dissolution, but above the moon all is eternal. For the Earth, which is in the ninth globe, and*

> *occupies the centre, is immovable, and being the lowest, all others gravitate towards it. ...”*
> [Selection from “*The Library of Original Sources*” Oliver J Thatcher, ed., modernized by Prof. J S Arkenberg]

The interesting thing about this vision is that it stresses the primacy of the Sun and has little to say about the other planets.

Table 6: Cicero’s “Dream of Scipio”

Planet	Property
Moon	Shines only in the reflected beams of the Sun
Mercury	Attends the Sun
Venus	Attends the Sun
Sun	Leader, governor, prince of the other luminaries, regulates and illumines
Mars	Fiery and terrible
Jupiter	Benign and salutary
Saturn	–

This was remedied by Macrobius in his fifth century CE commentary on the “Dream of Scipio” which described the descent of the soul into the world. The text contains translations of each of the planetary properties into Greek, which I have removed for the sake of clarity.

> *“In the sphere of Saturn it develops the powers of reason and theorising ... ; in that of Jupiter, the power of putting into practice ... ; in that of Mars, the power of ardent vehemence ... ; in that of the Sun, the nature of sensing and imagining ... ; in that of Venus, the motion of desire ... ; in the sphere of Mercury, the power of giving expression to and interpretation of feelings ... ; on its entrance into the sphere of the Moon it brings into activity ... the nature of making bodies grow and of moving them.”*
> [Selection from “*The Commentaries of Proclus on the Timaeus of Plato*” Thomas Taylor, trans.]

This continues with the seasonal planting theme for the Moon and the idea of Jupiter having associated with it the practical knowhow required by a ruler. Mercury is associated with intellect, the Sun with perception, and Saturn with a greater intellect.

Table 7: Macrobius' commentary on the "Dream of Scipio"

Planet	Property
Moon	Brings activity; nature of making bodies grow and of moving them
Mercury	Power of giving expression to and interpretation of feelings
Venus	Motion of desire
Sun	Nature of sensing and imagining
Mars	Power of ardent vehemence
Jupiter	Power of putting into practice
Saturn	Powers of reason and theorising

Negative planetary properties

Servius in his commentary on Virgil's Aeneid. VI. 714 writes:

> *"As the souls descend, they draw with them the torpor of Saturn, the wrathfulness of Mars, the concupiscence of Venus, the greed for gain of Mercury, the lust for power of Jupiter."*
> [Selection from "*The Gnostic Religion*" Hans Jonas]

It should be noted that Hermês was associated with commerce, hence "greed for gain" is quite appropriate as a negative property. Also, the property of "torpor" for Saturn refers to it being the slowest moving of the planets and representing the slowness of old age. The rationale behind omitting the Sun and Moon will be covered in Book iii, section 13 of the Tetrabiblos below.

Table 8: Servius' commentary on Virgil's "Aeneid"

Planet	Property
Moon	–
Mercury	Greed for gain
Venus	Concupiscence
Sun	–
Mars	Wrathfulness
Jupiter	Lust for power
Saturn	Torpor

In Corpus Hermeticum, Book I: Poemandres, The Shepherd of Men, Verse 25, there is a description of the ascent of the soul and the negative planetary accretions it has to divest itself of:

> *"And thus it is that man doth speed his way thereafter upwards through the Harmony.*
> *To the first zone he gives the energy of Growth and Waning; unto the second zone, Device of Evils now de-energised; unto the third, the Guile of the Desires de-energised; unto the fourth his Domineering Arrogance also de-energised; unto the fifth, unholy Daring and the Rashness of Audacity de-energised; unto the sixth, Striving for Wealth by evil means deprived of its aggrandisement; and to the seventh zone, Ensnaring Falsehood de-energised."*
> [Selection from "*Thrice Greatest Hermes: Studies in Hellenic Theosophy and Gnosis*" G R S Mead, trans.]

Note that the zones are equivalent to the planetary spheres. Tabulating the above:

Table 9: Poemandres "The Shepherd of Men"

Zone	Planet	Property
1	Moon	Growth and waning
2	Mercury	Device of evils
3	Venus	Guile of the desires
4	Sun	Domineering arrogance
5	Mars	Daring and the rashness of audacity
6	Jupiter	Striving for wealth by evil means
7	Saturn	Ensnaring falsehood

It is evident that only the Moon is not thought of as being evil, as here you only seek to harmonise with its cycles. Mercury is associated with utilising the intellect for evil rather than noble purposes.

Planetary properties from Orphic and Homeric Hymns, and mythology

In the chapters dealing with the seven planetary spheres, the Orphic and Homeric Hymns, and mythology have been included. The properties associated with the planetary deities from those hymns are summarised in the table below.

Table 10: Orphic and Homeric Hymns, and Mythology

Planet	Properties
Moon	Beauty, radiance, loving peace and vigilance, foe of strife. Excites lunacy. Connected with fertility.
Mercury	Good shepherd, priest, sage, celestial messenger, inducer of sleep and dreams, thief, prophet, psychopomp, gymnast and athlete, keeper of secrets, trickster and fraud, giver of gain both honest and dishonest. Can be wrathful. Associated with luck, divination, communication, inventiveness, cunning, commerce, science, magick, health and healing, fertility, memory, luck and grace.
Venus	Beautiful, joins the world with harmony, goddess of marriage, mother of love. Connected with fertility and nature. Binds in magic chains through mad desire. Prostitution.
Sun	Illuminating, all-seeing, the world's commander, rules seasons and years, summons the morning and the evening, punisher of the wicked, guiding righteousness, playing beautiful music. Connected with life, agriculture, divination.
Mars	God of war, unconquered, boisterous, strong warrior, doughty in heart, saviour and defender of cities, giver of dauntless youth, giver of boldness, drives away cowardice and deceitful impulses.
Jupiter	Omnipresent, omnipotent, omniscient, has all the attributes of divinity and kingship, father of the weather and the sky. Graces with power, wisdom, peace, health and wealth.
Saturn	Creator of Gods, men, beings and the world. Father of eternity. Permeating creation, governing birth and death. Source of counsel and possessing a subtle mind.

Planetary properties from Tetrabiblos

Between 130 and 170 CE, Ptolemy (Claudius Ptolemaeus, 100-178 CE) wrote the Tetrabiblos which has become the primary text of Western Astrology.

The beneficent and maleficent planets are outlined in Book i, section 5:

> *"... the ancients accepted two of the planets, Jupiter and Venus, together with the moon, as beneficent ..., and Saturn and Mars as producing effects of the opposite nature, ...; the sun and Mercury, however, they thought to have both powers, because they, have a common nature, and to join their influences with those of the other planets, with whichever of them they are associated."*
>
> [Selection from "*Ptolemy Tetrabiblos*" F E Robbins, trans.]

The theme of Mars and Saturn being maleficent energies permeates most astrological thought. As the preceding quotes show however, each planetary energy has a positive pole and a negative pole. The negative poles for Mars and Saturn are merely more obvious, just as the positive poles for the beneficent planets, Moon, Mercury, Venus and Jupiter, are more obvious. However, it must be remembered that the opposite poles are always there.

Detailed information about the nature of the planets is outlined in Book iii, section 13:

> *"If Saturn alone is ruler of the soul and dominates Mercury and the moon, if he has a dignified position with reference to the universe and the angles, he makes his subjects lovers of the body, strong-minded, deep thinkers, austere, of a single purpose, laborious, dictatorial, ready to punish, lovers of property, avaricious, violent, amassing treasure, and jealous; but if his position is the opposite and without dignity, he makes them sordid, petty, mean-spirited, indifferent, mean-minded, malignant, cowardly, diffident, evil-speakers, solitary, tearful, shameless, superstitious; fond of toil, unfeeling, devisers of plots against their friends, gloomy, taking no care of the body. ...*

If Jupiter alone has the domination of the soul, in honourable positions he makes his subjects magnanimous, generous, god-fearing, honourable, pleasure-loving, kind, magnificent, liberal, just, high-minded, dignified, minding their own business, compassionate, fond of discussion, beneficent, affectionate, with qualities of leadership. If he chances to be in the opposite kind of position, he makes their souls seem similar, to be sure, but with a difference in the direction of greater humility, less conspicuousness, and poorer judgement. For example, instead of magnanimity, he endows them with prodigality; instead of reverence for the gods, with superstition; instead of modesty, with cowardice; instead of dignity, with conceit; instead of kindness, with foolish simplicity; instead of the love of beauty, with love of pleasure; instead of high-mindedness, with stupidity; instead of liberality, with indifference, and the like. ...

Mars alone, given the domination of the soul, in an honourable position makes his subjects noble, commanding, spirited, military, versatile, powerful, venturesome, rash, unruly, indifferent, stubborn, keen, headstrong, contemptuous, tyrannical, active, easily angered, with the qualities of leadership. In a position of the opposite kind he makes them savage, insolent, bloodthirsty, makers of disturbances, spendthrifts, loud-mouthed, quick-fisted, impetuous, drunken, rapacious, evil-doers, pitiless, unsettled, mad, haters of their own kin, impious. ...

If Venus alone takes the domination of the soul, in an honourable position she makes her subjects pleasant, good, luxurious, eloquent, neat, cheerful, fond of dancing, eager for beauty, haters of evil, lovers of the arts, fond of spectacles, decorous, healthy, dreamers of pleasant dreams, affectionate, beneficent, compassionate, fastidious, easily conciliated, successful, and, in general, charming. In the opposite position she makes them careless, erotic, effeminate, womanish, timid, indifferent, depraved, censorious, insignificant, meriting reproach. ...

Mercury, by himself taking the domination of the soul, in an honourable position makes those who are born under him wise, shrewd, thoughtful, learned, inventive, experienced, good calculators, inquirers into nature, speculative, gifted, emulous, beneficent, prudent, good at conjecture, mathematicians, partakers in mysteries, successful in attaining their ends. In the opposite position he makes them utter rascals, precipitate, forgetful, impetuous, light-minded, fickle, prone to change their minds, foolish rogues, witless, sinful, liars, undiscriminating, unstable, undependable, avaricious, unjust, and, in general, unsteady in judgement and inclined to evil deeds.

While the foregoing is true as stated, nevertheless the condition of the moon itself also makes a certain contribution. For when the moon happens to be at the bendings of its northern and southern limits, it helps; with respect to the character of the soul, in the direction of greater versatility, resourcefulness, and capacity for change; at the nodes, in the direction of greater keenness, activity, and excitability; again, at rising and in the increases of its illumination,. towards greater natural endowments, renown, firmness, and frankness; and in the waning of its illumination, or its occultations, towards greater sluggishness and dullness, less fixity of purpose, greater cautiousness, and less renown.

The sun also aids, when it is familiar with the planet that governs the temperament of the soul, in an honourable position modifying it in the direction of justice, success, honour, dignity, and reverence for the gods, but in the contrary and alien position making it humbler, more industrious, less conspicuous, more savage, more obstinate, harsher, with a harder life, and in general less successful."

[Selection from "*Ptolemy Tetrabiblos*" F E Robbins, trans.]

It is evident that the actual rulers of the soul are the five planets, with the two luminaries (Moon and Sun) assisting. While this was not a view accepted by everyone, it was certainly the case in Servius' commentary on Virgil's Aeneid quoted above.

Table 11: Ptolemy's Tetrabiblos – Planetary Properties

Planet	Positive Properties	Negative Properties
Moon	greater versatility, resourcefulness, capacity for change, greater keenness, activity, excitability, greater natural endowments, renown, firmness, and frankness	greater sluggishness and dullness, less fixity of purpose, greater cautiousness, and less renown
Mercury	wise, shrewd, thoughtful, learned, inventive, experienced, good calculators, inquirers into nature, speculative, gifted, emulous, beneficent, prudent, good at conjecture, mathematicians, partakers in mysteries, successful in attaining their ends	utter rascals, precipitate, forgetful, impetuous, light-minded, fickle, prone to change their minds, foolish rogues, witless, sinful, liars, undiscriminating, unstable, unjust, undependable, avaricious, and, in general, unsteady in judgement and inclined to evil deeds
Venus	pleasant, good, luxurious, eloquent, neat, cheerful, fond of dancing, eager for beauty, haters of evil, lovers of the arts, fond of spectacles, decorous, healthy, pleasant dreamers, affectionate, beneficent, compassionate, fastidious, easily conciliated, successful, charming	careless, erotic, effeminate, womanish, timid, indifferent, depraved, censorious, insignificant, meriting reproach
Sun	justice, success, honour, dignity, and reverence for the gods	humbler, more industrious, less conspicuous, more savage, more obstinate, harsher, with a harder life, and in general less successful
Mars	noble, commanding, spirited, military, versatile, powerful, venturesome, keen, headstrong, active, with the qualities of leadership	rash, unruly, indifferent, stubborn, contemptuous, tyrannical, easily angered, savage, insolent, bloodthirsty, makers of disturbances, spendthrifts, loud-mouthed, quick-fisted, impetuous, drunken, rapacious, evil-doers, pitiless, unsettled, mad, haters of their own kin, impious
Jupiter	magnanimous, generous, god-fearing, honourable, pleasure-loving, kind, magnificent, liberal, just, high-minded, dignified, minding their own business, compassionate, fond of discussion, beneficent, affectionate, with qualities of leadership	greater humility, less conspicuousness, and poorer judgement; prodigality, superstition, cowardice, conceit, foolish simplicity, love of pleasure, stupidity, indifference
Saturn	lovers of the body, strong-minded, deep thinkers, austere, of a single purpose, laborious, dictatorial, ready to punish, lovers of property, amassing treasure	avaricious, violent, jealous, sordid, petty, mean-spirited, indifferent, mean-minded, malignant, cowardly, diffident, evil-speakers, solitary, tearful, shameless, superstitious; fond of toil, unfeeling, devisers of plots against their friends, gloomy, taking no care of the body

Planetary initiation from the Tetrabiblos and the PGM

In order to understand the nature of planetary initiation it is important to study Book iv, section 10 – Of the Division of Times:

> *"... For in the matter of the age-divisions of mankind in general there is one and the same approach, which for likeness and comparison depends upon the order of the seven planets; it begins with the first age of man and with the first sphere from us, that is, the moon's, and ends with the last of the ages and the outermost of the planetary spheres, which is called that of Saturn. And in truth the accidental qualities of each of the ages are those which are naturally proper to the planet compared with it, and these it will be needful to observe, in order that by this means we may investigate the general questions of the temporal divisions, while we determine particular differences from the special qualities which are discovered in the nativities.*
> *For up to about the fourth year, following the number which belongs to the quadrennium, the moon takes over the age of infancy and produces the suppleness and lack of fixity in its body, its quick growth and the moist nature, as a rule, of its food, the changeability of its condition, and the imperfection and inarticulate state of its soul, suitably to her own active qualities.*
> *In the following period of ten years, Mercury, to whom falls the second place and the second age, that of childhood, for the period which is half of the space of twenty years, begins to articulate and fashion the intelligent and logical part of the soul, to implant certain seeds and rudiments of learning, and to bring to light individual peculiarities of character and faculties, awaking the soul at this stage by instruction, tutelage, and the first gymnastic exercises.*
> *Venus, taking in charge the third age, that of youth, for the next eight years, corresponding in number to her own period, begins, as is natural, to inspire, at their maturity, an activity of the seminal passages and to implant an impulse toward the embrace of love. At this time particularly a kind of frenzy enters*

the soul, incontinence, desire for any chance sexual gratification, burning passion, guile, and the blindness of the impetuous lover. The lord of the middle sphere, the sun, takes over the fourth age, which is the middle one in order, young manhood, for the period of nineteen years, wherein he implants in the soul at length the mastery and direction of its actions, desire for substance, glory, and position, and a change from playful, ingenuous error to seriousness, decorum, and ambition.

After the sun, Mars, fifth in order, assumes command of manhood for the space of fifteen years, equal to his own period. He introduces severity and misery into life, and implants cares and troubles in the soul and in the body, giving it, as it were, same sense and notion of passing its prime and urging it, before it approaches its end, by labour to accomplish something among its undertakings that is worthy of note.

Sixth, Jupiter, taking as his lot the elderly age, again for the space of his own period, twelve years, brings about the renunciation of manual labour, toil, turmoil, and dangerous activity, and in their place brings decorum, foresight, retirement, together with all-embracing deliberation, admonition, and consolation; now especially he brings men to set store by honour, praise, and independence, accompanied by modesty and dignity.

Finally to Saturn falls as his lot old age, the latest period, which lasts for the rest of life. Now the movements both of body and of soul are cooled and impeded in their impulses, enjoyments, desires, and speed; for the natural decline supervenes upon life, which has become worn down with age, dispirited, weak, easily offended, and hard to please in all situations, in keeping with the sluggishness of his movements. ..."

[Selection from "*Ptolemy Tetrabiblos*" F E Robbins, trans.]

The properties of the ages ruled by each of the planets in the table below agree in broad terms with the planetary properties previously cited. Looking at the planets both ways enhances the overall understanding of what the energies truly represent.

Table 12: Ptolemy's Tetrabiblos – Planetary Initiation

Planet	*Ages (years)*	*Period (years)*	*Property*
Moon	1–4	4	Infancy, changeability
Mercury	5–15	10	Childhood, learning, physical exercise
Venus	16–24	8	Youth, awakening of libido
Sun	25–44	19	Young adulthood, life mastery, desire for glory
Mars	45–60	15	Adulthood, drive to beat obstacles in life
Jupiter	61–73	12	Old age, retirement, basking in earned glory
Saturn	74– ?	–	Old age, natural decline

It seems that Ptolemy was a difficult author to understand for the ancients, which necessitated the inclusion of an Anonymous commentary. The periods appear to be derived from a number of sources. The Anonymous commentary with the Tetrabiblos states that four years is assigned to the moon as its phases coincide again after that time. The Anonymous commentary states that half of twenty (being the age at which adulthood begins), is assigned to Mercury due to its "double" nature, which appears to refer to Hermês' attribution to reason and intellect as well as thievery and fraud. (While some readers may feel that this is a reference to Mercury Retrograde, I have been unable to find any ancient references to the astrological implications of retrograde motion, which was explained through epicycles.) The orbital period of Venus is a little under eight months. The period aspected to the sun appears to be the age at which young manhood ends, namely nineteen years. In the Michigan astrological treatise, the length of the period of Mars is associated with the age of boys at puberty, namely fifteen years. The orbital period for Jupiter is a little under twelve years. The period for Saturn extends until death.

There is evidence of the Graeco-Egyptian magickians being familiar with planetary attributions and applying them throughout life, indicating cycles within the major cycle outlined in the "Division of Times." This is shown in *PGM* IV. 835–49:

"From 53 years and 9 months on Hermês took the period up to 10 years and 9 months, from which he assigned to himself 20 months, which would be 55 years 5 months; then to Aphroditê 8 months, which would thus be 56 years 1 month; then to Hêlios 19 months, which would be 57 years 8 months. In this period assigned to Hêlios, that is to the 19 months, devote yourself to what you seek. After this he assigned to Arês 15 months, which would be 58 years 11 months. This is a hostile period. Then to Selênê 25 months, which would be 61 years. They are good. Then to Zeus, 12 months, which would be 62 years. They are good. Then to Kronos 30 months, which would be 64 ½ years. They are bad for the body; within them also are the dangerous points."
[*Tr.: W C Grese]

Table 13: PGM – Planetary Initiation

Planet	*Period (months)*	*Property*
Mercury	20	–
Venus	8	–
Sun	19	Devotion to what is sought in life
Mars	15	Hostile period
Moon	25	Good period
Jupiter	12	Good period
Saturn	30	Bad period containing dangerous points

The interesting points to note are that the magickian/astrologer has looked at a ten year, nine month period of a person's life and has assigned the seven planets to portions of this cycle. Periods in months have been assigned as opposed to years in the "Division of Times." In the case of Venus, Sun, Mars and Jupiter, the periods are an exact match. No time span is assigned to Saturn, so this cannot be compared. The period for Mercury has been doubled, so perhaps its "double" nature is not being considered. The period for the Moon has been greatly increased, although it is interesting that 25 months here is close to half that in the "Division of Times" if looked at in an absolute sense. Please note the remarks in my "Division of Times" commentary for the orbital periods of Venus and Jupiter. The orbital period for Saturn is a little under 30 years. For some unexplained reason, the Moon has been moved from where it should be to between Mars and Jupiter. The descriptions for the periods ruled by Mars and Saturn are consistent with their perception of being maleficent. It should be borne in mind that this appears to be a chart for a specific time period in a particular individual's life, and so we would need a detailed horoscope of the individual to make full sense of it.

I am satisfied that the two excerpts above give the time periods associated with Venus, Sun, Mars, Jupiter and Saturn. The Moon and Mercury are in doubt unless further information becomes available. A practical application of this is in determining the time period required to effectively complete planetary initiations. The numbers clearly represent multiples of a time unit associated with each planet. The time unit could be seen as a day, a week, a month, or even an hour (in the case of advanced magickians).

In the Ritual Preparation chapter, I left the matter of time periods for initiations up to the reader's discretion. I realize however, that certain readers may be happier with an absolute guide. In this case, I would suggest using intuition to determine when the initiation for the Moon has been completed. I would further suggest that beginners will need fairly long periods of time for the Moon and Mercury after which their progress will be somewhat easier. Thus, the time period for the Moon should be divided by twenty-five, to give the time unit. Then, use twenty time units for Mercury (that is, four fifths of the time period required for the Moon), followed by eight for Venus, nineteen for the Sun, fifteen for Mars, twelve for Jupiter and thirty for Saturn. More advanced readers should have fewer problems working with the Moon, and so should divide the time period by four. Then use ten time units for Mercury (that is, two and a half times the time period required for the Moon), followed by the same periods as above for the remainder.

Table 14: Planetary Initiation Time Periods

Planet	*Period (Beginners)*	*Period (Advanced)*
Moon	25	4
Mercury	20	10
Venus	8	8
Sun	19	19
Mars	15	15
Jupiter	12	12
Saturn	30	30

The general principles in these excerpts, especially the PGM excerpt, give a profound insight into the planetary initiation process. Portions of a person's life can be looked at in terms of planetary influences, which provide experiences and lessons. There is one planetary cycle from birth to death, another for the days of the week, and presumably a number of others, such as in the PGM excerpt above. Those who do not learn their lessons are condemned to repeat them.

The planetary initiation process detailed in the two excerpts greatly increases our understanding of the Saturn energy. Saturn is commonly thought of as being associated negatively with death and restriction and positively with the sage-like wisdom of old age. Most of humanity is caught in the cycle of birth, death and rebirth. Most people get swept along living their life similarly to everyone else. As they get older they start to prepare for death spiritually and financially, often fervently starting to attend religious services and ensuring that their relatives will be provided for. On their death bed they think back on their life, smiling over their successes and anguishing over their failures. At death they exit by the Saturn gate, only to re-enter by the Lunar gate and repeat the whole process again.

Truly it has been said that initiation is a preparation for death. Effectively the whole spiritual process within life is experienced by working through the seven planetary spheres. All that life has to offer can thus be experienced. Repetition of the planetary initiations is thus symbolic of the repetition of life after life.

Saturn represents a time of preparation for the transition of death into another existence.

With nothing left to learn, there is no reason for us to incarnate in another physical vehicle. Death is but a doorway. For the relatively small number who break free of the cycle of death and rebirth, Saturn becomes the doorway to the eighth and ninth spheres. This supremely important issue will be dealt with in my next book.

Overview of planetary properties

Combining the data, we produce the master table given at the beginning of this chapter. (See Table 2: Planetary Properties.)

Whilst extensive, this is not an exhaustive list. You could readily expand on it by studying the myths of the planetary deities and poring through various ancient texts. It is simply a matter of discerning the energies underlying the myths. This is indeed a worthwhile exercise, as you can never be too well informed.

However, such study should not be the main thrust of your efforts. This book is a practical text. Once you start invoking the planetary energies true understanding will follow.

Planetary Correspondences

Magick functions on sympathetic principles. In order to maximise the effectiveness of a ritual in which a planetary energy is being invoked, as many of the attributes of the corresponding deity as possible should be integrated. As a minimum, this entails using the names of power of the deity, the correct incense and the correct colour. The names of power will be dealt with in the chapters corresponding to the planetary deities.

The incenses, colours and gemstones used by the Graeco-Egyptian magickians are listed below:

Table 15: Planetary Correspondences

Planet	Incense	Colour	Gemstone/Metal
Moon	Myrrh	Silver	Silver
Mercury	Cassia	Orange	Turquoise/Amber
Venus	Spikenard	Blue	Lapis Lazuli
Sun	Frankincense	Gold	Gold
Mars	Costus	Red	Yellow-green Onyx / Garnet, Ruby
Jupiter	Indian bay leaf	Purple/White	Amethyst
Saturn	Storax	Black	Obsidian

The comment in the Planetary Properties chapter about not taking anything on faith is relevant here also. The remainder of this chapter is dedicated to showing where the correspondences are derived from.

Incense

A complete list of planetary incenses is found at *PGM* XIII. 17–20:

> *"The proper incense of Kronos is styrax, for it is heavy and fragrant; of Zeus, malabathron; of Arês, kostos; of Hêlios, frankincense; of Aphroditê, Indian nard; of Hermês, cassia; of Selênê, myrrh. These are the secret incenses..."*

The same incenses are given in *PGM* XIII. 353–354, but without their attributions:

*"The incenses are these: malabathron, styrax, nard, kostos, cassia, frankincense, myrrh." [*Tr.: Morton Smith]*

Table 16: Planetary Incenses

Planet	Incense
Moon	The Lunar incense is myrrh (Balsamodendron Myrrha or Commiphora Myrrha). The plant is indigenous to desert areas of North Africa and the Red Sea shores of Saudi Arabia, but the best quality comes from Somaliland. It was highly esteemed by the ancients as an unguent, perfume, temple incense and was used in embalming. Its association with the embalming process is the reason why it was used extensively in virtually all sub-lunar workings, which are for the underworld gods. Given that many of the Egyptian gods had underworld associations, it was used very extensively for the Egyptian pantheon.
Mercury	The Mercury incense is cassia or kasia (Cinnamomum cassia), and is also known as Chinese cassia, Bastard cinnamon, and Chinese cinnamon. The stem bark of the plant is used and it comes in quills or is rolled. Cassia grows in Burma and South China. Most of the cinnamon sold in North America is actually cassia. In Egypt it was used as part of the mummification process.
Venus	The Venus incense is Indian nard (Nardostachys jatamansi or Nardostachys grandiflora) and is also called Spikenard or Syrian nard. The root of the plant is used. In Sanskrit it is called jatamansi and this name is still widely used in India. It grows in the Alpine Himalayas in India, Nepal and Burma.
Sun	The Sun incense is frankincense or olibanum (Boswellia Thurifera). The gum resin is used. The plant grows in Southeast Arabia, Somalia, Ethiopia and India, but the best quality comes from Oman. It was highly esteemed by the ancients as a temple incense, perfume, and was used in embalming.
Mars	The Mars incense is kostos or costus (Sassurea lappa). The root is used. The plant grows only in the highlands of Kashmir.
Jupiter	The Jupiter incense was known as malabathron (Cinnamomum tamala or Cinnamomum tejpata) and is now known as Indian Bay-leaf. The leaves are used. The plant is native to India where it grows on the southern slopes of the Himalayas. In Sanskrit it was known as Tejapatra. In the Assami, Bengali, Hindi, Oriya and Punjabi dialects it is known as Tej pat, Tejpata or Tejpatra. In the Gujrati and Marathi dialects it is known as Tamaal patra. The common name, tamalapatra, was corrupted by the Greeks and Latins into malabatrum or malabathron.
Saturn	The Saturn incense is styrax or storax (Liquidambar orientalis) and is also known as Liquidambar imberbe, Styrax Praeparatus, Prepared Storax, Styrax liquidus, Flussiger Amber, Liquid Storax, and Balsam Styracis. The part used is the balsam obtained from the wood and inner bark. It grows in Asia Minor.

The striking thing about this list of incenses is that none of them are from northern Egypt. All were brought in by traders, and as such would have been expensive. The Graeco-Egyptian magickians obviously either had a penchant for the exotic or were keen to use the most appropriate incenses regardless of cost.

Having worked with these incenses for a number of years, I find them perfectly suited to the planetary Spheres. If used as perfumes, the incenses are very strong by modern standards. I suspect that strong fragrances may have come into vogue to mask poor personal hygiene (just as in 14th century Europe)!

Gemstones and Colour

Given that we are dealing with distinct planetary deities, each should have its own colour. *PGM* VII. 260–71 is a short spell titled "For ascent of the uterus" in which the instruction is to write the spell on a tin lamella and "clothe" it in seven colours. While the colours are not listed, it is clear that seven distinct colours are meant. The number seven suggests that the planetary colours are implied.

I have been able to find only one Graeco-Egyptian Magick text dealing with gemstones, and by extension, colour. If more were available then cross comparisons could be made.

> *"... a voice comes to you in conversation. Lay out the stars on the board in their natural order, with the exception of the sun and the moon. Make the sun gold, the moon silver, Kronos of obsidian, Arês of yellow-green onyx, Aphroditê of lapis-lazuli streaked with gold, Hermês of turquoise; make Zeus of a [dark blue] stone, but underneath of crystal."*
> *PGM* CX: 1–12 [*Tr.: Roy Kotansky]

The colours suggested by this list are tabulated below.

Table 17: PGM – Deities, Gemstones, Apparent Colours

Planet	Deity	Gemstone/Metal	Apparent colour
Sun	Hêlios	Gold	Gold
Moon	Selênê (Mênê)	Silver	Silver
Saturn	Kronos	Obsidian	Black
Mars	Arês	Yellow-green Onyx	Yellow-green
Venus	Aphroditê	Lapis Lazuli	Blue
Mercury	Hermês	Turquoise	Blue-green
Jupiter	Zeus	[Dark blue] and crystal	[Dark blue] and clear (?)

The first striking thing about this list is the absence of the colours red and orange. The second striking thing is the use of various shades of the colour blue for three of the planets. It should be noted that the square brackets around the first colour for Jupiter indicate that it was in doubt and consequently interpolated by the translator.

The use of gold as an attribution to the Sun appears almost universal because of its colour and great value. As mentioned repeatedly in this book, most of the ancients in late antiquity were Sun worshippers, as the Sun is the brightest object in the heavens.

The Moon is the second brightest object in the heavens. Silver appears to be universally attributed to the Moon because of its colour and value. It is interesting to note that silver is always considered to be inferior to gold, which is analogous to the Moon bringing far less light to the earth than the Sun.

Saturn in late antiquity was thought of as a dark and maleficent planet. Obsidian is a normally dark volcanic glass, that was used by the ancients for making tools such as sharp blades and arrowheads, tying it into the prehistoric Golden Age associated with Saturn (see Seventh Planetary Sphere – Saturn chapter).

It should be noted that red was the colour associated with Set. Most Egyptians during the decline of the Egyptian empire revered Osiris and hence avoided anything connected with Set. An examination of many Demotic magickal texts reveals numerous adjurations to avoid the colour red. This prohibition against the colour red was adopted for many centuries afterwards by Christians who viewed the devil as red in colour and regarded foreigners wearing items of red clothing with suspicion. A Graeco-Egyptian magickian who revered Osiris, or who worked for clients who revered Osiris would have been forced to look for an alternative for red. A number of animals were linked with Set including the red ox and the red donkey. In one festival, red donkeys were pushed off cliffs to symbolise the defeat of Set. It should be noted that red donkeys and red oxen are not actually red, but rather an orange-brown colour. Thus, in public, a Graeco-Egyptian magickian could conceivably have avoided the colours red and orange because of their association with Set.

Mars is the red planet, and was also thought of as maleficent by the ancients. Red is without a doubt the most appropriate colour for Mars, as it not only represents the colour of the planet, but the colour of the blood shed in battle by Arês, the god of war. However, as mentioned above, red was the colour associated with Set in late antiquity. Green is the flashing colour for red, meaning that if the colour green is focused on intently for a few minutes, red is seen once the eyes are closed. Yellow and green are colours of putrefaction which commonly resulted within a few days in wounds sustained on the battlefields. I think it reasonable to assume that those magickians who did not have a problem with Set would have used red for their private Mars rituals. A more appropriate gemstone for Arês than yellow-green onyx would have been one that was a deep red colour, such as garnet or ruby.

The Sumerians associated Inanna with Venus. Inanna was portrayed as tying small lapis beads around her neck, with double strands of beads falling to her breast, with a gold ring around her wrist, and a lapis measuring rod and line in her hand. Lapis lazuli is a blue stone with gold coloured iron pyrite intrusions. Clearly Venus, and hence Aphroditê, were being associated with Inanna by the choice of lapis lazuli. Thus we have the attribution of the colour blue with Venus, which indicates that the colour attributions for Mercury and Zeus are possibly in need of revision.

I will return to the planet Mercury, as there is insufficient information at this point to determine the colour properly attributed to it. However, as mentioned previously the red donkeys sacrificed to symbolise the defeat of Set were actually an orange-brown colour. We can thus treat orange and/or brown as possibilities for Mercury.

The Greeks, as well as the Jews, associated the colour purple with royalty. Hence, purple would be a very fitting colour for Zeus. The Sumerians, however, associated the colour white with royalty, as can been seen in the colour of the royal robe given to Inanna. The translation of the colour of the stone attributed to Zeus is in doubt and has been interpolated by the translator as dark blue, with crystal underneath. I am of the opinion that this is a mistake and that dark purple was meant. Even so, very dark blue and very dark purple can be difficult to distinguish. I believe that the gem meant by the Graeco-Egyptian magickian who wrote the text was amethyst. Very dark amethyst crystals feature dark purple points growing out of a crystal matrix. The crystal matrix actually appears white if a thick cross-section is viewed. If my theory is correct, a combination of purple and white, being the Greek and Sumerian colours of royalty, were sought in the one stone as an attribution to Jupiter.

As the available texts give no further clues as to the correct colours to be used, it is very relevant at this point to consider Babylonian planetary attributions. The Babylonians left behind a fantastic legacy in the form of their ziggurats. I was very excited when I came across references to some of the ziggurats having seven steps, each with a different colour. My research led to a bewildering array of colour schemes, and a lack of consistency in the attributions of the planets, suggested by a number of modern authors.

Herodotus is often mistakenly quoted as listing the colours of the steps in the great ziggurat in Babylon. A careful study of his writings relating to the Babylon ziggurat shows there were eight towers mounted on top of each other, and that the uppermost one was a temple largely of gold. I interpret this as referring to seven steps, surmounted by a temple (The History 1.181–1.183). The colours mentioned by Herodotus are actually those of the battlements of Ecbatana erected for Deioces by the Medes (The History 1.98). Regarding these, Herodotus, according to David Grene's translation, writes:

> *"The battlements of the first circle are white, the second black, the third scarlet, the fourth blue, the fifth orange. Thus the battlements of these five circles are painted with colours; but of*

the last two circles, the one had its battlements coated with silver, the other with gold."
[Selection from "*Herodotus: The History*" David Grene, trans.]

Scarlet is obviously a reference to red. I am focusing on primary and secondary colours.

Ernest Babelon in "*Manual of Oriental Antiquities*" states regarding the staged towers at Abu Shahrein in Chaldaea that:

"These towers always had, from the first, seven stages, each painted of a different colour, and connected with the workship of the sun (Samas), and the moon (Sin), and the five planets of the astronomical system of the Chaldeans."
[Selection from "*Manual of Oriental Antiquities*" Ernest Babelon]

See Appendix 1: Background to Graeco-Egyptian Magick for more information on the planetary deities of the Babylonians. In Babylon,

"... Nebuchadnezzar built, according to the testimony of his inscriptions, the famous tower of the Seven Lights."
[Selection from "*Manual of Oriental Antiquities*" Ernest Babelon]

A team of French archaeologists excavated the ziggurat of the palace at Khorsabad:

"The stages laid bare by the French excavations were still partly coloured by means of enamelled stucco, the lowest stage white, the second black, the third reddish purple and the fourth blue. Among the ruins of the remainder of the tower were found numerous fragments of enamelled bricks, coloured vermilion, silver grey and gold, which proves that the tower had seven stages of different colours."
[Selection from "*Manual of Oriental Antiquities*" Ernest Babelon]

Babelon subsequently discusses Herodotus's writings about the colours of the fortress of Ecbatana, in Media:

> *"The battlements of the first wall are white stone; those of the second of black stone; those of the fourth blue; those of the fifth vermilion. ... The two last walls are plated, the one with silver, the other with gold."*
> [Selection from "*Manual of Oriental Antiquities*" Ernest Babelon]

The reference to the third wall is unfortunately missing. Babelon refers to the fifth stage as being coloured vermilion. Comparing this to Grene's translation indicates that orange is meant.

Regarding the idea of a gold summit in Ecbatana and Khorsabad, Babelon points out that Nebuchadnezzar relates in his inscriptions that he overlaid the dome of the sanctuary of Bel Marduk "with plates of wrought gold so that it shone like the day." Also, among the ruins on the summit of the ziggurat at Abu Shahrein, were found:

> *"... a large quantity of thin plates of gold, still furnished with the gilded nails, which had served to fix them to the walls."*
> [Selection from "*Manual of Oriental Antiquities*" Ernest Babelon]

This is where things get interesting, as it can be seen that there is an almost direct correspondence between the colours of Herodotus and those found by the French archaeological expedition. If it is assumed that the ruins of the remaining three stages are orange, silver/grey and gold in ascending order, the following is found:

Table 18: Ecbatana and Khorsabad Ziggurat Colours

Step	Herodotus	Archaeological evidence
7	Gold	Gold
6	Silver	Silver/Grey
5	Orange	Orange
4	Blue	Blue
3	Red	Reddish purple
2	Black	Black
1	White	White

Reddish purple, making allowances for the ravages of time, is very close to scarlet, or red. It certainly appears that Herodotus has provided a list of planetary colours used by the Babylonians.

We know that gold and silver represent the Sun and Moon respectively. Blue was the colour attributed by the Sumerians and Babylonians to Inanna and hence, Venus. Red was the colour universally attributed to Mars. White was the colour attributed to Babylonian royalty and hence, Jupiter. Black was the colour associated with Saturn. By a process of elimination, this then leaves orange as the colour attributed to Mercury.

Let us consider the appropriateness of orange as the colour attributed to Mercury. The stone attributed by the Graeco-Egyptian magickians to Mercury was turquoise. Turquoise is a stone that normally ranges in colour from pale blue to bluish-green and is found throughout the Middle East and the Himalayas. Turquoise often has intrusions which are either black or orange in colour. To this day Himalayan craftsmen make jewellery combining Tibetan turquoise and amber. The amber used is a dull opaque orange colour, almost bordering on brown. It should be noted that just as in the case of Mars, where green and red are flashing colours, so for Mercury, blue and orange are flashing colours. As stated previously, the red donkeys associated with Set had an orange-brown colour, which is very reminiscent of amber. As stated earlier, the socially responsible Graeco-Egyptian magickian who avoided the colour red would have avoided the colour orange for good measure.

Thales (640?–547? BCE) of Miletus, Asia Minor, is credited with discovering that amber rubbed with wool or fur attracts light bodies of anything organic, such as small seeds, pieces of dry leaves, bits of straw, dust and pieces of cloth. Amber consequently was highly prized and thought of as magickal. All in all, it would seem that the Graeco-Egyptian magickians were implying orange as the colour, and possibly amber as the gemstone, attributed to Mercury.

I believe that another important key validating my usage of the colours quoted by Herodotus lies in the admonishment of the Graeco-Egyptian magickian (*PGM* CX: 1–12), who wrote "lay out the stars on the board in their natural order, with the exception of the sun and the moon." This implies the following order of planets: Sun, Moon, Mercury, Venus, Mars, Jupiter and Saturn. (This was known as the Platonic order of the planets. I shall be returning to the importance of this in a future chapter.) When these planets are listed in the order suggested by the text and the colour corrections detailed above are incorporated, we find:

Table 19: Graeco-Egyptian Planetary Colours

Planet	Deity	Graeco-Egyptian colour
Sun	Hêlios	Gold
Moon	Selênê (Mênê)	Silver
Mercury	Hermês	Turquoise blue/Orange
Venus	Aphroditê	Blue
Mars	Arês	Yellow-green/Red
Jupiter	Zeus	Dark purple and white
Saturn	Kronos	Black

It is then apparent that the order of planets is in perfect accord with the colour attributions given by Herodotus and the French excavations, for the upper five steps. The bottom two steps however, appear to have been interchanged. It is now appropriate to consider an essential difference between Greek and Sumerian cosmology. To the Greeks, Saturn/Kronos gave birth to Jupiter/Zeus and should precede him. To the Babylonians, Jupiter/Marduk was primary god, while Saturn/Ninurta was a god of vengeance subordinate to him. To the Babylonians it would have been logical to have the first step attributed to Jupiter/Marduk to symbolise their belief that he was the primary god. If the list provided by the Graeco-Egyptian magickians is amended by swapping Jupiter and Saturn, it becomes evident that the list of planetary attributions for the steps of the ziggurat is as follows:

Table 20: Babylonian Planetary Colours

Step	Colour	Planet
7	Gold	Sun
6	Silver	Moon
5	Orange	Mercury
4	Blue	Venus
3	Red	Mars
2	Black	Saturn
1	White	Jupiter

As an aside, I would recommend that should a series of invocations of the Babylonian gods be planned, it would be logical to start at the first step with Jupiter/Marduk. Each god should be invoked in sequence finishing with the Sun/Shamash. This could well be a very worthwhile exercise for the magickian prepared to experiment in order to determine the now forgotten proper pronunciation of the Babylonian god names.

Comparing the planetary colours of the Babylonians and the Graeco-Egyptian magickians:

Table 21: Comparison of Babylonian and Graeco-Egyptian Planetary Colours

Planet	Babylonian	Graeco-Egyptian
Moon	Silver	Silver
Mercury	Orange	Turquoise/Orange
Venus	Blue	Blue
Sun	Gold	Gold
Mars	Red	Yellow-green/Red
Jupiter	White	Purple/White
Saturn	Black	Black

Until more Graeco-Egyptian Magickal writings are found to verify or modify the Graeco-Egyptian colours listed above, I believe that the most accurate colours to use are those obtain by cross-referencing with those of the Babylonians. I am convinced that the Graeco-Egyptian magickians were very aware of the Babylonian colours as there are strong Sumerian and Babylonian influences in their spells.

Graeco-Egyptian Magick Opening Rite

This book represents a recreation of Graeco-Egyptian Magick. There were many Graeco-Egyptian magickians in the fourth and fifth centuries CE, and doubtless there were many approaches to working magick. Alas, most of the approaches are now lost to us, thanks to the pious efforts of the Church. What is available, however, I have incorporated into a "modular" system, beginning with the Opening Rite described in this chapter and ending with the Closing Rite described in the following chapter. The actual magickal working is slotted into the middle. As such, this modular system is suitable for all Graeco-Egyptian Magick applications of high magick.

The Opening Rite has been divided into segments for the sake of clarity. The bolded italic subtitles should obviously not be read out aloud when performing the rite. Instructions in the body of the ritual appear in italics.

Opening Rite

PGM XIII. 64–71 (First invocation of Aiôn)

"I call on you, who are greater than all, the creator of all,
you, the self-begotten, who see all and are not seen.
For you gave Hêlios the glory and all the power,
Selênê [the privilege] to wax and wane and have fixed courses,
yet you took nothing from the earlier-born darkness,
but apportioned things so that they should be equal.
For when you appeared, both order arose and light appeared.
All things are subject to you,
whose true form none of the gods can see;
who change into all forms.
You are invisible, Aiôn of Aiôn."

PGM XIII. 824–834 (Calling the Sevenths to induce equilibrium)

Face East – stretching out your right hand to the left
and your left hand, likewise to the left, chant "**A**"
Face North – putting forward only your right fist, chant "**E**"
Face West – extending both hands in front [of you], chant "**Ê**"
Face South – [holding] both on your stomach, chant "**I**"
Earth – face East, bending over, touching the ends of your toes, chant "**O**"
Air – face East, having your hand on your heart, chant "**U**"
Sky – face East, looking into the sky, having both hands on your head, chant "**Ô**"
Look straight ahead while facing East.

PGM XIII. 843–848 (First invocation of Ogdoas)

"I call on you, eternal and unbegotten, who are one,
who alone hold together the whole creation of all things,
whom none understands, whom the gods worship,
whose name not even the gods can utter.
Inspire from your exhalation (?), ruler of the pole,
him who is under you; create a ritual space."

PGM XIII. 849–851 (Homage to male-female duality)

"I call on you as by the voice of the male gods,
IÊÔ OUE ÔÊI UE AÔ EI ÔU AOÊ
OUÊ EÔA UÊI ÔEA OÊÔ IEOU AÔ.
I call on you, as by the voice of the female gods,
IAÊ EÔO IOU EÊl ÔA EÊ IÊ AI UO ÊIAU
EÔO OUÊE IAÔ ÔAI EOUÊ UÔÊI IÔA."

PGM XIII. 852–871 (Blasting open the portals with an expansion of the sevenths)

Face East and say
"I call on you, as the winds call you. I call on you, as the dawn,"
and chant "**A EE ÊÊÊ IIII OOOOO UUUUUU ÔÔÔÔÔÔÔ**"
Face South and say "I call on you as the South,"

and chant "**I OO UUU ÔÔÔÔ AAAAA EEEEEE ÊÊÊÊÊÊÊ**"
Face West and say "I call on you as the West,"
and chant "**Ê II OOO UUUU ÔÔÔÔÔ AAAAAA EEEEEEE**"
Face North and say "I call on you as the North"
and chant "**Ô AA EEE ÊÊÊÊ IIIII OOOOOO UUUUUUU**"
Earth – face East, look down and say "I call on you as the earth,"
and chant "**E ÊÊ III OOOO UUUUU ÔÔÔÔÔÔ AAAAAAA**"
Sky – face East, look straight ahead and say "I call on you as the sky,"
and chant "**U ÔÔ AAA EEEE ÊÊÊÊÊ IIIIII OOOOOOO"**
Cosmos – face East, look straight up, and say
"I call on you as the cosmos,"
and chant "**O UU ÔÔÔ AAAA EEEEE ÊÊÊÊÊÊ IIIIIII**"
Look straight ahead while facing East.

PGM XIII. 871–872 (Second invocation of Ogdoas)

"Create a vortex of energy, quickly.
I call on your name, the greatest among gods."

PGM XIII. 327–334 (Invocation of Aiôn and Hêlios)

"Open, open, four quarters of the cosmos,
for the lord of the inhabited world comes forth.
Archangels, decans, angels rejoice.
For Aiôn of Aiôn himself, the only and transcendant,
invisible, goes through this place.
Open, door! Hear, bar! Fall into two parts, lock!
By the name **AIA AINRUCHATH**,
cast up, Earth, for the lord, all things you contain,
for he is the storm-sender and controller of the abyss,
master of fire.
Open, for
ACHEBUKRÔM commands you!" *Repeat this line 8 times.*

[*Tr.: Morton Smith]

Commentary on Opening Rite

Most of the ancients venerated deities ascribed to the sun, including Attis, Shamash, Dionysus/Bacchus, Hercules/Hêraklês, Osiris, Mithras, Promêtheus, and Sarapis/Serapis. In homage to the sun, the Graeco-Egyptian magickians stood facing the East, with many rituals taking place at sunrise. The opening rite is no exception, and you should stand before an altar facing East.

In the case of a group ritual, I ask participants to take up positions in a circle around me, and also face East.

The bulk of the Opening Rite is taken from a lengthy invocation of Ogdoas (*PGM* XIII. 824–872), who is the god placed over the seven planetary spheres. Ogdoas rules the Ogdoad, which is the eighth sphere. He is described in *PGM* XIII. 742–746 as "the god who commands and directs all things, since to him angels, archangels, he-daimôns, she-daimôns, and all things under creation have been subjected."

Placed over Ogdoas is Aiôn, the Alexandrian god of eternity. The Opening Rite starts and finishes with an invocation to Aiôn as an additional safeguard. Aiôn is the god from whom all other gods emanated. (Both Ogdoas and Aiôn will be discussed fully in the sequel to this text.)

PGM XIII. 64–71 (First invocation of Aiôn)

The ritual begins with an invocation of Aiôn the god of gods for the purpose of protection. Most rituals in the PGM call on either the Sun (as Hêlios or Apollô), or the Moon (as Selênê or Mênê). This invocation highlights the fact that all deities, and indeed all of creation, have their origin in Aiôn. Truly someone having invoked the protection of Aiôn has nothing to fear and a protective circle is unnecessary.

PGM XIII. 824–834 (Calling the Sevenths to induce equilibrium)

In this portion of the Opening Rite, you are first brought into a state of equilibrium through "Calling the Sevenths" with chants directed in the seven directions. Each direction corresponds to a vowel. As each vowel chant is performed, a portal opening to the direction faced should be visualised. While singing each vowel is effective, harmonic chanting has been found to be even more effective.

It matters little how the portal is visualised so long as it is seen opening in the direction faced and stretching out to infinity. Participants in these rituals have seen portals as doorways, gates, elevator doors, tunnels and geometric shapes, just to name a few examples.

- Start by facing the East, look straight ahead, stretch out your right and left hands to the left, and chant "**A**." Visualise a portal opening to the East stretching out to infinity.
- Turn counter-clockwise through 90° to North, look straight ahead, put forward your right fist, leave your left arm by your side, and chant "**E**." Visualise a portal opening to the North stretching out to infinity.
- Turn counter-clockwise through 90° to West, look straight ahead, extend both hands in front of you, and chant "**Ê**." Visualise a portal opening to the West stretching out to infinity.
- Turn counter-clockwise through 90° to South, look straight ahead, hold both hands on your stomach, and chant "**I**." Visualise a portal opening to the South stretching out to infinity.
- Turn counter-clockwise through 90° to East, bend over, touch the ends of your toes, and chant "**O**." Visualise a portal opening to the depths of the Earth. Feel grounded and stable.
- Stand up straight, look straight ahead, have your right hand on your heart and your left hand by your side, and chant "**U**." Visualise a portal opening to the very Centre of your being. I personally like to focus on my heart. Feel yourself in the

present moment, the here and now. (It has been said that the past is a memory, the future is uncertain, and all you have to work with is the razor edge of the present.) The present moment is where you are truly powerful.

ξ Look straight up into the sky, place both hands on your head, and chant "**Ô**." Visualise a portal opening to the Cosmos stretching out to infinity connecting you with the depths of the universe.

In a group setting I ask participants to chant with me while facing the appropriate directions as detailed above.

PGM XIII. 843–848 (First invocation of Ogdoas)

Ogdoas is praised and described as the most important force in the universe. In the northern hemisphere, the heavens appear to rotate about the Pole Star. Ogdoas' identification as the ruler of the Pole reinforces his pivotal role in the Cosmos.

The original text after Ogdoas' praise reads "accomplish for me the NN thing" which has been incorporated into the structure of the spell to enable the adaptation of it for specific requirements. I have substituted a request to create a ritual space.

PGM XIII. 849–851 (Homage to male-female duality)

Homage is then paid to the duality of masculine and feminine polarity with a series of chants ascribed to the male and female deities.

A solitary practitioner would chant all of the vowels, while a male – female couple could share the chants.

In a group setting, I ask the male participants to hold a tone while I chant the "voice of the male gods" and I then ask the female participants to hold a tone while I chant the "voice of the female gods." The chants can take on a surreal quality in a group setting when performed this way.

PGM XIII. 852–871 (Blasting open the portals with an expansion of the sevenths)

The portals to the seven directions are revisited. This time the portals are visualised as totally open with maximum energy flowing unimpeded between you and your magickal universe, while chanting a lengthy series of vowels.

In my group rituals, participants visualise the process differently. Some feel themselves drawn into the portals as they are opened. Some participants have reported hearing spirit voices joining in the chanting.

The chants are seven uniquely distinct permutations of the seven vowel sounds, with the first vowel being chanted once, the second twice and so on. The length of the chant in each direction is indicative of the determination of the Graeco-Egyptian magickians to ensure that the portals were fully open. I affectionately refer to this process as "blasting" the portals open.

The Graeco-Egyptian magickians often inscribed magickal formulas to form geometric shapes. It is evident that the magickian who put together this ritual had a love of mathematics, geometry, and symmetry. The chant to the East could be visualised as follows:

A
E E
Ê Ê Ê
I I I I
O O O O O
U U U U U U
Ô Ô Ô Ô Ô Ô Ô

It will be remembered that when equilibrium was being attained, you moved counter-clockwise through the cardinal points. In order to balance this counter-clockwise movement, you will now move clockwise. This balancing of clockwise and counter-clockwise rotations is a recurring theme in Graeco-Egyptian Magick as will be seen in the Closing Rite chapter and in Appendix 3: Rotation and Counter-Rotation. While it has been lost in modern witchcraft and magick there are still solitary practitioners who intuitively draw their circles twice – clockwise and counter-clockwise.

Start with the East and move clockwise, stopping at each of the cardinal directions and "blasting" open the portals. As there are no instructions provided as to any postures to be assumed, I normally have my hands by my sides. Always be attentive to your intuition – if you feel moved to adopt a particular posture, do it.

To call Earth, turn to the East and look downwards. To call the Centre, referred to as Sky, continue to face the East and look straight ahead. To call the Cosmos, continue to face the East and look upwards.

In a group setting I ask participants to chant with me while facing the appropriate directions as detailed above.

PGM XIII. 871–872 (Second invocation of Ogdoas)

The original text states "Accomplish for me NN thing, quickly. I call on your name, the greatest among gods." I have substituted a request to create a vortex of energy. This is to energise the previously created ritual space.

PGM XIII. 327–334 (Invocation of Aiôn and Hêlios)

At the end of this segment of the Opening Rite, the original text contains the instruction "[Say **ACHEBUKRÔM**] 8 times; [it is] the name of Hêlios." This clearly identifies **ACHEBUKRÔM** as the word of power for Hêlios. *PGM* XIII. 446 similarly explains that this word of power "signifies the flame and radiance of the disk."

This segment can be seen as a request to Aiôn and Hêlios to open the four quarters of the cosmos. While Aiôn was seen as the principle god, Hêlios (representing the sun) was visible, accessible, and popularly considered as second in power only to Aiôn. To identify Hêlios with Aiôn is an example of the magickal use of flattery by the Graeco-Egyptian magickians.

It is important to note that this reverence of Hêlios is in contradiction to the classical Greek perception of Zeus being the most powerful of the gods and Hêlios being his subordinate.

The segment is ostensibly a spell to open doors, hence the statement "Open, door! Hear, bar! Fall into two parts, lock!" I believe that its use for opening doors was a later adaptation and that its original use was as part of an Opening Rite, hence its inclusion.

The original spell instructs you to "[Say **ACHEBUKRÔM**] 8 times." I find this vague, and actually repeat "**ACHEBUKRÔM** commands you" eight times. Eight is the number of the Ogdoad and hence represents an attempt to transcend the seven planetary spheres in order to be able to master them.

At this point the invocation to the planetary Sphere should be performed.

Abbreviated Framework Rite Based on the Sevenths

The Opening Rite is certainly ideal for all Graeco-Egyptian Magickal workings, especially in a group scenario. It is however, time consuming.

What if you wish to quickly assume a spiritually receptive frame of mind, perhaps for a divination, or a daily adoration? Experimentation has shown that the Opening and Closing Rites can be abbreviated to an expansion of the segment of the Opening Rite where the Sevenths are called:

- ξ Face East, contemplate Aiôn with heart and mind.
- ξ Call the Sevenths while rotating counter-clockwise from cardinal point to cardinal point.
- ξ Rotate 360° clockwise to restore balance, while asking Aiôn to create a ritual space.
- ξ Perform the magickal working.
- ξ Call the Sevenths again while rotating counter-clockwise from cardinal point to cardinal point, but this time visualise the portals closing.
- ξ Rotate 360° clockwise to restore balance, while giving thanks to Aiôn.

This Abbreviated Framework Rite can be performed physically, astrally or visualised. It is thus quick and discrete.

Note: This Abbreviated Framework Rite is both an opening and a closing rite, with the difference being in whether the portals are visualised opening or closing whilst chanting.

Graeco-Egyptian Magick Closing Rite

Once the deity being invoked has been dismissed, it is necessary to close down the energy in the ritual space. The Closing Rite is taken from the end of a lengthy self-initiation rite dedicated to Aiôn.

Closing Rite

PGM XIII. 641-646

Having drawn in spirit with all your senses
Face East and with one breath chant "**ÔAÔÊ ÔÔ EOÊIAÔ**."
Face South and chant "**III**."
Face North and chant "**AAÔ**."
Face West and chant "**THÊ**."
Kneel to the left on your right knee,
Stand, and keep rotating until East is again faced.
Look down at the Earth and chant "**THOU**."
Look up at (or visualise) the Moon and chant "**THÊ**."
Look up at (or visualise) the Water and chant "**AATHÔ**."
Look up at the Sky (cosmos) and chant "**ATHÊROUÔ**."
[*Tr.: Morton Smith]

Commentary on Closing Rite

Start by facing the East and sequentially close off the portals by chanting words of power while visualising them closing. The shape of the portal being visualised is unimportant, so long as it is seen and felt to close.

The initial instruction states that you must be infused with spiritual energy through all the senses. This means that the energy must be tangible – it should be seen, heard, felt, smelt and tasted. I suggest breathing in with the eyes closed and visualising the energy to be as tangible as possible.

Facing East chant "**ÔAÔÊ ÔÔ EOÊIAÔ**," with one breath while visualising the portal closing.

Turn 90° clockwise to South and chant "**III**" while visualising the portal closing.

Turn 180° clockwise to North and chant "**AAÔ**" while visualising the portal closing.

This makes a total clockwise rotation of 270°.

Turn 90° counter-clockwise to West and chant "**THÊ**" while visualising the portal closing.

Turn 90° counter-clockwise to South, kneel down on the right knee once, stand up and turn a further 90° counter-clockwise to East and look down to the depths of the Earth, and chant "**THOU**" while visualising the portal closing.

This makes a total counter-clockwise rotation of 270°.

It should be noted here that in the Opening Rite, you turned 360° counter-clockwise during the equilibrium attainment and then 360° clockwise while "blasting" (see Opening Rite Chapter for clarification) to balance the rotation. Here you turn 270° clockwise and then 270° counter-clockwise. As you are not working within a circle, the emphasis is to access all seven directions while maintaining rotational balance. (The balancing of clockwise and counter-clockwise movements is a recurring theme in Graeco-Egyptian Magick and is discussed in Appendix 3: Rotation and Counter-Rotation.)

The centre is not visualised as a single direction in this rite. It is divided between Moon and Water. This is quite appropriate as the Moon represents the subconscious and dreams, while Water represents the emotions.

Face (or imagine) the Moon, visualise a portal to it, and then visualise this closing, and chant "**THÊ**."

Face (or imagine) a body of Water, visualise a portal to it, and then visualise this closing, and chant "**AATHÔ**."

The only problem that has been reported with this Rite is occasional difficulty in disconnecting from the Moon and Water portals. The easiest way to overcome this is through a conscious awareness of the equivalence of these portals with the Centre portal of the Opening Rite.

Finally, look straight up and visualise the portal to the Cosmos (referred to as Sky) closing, and chant "**ATHÊROUÔ**."

Once the portals are all closed off, any energy not absorbed or channelled should be grounded. This can be as simple as visualising the energy going back into the Universe from whence it came, and exercising will power to ensure that it happens. Once the ambient energy is at its pre-ritual level, you may leave the area.

At the end of the original spell, the scribe attached the note "(36 letters)." A count of the number of letters in the Closing Rite confirms that are indeed 36 letters used in the words of power (remembering that TH is Theta). While some scholars believe that such notes were a quick check for the scribe to confirm that the words of power had been transcribed correctly, the widespread use of isopsephy suggests that this may not be the case. For information about isopsephy, see the Greek Thread section of Appendix 1: Background to Graeco-Egyptian Magick.

Here, the numerological significance of 36 possibly refers to the Decans. (Decan comes from the Greek word for "ten.") The Decans are the 36 deities each of whom presides over 10° of the ecliptic. These are belts of stars extending around the heavens, the risings of which followed each other by ten days or so. The Decans were originally prominent in Egyptian tradition.

E A Wallis Budge provides a list of the Decans and the Gods of the Decans in "*The Gods of the Egyptians.*" While interesting, knowledge of the Decans is not essential to successfully practising the Closing Rite.

In a group ritual, I ask the participants to face the same directions as I do and visualise the portals closing.

Not surprisingly, performing this rite near a stream or at the seaside under a full moon leads to breathtaking experiences.

Journalise results as soon as possible after the ritual so that nothing is forgotten.

First Planetary Sphere – Moon

This Sphere marks the beginning of the spiritual path and the first stirrings of awareness. It is here that you first start to explore the hidden realms through dreams. The connection between sexuality and spirituality becomes understood. Cycles and change start to become more apparent.

Apart from the Sun, no other celestial object has as much of an effect upon the Earth and its inhabitants as the Moon. The lunar cycles are linked with the tides and menstruation, and have been traditionally used by farmers to optimise times for planting and reaping. The full moon has been linked with behavioural changes in humans and animals.

Of all of the planetary energies, the lunar energy is the easiest to discern. It is thus fitting that the spiritual path should begin here.

Goddess Invoked	Selênê (Mênê)
Key properties	Beginning of the spiritual path. Sleep, fertility, cycles, change.
(+)	Generation, growth and movement, sleep and dreams.
(–)	Energy of waning, inability to adapt to change.
Fragrance	Myrrh
Colour	Silver
Gemstone/Metal	Silver

Mythology

The moon goddess, Selênê (otherwise known as Mênê) was the sister of the sun god, Hêlios. Selênê's golden crown illuminated the night sky. Every night Selênê would begin her journey across the heavens after her brother had finished his. She was portrayed as clad in splendid robes riding across the sky in a chariot drawn by two white horses, mules or cows. Sometimes she was portrayed as mounted on a horse, a mule or a bull. The horns of the bull and cows symbolised the crescent moon.

Her beauty attracted Zeus the greatest of the Olympic gods. Through Selênê, Zeus fathered three daughters: Pandia, Erse and Nemea. In one legend, the Nemean Lion, which fell from the moon to the earth, was also reputed to be born to them.

The best known legend of Selênê is that of her love for Endymiôn. One version has Endymiôn as a young prince who, tired from hunting, fell asleep in a cool grotto. When Selênê saw him, she was captivated by his beauty and stole a kiss. Endymiôn asked Zeus to grant him immortality and eternal youth. Zeus agreed on the condition that Endymiôn remain eternally asleep. Selênê then came silently every night to contemplate her sleeping lover.

In Nonnus' *Dionysiaca*, Selênê was described as ruling "distracted madness" and exciting lunacy equally with Bakkhos (Bacchus). Bakkhos was the Roman god of drunks and lunatics who was equated with the Greek god, Dionysus.

In later legends, Selênê was identified with Artemis, Hekatê, Persephonê and other lunar goddesses. She became regarded as a huntress and archer. In most classical literature, Selênê was referred to as the only moon goddess.

Selênê had a number of titles:

- Aiglê – moon-light, gleam, radiance
- Eileithyia – come to aid or relieve childbirth
- Pasiphae – all-shining

Orphic Hymn VIII: To Selênê (Mênê)

Hear, Goddess queen, diffusing silver light,
Bull-horned and wandering through the gloom of Night.
With stars surrounded, and with circuit wide
Night's torch extending, through the heavens you ride:
Female and Male with borrowed rays you shine,
And now full-orbed, now tending to decline.
Mother of ages, fruit-producing Moon,
Whose amber orb makes Night's reflected noon:
Lover of horses, splendid, queen of Night,
All-seeing power bedecked with starry light.
Lover of vigilance, the foe of strife,
In peace rejoicing, and a prudent life:
Fair lamp of Night, its ornament and friend,

Who gives to Nature's works their destined end.
Queen of the stars, all-wise Artemis hail!
Decked with a graceful robe and shining veil;
Come, blessed Goddess, prudent, starry, bright,
Come moony-lamp with chaste and splendid light,
Shine on these sacred rites with prosperous rays,
And pleased accept your suppliant's mystic praise.

[Selection from "*The Hymns of Orpheus*" Thomas Taylor, trans.]

Homeric Hymn XXXII: To Selênê (Mênê)

And next, sweet voiced Muses, daughters of Zeus,
well-skilled in song, tell of the long-winged Moon.
From her immortal head a radiance is shown
from heaven and embraces earth;
and great is the beauty that ariseth from her shining light.
The air, unlit before, glows with the light of her golden crown,
and her rays beam clear,
whensoever bright Selênê having bathed her lovely body
in the waters of Ocean,
and donned her far-gleaming, shining team,
drives on her long-maned horses at full speed,
at eventime in the mid-month:
then her great orbit is full
and then her beams shine brightest as she increases.
So she is a sure token and a sign to mortal men.
Once the Son of Kronos was joined with her in love;
and she conceived and bare a daughter Pandia,
exceeding lovely amongst the deathless gods.
Hail, white-armed goddess, bright Selênê, mild, bright-tressed queen!
And now I will leave you and sing the glories of men half-divine,
whose deeds minstrels, the servants of the Muses, celebrate with lovely lips.

[Selection from "*Hesiod, Homeric Hymns, Epic Cycle, Homerica*" Hugh G Evelyn-White, trans.]

Graeco-Egyptian Magick Invocation to Selênê (Mênê)

Either face East, or turn to face the Moon (if it is visible). Burn myrrh resin, anoint your forehead with myrrh oil and chant "**AKTIÔPHIS**."

PGM VII. 756–94

"I call upon you who have all forms and many names,
double-horned goddess, **MÊNÊ**, whose form no one knows
except him who made the entire world,
IAÔ, the one who shaped [you]
into the 28 shapes of the world
so that you might complete every figure
and distribute breath
to every animal and plant, that it might flourish,
you who wax from obscurity into light
and wane from light into darkness.

Say the following words and articulate the corresponding sounds:

And the first companion of your name is silence,
The second a popping sound,
The third groaning,
The fourth hissing,
The fifth a cry of joy,
The sixth moaning,
The seventh barking,
The eighth bellowing,
The ninth neighing,
The tenth a musical sound,
The eleventh a sounding wind,
The twelfth a wind-creating sound,
The thirteenth a coercive sound,
The fourteenth a coercive emanation from perfection."

Say the following words and visualise them sequentially:

"Ox, vulture, bull, beetle, falcon, crab, dog,
wolf, serpent, horse, she-goat, asp, goat, he-goat,

baboon, cat, lion, leopard, fieldmouse, deer, multiform,
virgin, torch, lightning, garland, a herald's wand, child, key.

I have said your signs and symbols of your name
so that you might hear me, because I pray to you,
mistress of the whole world.
Hear me, you, the stable one, the mighty one,
**APHEIBOÊÔ MINTÊR OCHAÔ PIZEPHUDÔR
CHANTHAR CHADÊROZO MOCHTHION
EOTNEU PHÊRZON AINDÊS LACHABOÔ
PITTÔ RIPHTHAMER ZMOMOCHÔLEIE
TIÊDRANTEIA OISOZOCHABÊDÔPHRA**."
[*Tr.: W C Grese]

Meditation

Experience the planetary energy through meditation. Eyes may be open or shut. Certain tangible things will happen which should not be feared but embraced. Let your intuition guide you as to how long you should stay in this state.

Eucharist

Consume the eucharist so as to absorb additional lunar energy. See the Ritual Preliminaries chapter for more details.

Dismissal

"I have said your signs and symbols of your name
so that you might hear me, because I pray to you,
mistress of the whole world.
Hear me, you, the stable one, the mighty one,
**APHEIBOÊÔ MINTÊR OCHAÔ PIZEPHUDÔR
CHANTHAR CHADÊROZO MOCHTHION
EOTNEU PHÊRZON AINDÊS LACHABOÔ
PITTÔ PIPHTHAMER ZMOMOCHÔLEIE
TIÊDRANTEIA OISOZOCHABÊDÔPHRA**.
I thank you for having come to me, **MÊNÊ**,
and may you always be a part of my life."
[*Tr.: W C Grese]

Commentary on Graeco-Egyptian Invocation to Selênê (Mênê)

The word to be chanted while anointing your forehead with myrrh oil is "**AKTIÔPHIS**." This word of power appears a number of times in the PGM and refers to Selênê, as explicitly shown below in two very similar spells:

> *"But you, **AKTIÔPHIS**, Mistress, Selênê, Only Ruler, Swift Fortune of daimôns and gods..."*

PGM *IV. 2602*

> *"But you, **AKTIÔPHIS**, Mistress, Selênê, Only Ruler, The Fortune of daimôns and gods..."*

PGM *IV. 2664*

The connection between Selênê and Mênê is shown explicitly below:

> *"And heed my prayers, Selênê,*
> *Who suffer much, who rise and set at night,*
> *O triple-headed, triple named **MÊNÊ MARZOUNÊ**..."*

PGM *IV. 2545–2548*

PGM VII. 756–94

In the first paragraph, the word of power used is **IAÔ**, who is referred to as the creator of the world. This is a common magickal name originally derived from the Hebrew god, known as YHWH (often erroneously transliterated as Yahweh or Jehovah) in the Torah or Old Testament, and traditionally referred to as the Tetragrammaton by those who practice magick. In *PGM* V. 24-30 [*Tr.: W C Grese], there is an interesting performance instruction that **IAÔ** should be pronounced "to earth, to air, to heaven." This appears to link the magickian with the underworld and heaven.

After this, Mênê is described as being aspected to "the 28 shapes of the world" which is a reference to the 28 days of the lunar month. (This technique is also used in a number of solar invocations, where there are characteristics associated with each of the 12 hours of the day.)

Mênê is described as one who will "distribute breath to every animal and plant" which is a reference to her connection with fertility and the cycles of menstruation and planting.

"You who wax from obscurity into light and wane from light into darkness," is a reference to the waxing and waning of the moon.

The theme of 28 is resumed, as the spell requires making 14 sounds and then visualising 28 objects. Half a lunar month is of course 14 days. All of the sounds and visualisations are of things that were familiar to the magickians of Alexandria, so wherever possible you should be mindful of their world.

I have performed this ritual with numerous groups and some of the sounds invariably lead to embarrassment or amusement. The end result however, justifies any negative feelings during the ritual.

14 sounds

The explanation of the sounds that I use within my group rituals follows:

1 silence.
2 popping sound – forcibly separate pressed lips.
3 groaning – as if exerting (to distinguish it from "moaning").
4 hissing – simulate a snake.
5 cry of joy – laugh out loud.
6 moaning – as if in pain (should be distinguished from "groaning").
7 barking – simulate a dog.
8 bellowing – roar like a bull.
9 neighing – simulate a horse.
10 musical sound – humming noise or singing a note (but not whistling).
11 sounding wind – simulate the wind whistling through the trees.
12 wind-creating sound – blowing sound (which results in the wind whistling).
13 coercive sound – cry "Oiy!" in a commanding fashion.
14 coercive emanation from perfection – a spontaneous sound (such as a sigh) made whilst experiencing something wondrous which entices others to also wish to share it. A good example is climbing to the top of a cliff or hill top and beholding a magnificent view.

28 visions

The explanation of the visions that I use within my group rituals follows:

1. ox
2. vulture – the goddess Nekhbet
3. bull – the Apis bull
4. beetle – the scarab beetle
5. falcon – the god Horus
6. crab – the Nile crab
7. dog – the Saluki
8. wolf
9. serpent – Apophis/Apep (or any Egyptian snake except a cobra to distinguish from an "asp")
10. horse
11. she-goat – nanny goat (to distinguish from "goat" and "he-goat")
12. asp – the Egyptian cobra, perhaps the goddess Wadjet
13. goat – a kid (to distinguish from "she-goat" and "he-goat")
14. he-goat – billy goat (to distinguish from "she-goat" and "goat")
15. baboon – the dog-faced baboon form of the god Thoth
16. cat – the goddess Bast
17. lion – the god Aker or the goddess Sekhmet
18. leopard
19. fieldmouse – (these were familiar in households and often used in magick)
20. deer
21. multiform – compound animal, such as a griffin, basilisk, or chimera
22. virgin – vestal virgin in diaphanous robes
23. torch – similar to the Olympic torch
24. lightning
25. garland – laurel wreath
26. herald's wand – short wand held by messengers which gave them the authority to speak; it consisted of three shoots, one of which formed the handle, the other two being knotted at

the top; the knot was later replaced by serpents to form the caduceus (kerykeion)

27. child
28. key

Some of the visions in this ritual are also used in an invocation of Hekatê Ereschigal (*PGM* LXX.9–11). Hekatê is the goddess of the dark moon. She was often associated with Ereschigal (Erisch-ki-gal), who was a Babylonian underworld goddess. In this invocation, Hekatê Ereschigal is called upon to protect against punishment in the underworld. The required visions are – "Ereschigal, virgin, bitch, serpent, wreath, key, herald's wand, golden sandal of the Lady of Tartaros." Such an overlap is not unexpected given that both invocations are for lunar energies. (Hekatê will be experienced in the sequel to this book.)

Meditation and Eucharist

For the remaining Planetary Spheres chapters I have referred to the Ritual Performance and Ritual Preparation chapters for more information on Meditation and Eucharist.

Spells not used

There are a number of lunar spells which I have not incorporated into this ritual. These spells are *PGM* IV. 2241–2358, *PGM* IV. 2446–2621, *PGM* IV. 2622–2707, *PGM* IV. 2708–84, and *PGM* IV. 2785–2890.

These have very few words of power and employ symbolism which is not readily understood. With one exception, each of these spells call on more than one lunar goddess, from the following: Selênê, Mênê, Korê, Persephonê, Hekatê and Artemis. (Artemis will be experienced in the sequel to this book.)

Procedure for initiation

To summarise the process in the Ritual Preparation chapter, you should:

- ξ dress in as much silver or grey as possible,
- ξ wear silver jewellery,
- ξ anoint with myrrh oil and burn myrrh incense,
- ξ study the mythology of Selênê,
- ξ recite the Orphic and Homeric Hymns to Selênê.

These processes are synergistic and wearing the clothing, jewellery and essential oil on a daily basis should intensify their influence. For the remaining Planetary Spheres chapters I have not specifically stated the above summary information but have indicated "Bringing the planetary energies into everyday life" in the Ritual Performance chapter for a summary of these procedures.

When you feel ready, the Graeco-Egyptian Magick Invocation of Selênê (Mênê) should be performed. This ritual works particularly well when the Moon is full. The Practical requirements for Graeco-Egyptian Magick rituals section in the Ritual Performance chapter detail how this should be done. Here, the practical and theoretical requirements come together and the initiation process is greatly accelerated.

The invocation opens wide a door for lunar energy to enter your life, leading to gifts as well as challenges. It is important to repeatedly invoke the lunar energy until no further directly attributable changes occur in life and everything has been assimilated and understood. The lunar gifts and challenges will not end at this point, but may well be intensified as the energies of subsequent planetary Spheres are experienced.

Results

If you are reading this portion of the chapter, I assume that you have already invoked Selênê (Mênê) with the ritual above. If you haven't, stop reading and do so now!

The Graeco-Egyptian Magick Invocation of Selênê (Mênê) opens wide a door for lunar energy to enter your life. For those who have little previous magickal experience, the first stirrings of spirituality are felt, and for those who had doubts as to the reality of spiritual phenomena tangible proof manifests. This tangible proof can take the form of feeling temperature fluctuations, feeling your body being moved by an unseen force, and in the case of group rituals, sharing similar visions with other participants.

Sometimes the results obtained do not immediately appear to be directly related to the lunar sphere, but rather are indicative of increasing spiritual awareness. For example, a couple met just before a lunar ritual and moved in together shortly afterwards. Their spiritual compatibility was a major factor. Another couple realised the importance of listening to their intuition and bought a successful business together.

Dreams, whilst asleep and daydreams whilst awake, become more intense and normally hidden realms are explored. Dreams should be recorded in a journal and examined for meanings. Sometimes meanings are not clear at the time, but become so in the context of events and subsequent dreams.

The lunar energy is connected with sensuality. The way sensuality ties in with spirituality should be explored. This is a very personal journey.

There is a greater awareness of cycles in life and in nature. Harmonising with these cycles is invariably more productive than fighting against them.

The lunar energy has a negative side which result in tests. Any resistance to change must be fought against. There may also be experiences of delusion, and so any insights or visions should be scrutinised carefully.

Specific results which have occurred in group rituals invoking Selênê (Mênê) include:

The 28 visions

- ξ There was no general rule for how the 28 visions were perceived. Some participants had difficulty seeing all of them.

For some they were the same size and crystal clear. Some participants saw the animals as quite active and constantly in movement. Some saw the animals transform into each other. Some saw the animals individually, while others saw them as interacting with each other and even running into the ritual area to join the participants. On cold days, the animals were sometimes seen brushing up against participants to keep warm.

Presence of energy in ritual area

- ξ Sometimes the lunar energy came into the ritual area as a burst of wind even though the day was calm. If the day was already windy, the wind whipped up and become stronger. The wind sometimes came from a different direction to normal.
- ξ On cold days, some participants felt the cold before the invocation, but then warmed when the lunar energy came in. This warmth sometimes encompassed the whole body or was sometimes limited to the feet or hands. Many associated this feeling of warmth with having the potential to heal.
- ξ Some participants experienced the energy as a light that surrounded and encompassed them. For others, it was a spiral of energy that embraced them. Some actually perceived arms reaching out, rocking them gently and comforting them.
- ξ Many participants swayed during the ritual. The swaying was usually a circular movement, but sometimes was a rocking motion either backwards and forwards or from left to right. The swaying varied in intensity from participant to participant. Some participants were spun around in different directions. Some worried that they would fall over, but in six years of rituals, no participant has. Some found themselves interacting with the lunar energy in a physical way by moving with it. Occasionally a participant felt a need to dance.
- ξ Some participants experienced a peaceful feeling of wanting to lie or sit on the ground. Others were forced and felt as if their legs were shaking and they had a need to kneel, squat or lay down. Sometimes, this came as a feeling of being prodded, or

some other pain that forced them to bend down. Some felt that they were almost knocked to the ground. For some participants there was a feeling of having no control over what was happening which led to fear. Some tried to relax but strove too hard and obtained less than optimal results. Some participants, who resisted the energy coming in, felt their bodies starting to shake.

- Participants often felt that their legs were like lead and rooted to the spot. Their upper body felt light as if it would float away. Some participants felt their arms raising up or moved their hands in circles.
- Many participants reported feeling empowered.

Quality of energy

- The lunar energy was quite youthful, with some perceiving it as having a light dancing quality.
- Participants felt loved, comforted, at peace, secure and safe, calm, and very mellow. There was often an absence of fear and a feeling of freedom.
- Some participants experienced Selênê in a very sensual way, and even perceived her as a temptress figure. Participants reported feeling a woman's hair blowing on their face. Others felt as though they were being stroked down their backs or across their faces. Some participants were filled with an overwhelming desire to kiss someone, or felt themselves being kissed by Selênê on the mouth. In some this progressed to more erotic feelings. A small number of participants have experienced an orgasmic release during this ritual, while a few have approached this state.

Experiences through physical senses

- A number of participants saw the Moon become brighter, bigger, or actually drawn down in front of clouds. Some participants saw a bright light or flame around the moon.

- Some participants saw a second moon, a spiritual moon. Those who normally see the second moon perceived it as having moved further way.
- Some participants saw the stars change colours.
- Some participants saw things with their peripheral vision. They perceived things occurring amongst the shadows in the dark.

Experiences through non-physical senses

- Things became most interesting when the eyes were closed. Some participants had rapid flashes of visions. Some of these visions were very erotic.
- Some participants saw a temple or the steps of a temple. The temple had a white marble floor and columns reaching up to the sky.
- At the beginning of a ritual one participant saw lava streams through the earth portal, and at the end saw hands coming up not wanting the portal closed. Two people did not participate in this particular ritual as they felt nausea before it started. A few hours after the ritual there was an earthquake. These incidents highlighted the strong connection that some participants have with the earth.
- Occasionally, participants felt a strong connection with water to the extent that they either visualised it or felt themselves under water. A few heard or smelt the ocean despite not being anywhere near it. Some had visions of scrying in water.
- Many participants felt someone moving around the ritual or saw someone either moving or dancing around the ritual area.

Visions of Selênê (Mênê)

- Elements of Selênê seen included a young beautiful woman, long dark hair, dark face, the epitome of female sexuality, luscious full lips, dark eye makeup, horns on her head, wearing an Isis crown with the lunar crescent, white dress, sometimes with silver accents, wearing a cape, sometimes dancing down the steps of her temple.

Messages received

- ξ Because this was their first Graeco-Egyptian ritual, some participants asked for confirmation that they were on the right path.
- ξ Many participants sought to realise who they are and visualised layers peeling away, revealing what they believed to be their true self.
- ξ Some participants saw reflections of themselves in a mirror or in a body of water, leading to an understanding of themselves and a sense of clarity.
- ξ Some made requests or asked for inner peace. Some visualised being given gifts which they had to interpret or were given instructions such as needing to develop more focus. Others sought an understanding of the effects of lunar phases on people.

Astral experiences

- ξ Because the lunar energy is connected with the astral, some participants asked for help when going into the astral, or felt a strong desire to go on a journey.
- ξ Some experienced the early stages of astral projection, such as the activation of the astral senses. This involved seeing the moon and their immediate environment clearly even though their eyes were closed.
- ξ Some participants who wanted to astral travel experienced a test where fear needed to be overcome. Faith needed to be developed that these tests would not harm. As an example, sensations of bugs and spiders crawling on the body were experienced. Distractions and fears are a sure way of ending an astral journey, or of preventing it from happening.
- ξ Some participants felt themselves pulled out of their body. Some had a sensation of travelling through space, and seeing numerous colours. Some were drawn to places on high, and perceived themselves floating over mountains, around the world, into the solar system, or beyond into the cosmos.

The gifts and challenges of the Lunar Sphere never actually come to an end. As the energies of subsequent planetary spheres are experienced, the gifts of the Lunar Sphere may well be intensified. Dreams eventually give way to lucid dreaming and astral projection experiences. The exploration of sensuality develops into a profound understanding of its function in spirituality. The scrutiny of insights and visions eventually develops into a keen sense of discrimination and intuition.

Second Planetary Sphere – Mercury

This Sphere marks acquiring wisdom and applying it to the lessons of the Lunar Sphere. The wisdom obtained facilitates healing, communication and travel. Spiritual abilities are honed to the extent that the first steps towards becoming a magickian are taken.

God Invoked	Hermês
Key properties	Intellect, knowledge, commerce, travel, healing and magick.
(+)	Communication, travel, reason, intellect to express and interpret.
(-)	Fraud, greed for gain, using intellect for evil.
Fragrance	Cassia
Colour	Orange
Gemstone/Metal	Turquoise (or amber)

Mythology

Legend has it that Hermês was the son of Zeus and Maia. Maia was a Naiad and the daughter of Atlas. (For more information about Zeus see the Sixth Planetary Sphere – Jupiter chapter.) Hermês was born one morning, invented the lyre by noon, stole fifty head of cattle from his brother Apollô which he hid in a cave, and returned to his crib.

Apollô by means of his prophetic power, divined that Hermês was responsible and took him before Zeus. Hermês so impressed Apollô with his playing of the lyre, that in exchange for the lyre, Apollô allowed Hermês to keep the cattle and gifted him the golden staff of fortune and riches, and with some small ability in divination and prophecy. Zeus made Hermês herald to the gods and guide of the dead in Hadês. Hermês' attributes are seen here as inventiveness, versatility, trickery and cunning.

In Arcadia, Hermês was seen as a god who ensured the fertility of pastures and herds. Elsewhere, he was a god of crops, as well as mining and seeking buried treasure.

Hermês was a god of roads and a patron of travellers. This role included conducting the souls of the dead into the afterlife, as a psychopomp. His chthonic aspect (meaning that he was associated with the underworld) was particularly evident in the Curse Tablets, where he was often associated with Dêmêter and Hekatê, and was referred to as "Hermês of the Underworld" and "Hermês the Restrainer" ("*katochos*").

As travel was normally engaged in for trading, Hermês became associated with commerce, and hence profit. The idea of profit was then extended to include thievery, trickery and games of chance. Successful trading requires good communication skills and so this also became the province of Hermês.

These characteristics of Hermês made him well suited to a role as the messenger of the gods, a task that he carried out with great diplomacy and tact. In this role, he was associated with learning, mental and physical agility, and was honoured by athletes.

Hermês was particularly adept at carrying out Zeus' commands, as demonstrated when he slew Argos. Hermês was the sacrificial herald of the gods, and in imitation of this, heralds would assist in sacrifices.

In later times, Hermês became known as the inventor of writing, mathematics, astronomy and music. He was generally thought of as the archetypal magickian. He was the god of sleep and dreams. In the PGM writings Hermês was often seen as a sender of dreams and a means of making businesses more successful.

Hermês had a capricious side to his nature as shown in a number of myths where he punished various people who had displeased him by magickally transforming them into stones, birds and a tortoise.

The earliest representations of Hermês were of a mature man with long beard and long hair. Later he was portrayed as a young athletic runner, wearing a round winged hat and winged sandals. He carried the caduceus (kerykeion), a long staff around which two serpents were entwined, symbolising good health and healing.

Hermês had a number of cult titles. The following is a selection of titles:

- Agoraios – of the market place
- Dolios – of crafts, of wiles

- ξ Enagônios – of the games
- ξ Epimêlios – keeper of the flocks
- ξ Herméneutês – interpretor, translator
- ξ Promakhos – champion

Orphic Hymn XXVII: To Hermês

Hermês, draw near, and to my prayer incline,
Angel of Zeus, and Maia's son divine;
Studious of contests, ruler of mankind,
With heart almighty, and a prudent mind.
Celestial messenger, of various skill,
Whose powerful arts could watchful Argus kill:
With winged feet, it is yours through air to course,
O friend of man, and prophet of discourse:
Great life-supporter, to rejoice is yours,
In arts gymnastic, and in fraud divine:
With power endued all language to explain,
Of care the loosener, and the source of gain.
Whose hand contains of blameless peace the rod,
Corucian, blessed, profitable God:
Of various speech, whose aid in works we find,
And in necessities to mortals kind:
Dire weapon of the tongue, which men revere,
Be present, Hermês, and your suppliant hear;
Assist my works, conclude my life with peace,
Give graceful speech, and memory's increase.

[Selection from "*The Hymns of Orpheus*" Thomas Taylor, trans.]

Homeric Hymn XVIII: To Hermês

I sing of Cyllenian Hermês, the Slayer of Argus,
lord of Cyllene and Arcadia rich in flocks,
luck-bringing messenger of the deathless gods.
He was born of Maia, the daughter of Atlas,
when she had made with Zeus, – a shy goddess she.
Ever she avoided the throng of the blessed gods
and lived in a shadowy cave,
and there the Son of Kronos used to lie
with the rich-tressed nymph at dead of night,

while white-armed Hêra lay bound in sweet sleep:
and neither deathless god nor mortal man knew it.
And so hail to you, Son of Zeus and Maia;
with you I have begun: now I will turn to another song!
Hail, Hermês, giver of grace, guide, and giver of good things!

[Selection from "*Hesiod, Homeric Hymns, Epic Cycle, Homerica*" Hugh G Evelyn-White, trans.]

Graeco-Egyptian Magick Invocation to Hermês

Face East.

Burn powdered cassia bark, anoint your hair with cassia oil and chant: "**PSUCHOPOMPOIAPS**."

PGM VIII. 1–63

"Come to me, lord Hermês,
as foetuses do to the wombs of women.
Come to me, lord Hermês,
who collect the sustenance of gods and men;
[come] to me, lord Hermês,
and give me favour, sustenance, victory, prosperity, elegance, beauty of face, strength of all men and women.
Your names in heaven:
LAMPHTHEN OUÔTHI OUASTHEN OUÔTHI OAMENÔTH ENTHOMOUCH.
These are the [names] in the four quarters of heaven.

I also know what your forms are:
in the East you have the form of an ibis,
in the West you have the form of a dog-faced baboon,
in the North you have the form of a serpent,
and in the South you have the form of a wolf.

Your plant is the grape which is the olive.
I also know your wood: ebony.
I know you, Hermês who you are and where you come from and what your city is: Hermopolis.
Come to me, lord Hermês, many-named one,
who know the things hidden beneath heaven and earth.

Come [to me], lord Hermês;
serve well, benefactor of the world.
Hear me and make me agreeable
to all the forms throughout the inhabited world.
Open up for me the hands of everyone who [dispenses gifts]
and compel them to give me what they have in their hands.
I also know your foreign names:
'**PHARNATHAR BARACHÊL CHTHA**.'
These are your foreign names.

Whereas Isis, the greatest of all the gods,
invoked you in every crisis, in every district,
against gods and men and daimôns,
creatures of water and earth and held your favour,
victory against gods and men
and [among] all the creatures beneath the world,
so also I invoke you.
Wherefore, give me favour, form, beauty.
Hear me, Hermês, benefactor, [inventor] of drugs;
be easy to talk to and hear me,
just as you have done everything in the form
of your Ethiopian dog-faced baboon,
the lord of the chthonic daimôns.
Calm them all and give me strength, form,
and let them give me gold and silver
and every sustenance which will never fail.
Preserve me always, through all eternity,
from drugs and deceits, every slander and evil tongues,
from every daimônic possession
from every hatred of both gods and men.
Let them give me favour and victory and business and prosperity.

For you are I, and I am you;
your name is mine, and mine is yours.
For I am your image.
If something should happen to me
during this year or this month or this day or this hour,

it will happen to the great god **ACHCHEMEN ESTROPH**,
the one inscribed on the prow of the holy ship.

Your true name has been inscribed on the sacred stele
in the shrine at Hermopolis where your birth is.
Your true name: **OSERGARIACH NOMAPHI**.
This is your name with fifteen letters,
a number corresponding to the days of the rising moon;
and the second name with the number 7,
corresponding to those who rule the world,
with the exact number 365,
corresponding to the days of the year.
Truly: **ABRASAX**.
I know you, Hermês, and you know me.
I am you, and you are I.
And so, do everything for me,
and may you turn to me
with Good Fortune and Good Daimôn,
immediately, immediately; quickly, quickly."
"**PHTHORON PHTHIONÊ THÔUTH**"
"**IAÔ SABAÔTH ADÔNAIE**
ABLANATHANALBA AKRAMMACHAMAREI,
365, give to me business, favour, prosperity, elegance,
immediately, immediately; quickly, quickly."

[*Tr.: E N O'Neil]

Either remain facing the East, or turn to face Mercury if it is visible.

PGM VII. 919–24

"**THÔOUTH** give me victory, strength, influence."

[*Tr.: R F Hock]

PGM VII. 664–85

The following spell is to be repeated seven times:

"Hermês, lord of the world, who're in the heart,
O circle of Selênê, spherical and square,
The founder of the words of speech,
Pleader of Justice's cause,

Garbed in a mantle, with golden sandals,
Turning airy course beneath earth's depths,
Who hold the spirit's reins, the sun's,
And who with lamps of gods immortal
give joy to those beneath earth's depths,
To mortals who've finished life.
The Moirai's fatal thread and Dream divine you're said to be,
Who send forth oracles by day and night;
You cure pains of all mortals with your healing cares.
Hither, O blessed one, O mighty son of the goddess
who brings full mental powers,
By your own form and gracious mind.
And to me reveal a sign and send me your true skill of prophecy,
OIOSENMIGADÔN ORTHÔ BAUBÔ
NIOÊRE KODÊRETH DOSÊRE SURE SUROE
SANKISTÊ DÔDEKAKISTÊ AKROUROBORE
KODÊRE RINÔTON KOUMETANA ROUBITHA
NOUMILA PERPHEROU AROUÔRÊR AROUÊR."

[*Tr.: E N O'Neil]

PGM IV. 2359–72

"**CHAIÔCHEN OUTIBILMEMNOUÔTH ATRAUICH**."

[*Tr.: R F Hock]

Curse Tablet

"...Hermês of the underworld
ARCHEDAMA PHÔCHENSE PSEUSA RERTA THOUMISON..."

[Selection from "*Curse Tablets and Binding Spells from the Ancient World*" John Gager, trans.]

PGM V. 424–435

The following spell is to be said three times:
"**UESENNIGADÔN ORTHÔ BAUBÔ**
NOÊRE KODÊRE SOIRE SOIRE
SANKANTHARA ERESCHIGAL
ANKISTÊ DÔDEKAKISTÊ

**AKROUROBORE KODÊRE SÊMEA
KENTEU KONTEU KENTEU KÊRIDEU
DARUGKÔ LUKUNXUNTA KAMPUCHRÊ
IRINÔTON LOUMANATA ... ION KOMANDRON
CHREIBACHA NOUBACHA NOUMILLON
EROUPHI TEROUPHI LIBINOU NOUMILLON
CHANDARA TON PHERPHEREU DROUÊR
MAROUÊR.**"

PGM V. 436–439 (Spell of compulsion)
"**OUKRA NOUKRA PETIRINODE TMAISIA,**
terrible-eyed,
**DRUSALPIPS BLEMENNITHEN BANDUODMA
TRIPSADA ARIBA ... TA KRATARNA.**"

PGM V. 440–446 (Another spell of compulsion)
"**IOUKRAIÔNIOU ÔCHMARMACHÔ
TONNOURAI CHRÊMILLON DERKUÔN NIA IAÔ
SOUMPSÊPHISON SOUMPSÊNIS SIASIAS IAÔ,**
you who shake the world, come in
THOIS KOTOTH PHTHOUPHNOUN NOUEBOUÊ."
[*Tr.: E N O'Neil]

Meditation and Eucharist

See Ritual Performance and Ritual Preparation chapters for more information on Meditation and Eucharist.

Dismissal

"Your names in heaven:
**LAMPHTHEN OUÔTHI OUASTHEN
OUÔTHI OAMENÔTH ENTHOMOUCH.**
Lord Hermês I thank you for having come to me,
and may you always be a part of my life."
[*Tr.: E N O'Neil]

Commentary on Graeco-Egyptian Invocation to Hermês

To understand this invocation, it is important to note that in Egypt, the Greeks identified Hermês with Thoth. Thoth was the scribe of the gods. He had complete knowledge and wisdom, he invented all the arts and sciences. Thoth was represented in two forms – the sacred ibis and the dog-faced baboon (*Papio Cynocephalus*). He can be depicted as these appear in nature or in the case of the ibis, anthropomorphic with the bird's head. (Thoth will be experienced in the sequel to this book.)

A number of the spells used in the ritual involve the preparation of statues. These are not necessary to the success of the ritual and I have included the steps involved for information purposes only.

This ritual is quite lengthy and should be performed in its entirety the first few times. If, however, Hermês is intuited as manifesting partway through the ritual there is no need to say the ritual in its entirety.

During the anointing with cassia, chant "**PSUCHOPOMPOIAPS**" (See *PGM* CI. 29 and John Gager's "*Curse Tablets and Binding Spells from the Ancient World*," Tablet number 30). This name of power is related to the Greek "guide of souls" or psychopomp, a traditional epithet of Hermês. This is Hermês in his chthonic form and has no reference to Thoth whatsoever. While normally the forehead is anointed with the aspected essential oil, the skin of many people is sensitive to cassia and it may burn. A safer option is to put a small dab on the hair. Be very careful with cassia oil.

PGM VIII. 1–63

Hermês was often associated with commerce. This invocation conveys business, favour, prosperity, and elegance for a shop owner. A carved statue is prepared which is left in the middle of the shop, to ensure good business.

The statue is to be carved out of olive wood, and should be of a small dog-faced baboon sitting down, wearing the winged helmet of Hermês, and with a box on its back. The name of Hermês

(PHTHORON PHTHIONÊ THÔUTH) is to be written on papyrus using myrrh ink and placed in box. Also to be written on the papyrus is: "**IAÔ SABAÔTH ADÔNAIE ABLANATHANALBA AKRAMMACHAMAREI**, 365, give to the workshop business, favour, prosperity, elegance, both to NN himself and to his workshop, immediately, immediately; quickly, quickly."

Myrrh ink is used extensively in the magickal papyri. While myrrh ink would certainly add authenticity to a Graeco-Egyptian ritual, none of the rituals in this book require any writing at all.

The ingredients for myrrh ink are given in *PGM* I. 244–7:

> *"myrrh troglitis, 4 drams; 3 karian figs, 7 pits of Nikolaus dates, 7 dried pinecones, 7 piths of the single-stemmed wormwood, 7 wings of the Hermaic ibis, spring water. When you have burned the ingredients, prepare them and write."*
> [*Tr.: E N O'Neil]

In *PGM* XII. 401–44 there is a list of the "names" of ingredients used in magick spells and what they really are. This was a precautionary device to prevent the masses from practising magick.

In Egypt, the ibis was sacred to Thoth, and by extension, Hermês. If a spell calls for "a bone of an ibis" then it is really calling for buckthorn. The wing of an ibis required in the myrrh ink would thus correspond to a part of the buckthorn plant, perhaps a leaf.

THÔUTH is another variation on the name Thoth.

SABAÔTH in Hebrew is the plural form of "host" or "army." It is normally used in conjunction with the Divine name as a title of majesty, and refers to the hosts of heaven, the angels, and by extension the stars and the entire universe.

ADÔNAIE, or Adonai, means "Lord" and is used as an epithet of the Hebrew god, YHWH. In Gnostic and magickal writings it is used as the name of an angelic figure. The name is sometimes corrupted to Adonaêl and Adonaios.

ABLANATHANALBA is a very popular palindrome in magickal writings used for beneficent results. It possibly originates from the Hebrew "father (*ab*) come to us (*lanath*)."

AKRAMMACHAMAREI is another popular name in magickal writings. According to Gershom Scholem, it consists of two

Aramaic words. The verb *'aqar* means "to uproot" and is used in the context of the destruction of evil spirits. The noun *makhmarei* originally meant "nets" and acquired the meaning of a magick spell cast like a net upon a person. Hence the meaning is "uproot the magick spells." In the Pistis Sophia the name is used for the first of a divine triad, while on a curse tablet it refers to the master and ruler of the heavenly firmament.

The number 365 is a reference to Abraxas or Abrasax. This god is discussed below.

The names of Hermês in the four quarters of heaven are intoned. The fourfold theme is then continued with the visualisation of four animals:

- While facing East, visualise an ibis.
- Turn 180° clockwise to face West, and visualise a dog-faced baboon.
- Turn a further 90° clockwise to face North, and visualise a serpent.
- Turn anti-clockwise 180° to face South, and visualise a wolf.
- Turn a further 90° anti-clockwise to return to the East.

This makes a total of 270° clockwise and 270° anti-clockwise rotations. See Appendix 3: Rotation and Counter-Rotation for more information on this characteristic of Graeco-Egyptian Magick.

Now contemplate all four animals simultaneously:

- East (straight ahead) – ibis (a form of Thoth)
- West (behind) – dog-faced baboon (another form of Thoth)
- North (left) – serpent (Uto, Apophis, Agathos Daimôn or Ouroboros)
- South (right) – wolf (Anubis or Ap-uat)

As stated previously, the Greeks identified Hermês with Thoth, and so the attributions for East and West are understandable.

The PGM commentary suggests that Uto is often in the north, and is thus the goddess associated with the serpent. Uto, the cobra goddess, is a protectress, but has no clear link to Hermês. Apophis (Apep), the underworld serpent deity, threatens the sun god by night in his passage through the underworld. Apophis can be seen as corresponding to the chthonic aspect of Hermês, with his location being with the sun by night, which is in the north. Agathos Daimôn or Agathodaimôn, is the serpent god who served as the protector of Alexandria (he will be met in the sequel to this book), which is in the north of Egypt. The Ouroboros serpent is the least likely candidate, as it does not have an explicit link to Hermês. My choice is Agathos Daimôn, as he ties in with the caduceus (see below), and is located in the north.

The PGM commentary suggests that Anubis is often in the south, and is thus the god associated with the wolf. Anubis is the jackal god of the underworld (and will be met in the sequel to this book). Sharing Anubis' role of psychopomp in the Egyptian underworld, is Ap-uat (Wepwawet), another jackal god, whose name means "opener of the ways." Anubis and Ap-uat obviously tie in with the psychopomp aspect of Hermês. Anubis is the opener of the roads of the North, personifying the Summer Solstice, while Ap-uat is the opener of the roads of the South, personifying the Winter Solstice. Of the two jackal gods, Ap-uat is the more likely candidate, as he is associated with the south.

Next, demonstrate your knowledge of Hermês by naming the plant, wood and city associated with Hermês. The reference to Hermês as one who knows "the things hidden beneath heaven and earth" refers to his abilities in divination, and to his frequent visits to the underworld as a psychopomp. Hermês is then identified with Thoth as Isis' chief helper. This is followed with a request for material goods, various physical endowments, success and protection.

Then, assert mutual identity with Hermês: "For you are I, and I am you; your name is mine, and mine is yours. For I am your image."

Thoth's cult centre was at Hermopolis, which means "city of Hermês."

Call on the true name of Hermês, **OSERGARIACH NOMAPHI**, saying that it consists of fifteen letters which corresponds to "the days of the rising moon." The translator of the PGM has flagged this as a mistake in the original manuscript as the name actually consists of sixteen letters. The intention however, was to associate Hermês with the moon, as Thoth was worshipped throughout Egypt as a moon god. In the sequel to this book I will be dealing with the difficulty of unambiguously assigning Egyptian deities to a single celestial body.

Then call on what is described as the second name of Hermês, **ABRASAX**. Abrasax or Abraxas, was one of the main Gnostic gods. According to Irenæus, he was the Basilidian ruler of the 365 heavens. He was portrayed as snake footed, armoured, and with the head of a rooster. The number of letters in Abrasax or Abraxas is seven, corresponding to "those who rule the world," referring to the seven planetary spheres. Numerologically the value of the name is 365, corresponding to the days of the year. This is an example of the magickal use of flattery, as Abrasax or Abraxas was considered to be far superior to Hermês.

Then assert mutual identity with Hermês. "I am you, and you are I." Again the goal is empowerment.

The reference to Good Daimôn, is a reference to Agathos Daimôn. This is an example of the use of one god to call on another god.

The spell ends by intoning the words of power written on the papyrus placed within the statue.

The spell is actually titled "Binding love spell of Astrapsoukos." Astrapsoukos was the name of one or more Persian magickians. The spell clearly has no connection with love, and so its attribution to Astrapsoukos is uncertain.

PGM VII. 919–24

This spell is known as Hermês' Wondrous Victory Charm.

A number of characters are to be inscribed on a gold lamella, which is then kept in your sandals. The words to be recited are "**THÔOUTH**, give victory, strength, influence to the wearer." I have modified these slightly.

PGM VII. 664–85

This spell is a request for a dream oracle.

The spell instructs that a query is written in myrrh ink on linen which is wrapped around an olive branch. Lay down to sleep on a pure rush mat on the ground, and place the branch beneath the left side of your head. Face a lamp and repeat the invocation seven times.

The lamp is a vessel filled with oil into which a wick has been placed. These were used throughout the ancient world. Whenever a light source is stipulated in the Graeco-Egyptian Magickal writings it is invariably an oil lamp and not a candle, even though tallow candles were known at the time.

The instruction stipulates that this spell is to be repeated seven times. I would recommend this the first few times; however, eventually just saying the spell once should be sufficient. Let your intuition guide you.

There are a number of references to Hermês as a psychopomp: "Turning airy course beneath earth's depths ... And who with lamps of gods immortal give joy to those beneath earth's depths, to mortals who've finished life."

The Moirai are the Greek goddesses of Fate, who hold unlimited sway over men and gods. They are Klôthô (the Spinner) who spins the thread of life, Lakhesis (Disposer of Lots) who determines its length, and Atropos (Inevitable) who cuts it off.

By comparing this spell with *PGM* V. 370–446, it is evident that when Hermês is described as "O mighty son of the Goddess," the goddess in question is Memory.

Just prior to the words of power at the end of the spell, the original text has "And to an uncorrupted youth reveal a sign and send him your true skill of prophecy." I have amended this to "And to me reveal a sign and send me your true skill of prophecy." Magickians in the ancient world, and indeed the medieval world, often employed young virginal boys to act as seers. Being pure, the young boys were thought of by magickians as being far more receptive to visions than they were.

Prophecy is just one of the gifts that Hermês reputedly can bestow. Others include healing and intellect. Aptitude for prophecy will vary amongst people, but there is no reason to use a substitute as a seer. You should be interested in developing your own abilities.

Dôdeka is the number twelve and *kistos* means basket. John Gager suggests that **DÔDEKAKISTÊ** could mean "the one (female) who encompasses the twelve (gods)."

AKROUROBORE in Greek means "eater of the tip of your tail," and is a reference to the Ouroboros serpent.

AROUÊR in Egyptian means, "Horus the great."

PGM IV. 2359–72

This is a spell to bring continuous business to a shop.

The instruction for this spell is to take orange beeswax, the juice of the aeria plant and ground ivy and mix them. Fashion a figure of Hermês grasping in his left hand a herald's wand and in his right a small bag. Leave a hollow base in the statue.

On hieratic papyrus write "**CHAIÔCHEN OUTIBILMEMNOUÔTH ATRAUICH**. Give income and business to this place, because Psentebeth lives here." Psentebeth means "the son of the female falcon."

Place the papyrus in the hollow base of the statue and seal it with more of the beeswax mixture. Finally, the statue should then be placed inconspicuously in a wall, and offerings made to it. A lamp should be lit to Hermês that is not coloured red (and hence not connected to Set).

Curse Tablet

A lead tablet from Alexandria in the third century CE, seeks to bind a man by appealing to a number of underworld gods (repeatedly using the same names of power), including Hermês. Hermês was often appealed to in curse tablets due to his connection with the underworld. The tablet quoted from preserves some of the names of power associated with Hermês not attested elsewhere. "...Hermês of the underworld **ARCHEDAMA PHÔCHENSE PSEUSA RERTA THOUMISON...**" is repeated four times on the tablet. This name of power refers to Hermês in his chthonic form, rather than a name that includes a reference to Thoth, as so many of the other spells do. (See John Gager's "*Curse Tablets and Binding Spells from the Ancient World*," Tablet number 110.)

PGM V. 370–446 incorporating PGM V. 424–435, PGM V. 436–439 and PGM V. 440–446

This spell instructs that a figure of Hermês is made out of dough into which a number of plant materials and the liquid of an ibis egg have been mixed. (The ibis is connected with Thoth, as discussed above.) Hermês is to be portrayed wearing a mantle and holding a herald's staff. The figure is placed in a lime wood shrine. To use the spell, burn incense, earth from a grain-bearing field and a lump of rock salt, and then lay down with the shrine beside your head. It is important to not talk to anyone during the procedure.

The spell begins with the poem to Hermês from *PGM* VII. 664–85. The wording is almost identical, and I have not incorporated it into the ritual a second time.

PGM V. 424–435

This is followed by words of power which are fairly similar to those at the end of *PGM* VII. 664–85, but have a number of additional words. The instruction with this spell is that these words are to be repeated three times. Again, as stated earlier, I would recommend this the first few times, however, eventually just saying the spell once should be sufficient. Let your intuition guide you.

Amongst the additional words is **ERESCHIGAL**, which is the name of a Babylonian underworld goddess. Her name is often associated with the Greek goddess, Hekatê, and the word of power, Neboutousoualêth.

PGM V. 436–439 (Spell of compulsion)

The first spell of compulsion ends with the instruction to say "the hundred-lettered name of Hermês." This has unfortunately not been preserved.

PGM V. 440–446 (Another spell of compulsion)

The second spell of compulsion includes the instruction to say **IOUKRAIÔNIOU** to a lamp. Towards the end, the original text has "**IAÔ**, you who shake the world, come in and prophesy concerning the NN matter, **THOIS**." I have removed the reference to prophesying, as the goal is to have Hermês manifest.

PGM IV. 2373–2440 – not used

This is another spell for bringing customers into a shop.

The instruction for this spell states that out of unheated beeswax fashion a man dressed in a girdle, with his right hand in the position of begging, and in his left hand a bag and a staff. The staff should have a coiled snake around it, so as to symbolize the caduceus, and the man should be standing on a sphere that has a coiled snake. The coiled snake is identified with Agathos Daimôn. The statue should be placed into a single block of hollowed-out juniper, with an asp covering the top. The spell includes a number of words of power to be repeated four times over various parts of the anatomy of the statue.

I have omitted this spell as it would necessitate the construction of a statue. The previous spells are perfectly adequate without the need for props.

Procedure for initiation

See "Bringing the planetary energies into everyday life" in the Ritual Performance chapter for a summary of these procedures.

Results

If you are reading this portion of the chapter, I assume that you have already invoked Hermês with the ritual above. If you haven't, stop reading and do so!

While the first stirrings of magickal ability were experienced in the lunar Sphere, these become less mysterious as knowledge is acquired. You should also begin to access the all-pervading energy reservoir, the life force, and use it for healing.

The Mercury energy is connected with the afterlife through the psychopomp aspect of Hermês. Knowledge of the certainty of an afterlife diminishes a fear of death for some, and helps others who are grieving for loved ones that have passed over.

The Mercury energy has a negative side which result in tests. There is a temptation to misuse the gifts of the Mercury Sphere for personal gain.

Hermês has a trickster aspect and so a lot of things seem to go wrong in the life. These should be viewed as challenges and opportunities for further growth rather than obstacles.

The Mercury energy is connected with the intellect and is excellent to call upon when studying. The acquisition of knowledge can have an obsessive quality to it, and many academics remain in the Mercury Sphere, and never grow beyond.

Specific results which have occurred in group rituals invoking Hermês include:

The 4 animals

- There is no general rule for how the 4 animals are perceived. For some participants the animals disappear after being visualised, while for others, they stay throughout the ritual. The animals which feature most prominently in the interactive experiences of participants are the wolf and the serpent. It is possible that these animals are more familiar to modern participants than the ibis and the baboon. It would be interesting to run this ritual with African participants for a comparison.

Presence of energy in ritual area

- The Mercury energy was sometimes experienced coming into the ritual area as a wind or as a light. The energy was felt as tingles, shivers, shakes, or goose pimples. Others felt the energy as varying degrees of warmth, either in the whole body or hands and feet. For some participants, the energy came in quickly and stayed for only a short time. Some participants reported that when the energy left their body, it left through various chakras.

- As with the lunar invocation, a number of participants felt heavy from the waist down, but light from the waist up. There was a lot of swaying, usually in circles, but sometimes in a figure eight motion.
- Many participants felt a need to sit down, crouch or lie down during the ritual. Those participants who resisted this were compelled through not being able to stand still; pains and tightness in the calves; heaviness or cramping in the legs; a light head; aches and pains; nausea; pressure on upper body; or sensation of being hit by a force.

Quality of energy

- Most participants felt the energy as a combination of youthful, friendly, smiling, jovial, joking, streetsmart, natural, nice, safe and positive.
- Some participants perceived the energy as being connected with wisdom and had numerous thoughts throughout the ritual. Many asked for help with communication.
- Some perceived the energy as having healing properties. Some asked for help with the healing arts while others obtained pain relief.

Experiences through physical senses

- Some participants experienced a heightened sense of awareness. Quite often animals and insects were heard making various sounds during the ritual as they usually respond to spiritual phenomena. A number of participants saw auras around trees.

- ξ One ritual started with clouds overhead. By the end, the clouds were around the horizon, and there was clear sky overhead.

Experiences through non-physical senses

- ξ Participants often saw people from their past. Some relived childhood memories.
- ξ Some participants saw rapid visuals of places and people they could not identify. A number of participants experienced visions of nature or distinctly Greek vistas.
- ξ Some participants experienced underworld visions in keeping with Hermês' function as a psychopomp. These often involved journeying through caves and sometimes encountering faces or souls.
- ξ For a number of the visions above, Hermês was present as a guide.

Visions of Hermês

- ξ Elements of Hermês seen included a young man; a naked muscular man; golden coloured with a big white light around him; with a lot of gold around his head; with his staff held out from his body; gold helmet with wings; winged sandles; the magickian card in tarot decks; an elderly man with a staff; a Native American Indian.
- ξ Some participants saw Hermês as a trickster, but not a malevolent trickster. As an example, one participant asked Hermês if she could sit down. She was initially denied, but eventually permitted.

Messages received

- ξ Some participants felt that they acquired knowledge or obtained insights. Some revisited past events to learn from them. Some were given words of encouragement.

Astral experiences

- Some participants exteriorised their astral bodies briefly during the ritual.

Fears

- Most participants did not feel frightened or threatened. One inexperienced participant felt terrified and reported that his hands went heavy and numb. He overcame his fears and went on to safely complete numerous additional rituals.
- Some participants experienced a sensation of being watched from outside the ritual area. This fear left them in subsequent rituals when they realised that there was nothing to fear.

The influence of the Mercury Sphere continues through the remaining Spheres with progressively more wisdom and healing ability being acquired.

Third Planetary Sphere – Venus

This Sphere marks coming to terms with the emotions and applying this to the lessons of the previous Spheres. The sensuality of the Lunar Sphere matures into love. The rationality of the Mercury Sphere finds balance as the emotions are understood and mastered. There is an appreciation of beauty in art and life in general, leading to greater zest for the joy of living.

The Lunar Sphere marked the beginning of the spiritual journey while the Mercury Sphere developed a better understanding in an impassive intellectual way. Now the Venus Sphere continues the journey by adding empathy and mastery of the emotions to the mix.

Goddess Invoked	Aphroditê
Key properties	Mastering emotions. Love, graciousness, beauty, success in romance and the arts.
(+)	Desire, harmony, physical and spiritual unions.
(–)	Concupiscence, depravity, guile of the desires.
Fragrance	Spikenard
Colour	Blue
Gemstone/Metal	Lapis Lazuli

Mythology

Aphroditê appears to be of Phoenician origin. Her cult passed from Kythêra – a Phoenician trading post – to Cyprus, and then on to Greece. She was originally a fertility goddess whose domain encompassed all of nature.

There are a number of myths concerning the origins of Aphroditê. To the earliest Greeks, she was the daughter of Zeus and Diônê, the Titan goddess of the oracle of Dodona.

In Hesiod's "Theogony," however, the world emerged from chaos, followed by the birth of the 12 Titans, whose parents were Ouranos, the sky, and Gaia, the earth. Unprepared for fatherhood,

Ouranos hid his offspring inside Gaia's body. In pain Gaia cried out for help, whereupon Kronos, the youngest, responded by castrating Ouranos and tossing his genitals into the Mediterranean Sea.

The genitals were enveloped in a mist of white foam from which a beautiful maiden appeared. She was transported on a scallop shell to the Greek island, Kythêra, where she was called Kythêrea. She then travelled to Cyprus, which had a long tradition of goddess worship. At Cyprus she was first worshipped, and was named Aphroditê, which means "she who comes from foam." When she first walked on Cypriot soil, grass sprung up under her feet and she was affirmed as a fertility goddess who revitalised the earth.

Aphroditê was a power of nature. As goddess of the shifting gale and changeful sky, she was Aphroditê Urania, the heavenly or celestial, the moral conception of which came to encompass pure and ideal love. As goddess of storm and lightning, she was represented as Aphroditê Hôplismenê (armed), which may explain her connection with Arês (Aphroditê Areia) and her perception as Aphroditê Nikêphoros (bringer of victory). She presided over marriage as Aphroditê Genetrix, Migôntis (marital union) and Nymphia (bridal). As Aphroditê Pandêmos (common to all the people) and Aphroditê Porne (courtesan) she was the goddess of love and prostitution. Aphroditê Pelagia or Pontia was a marine deity.

Aphroditê's temple at Corinth was renowned for its priestesses who performed initiation rites and provided sexual services to incoming sailors. As time went on, Aphroditê's role of a goddess of love overshadowed her role as a fertility deity. In Hesiod's "Works and Days", Zeus assigns the roles of the Olympic deities. Aphroditê's role was that of goddess of love and beauty, while her former role as a goddess of agriculture was given to Dêmêtêr.

Aphroditê had a wrathful side to her nature as shown in numerous myths where she punished people who failed to give her due worship or failed to honour pledges made to her by causing them to fall in love within destructive relationships, denying them of love by making them sexually repulsive, or by magickally transforming them into various objects.

Among plants, the myrtle, rose and apple were sacred to Aphroditê; while among animals, the ram, he-goat, hare, dove and sparrow were sacred to her; as sea-goddess, the swan, mussels and dolphin; as Urania, the tortoise.

In art, Aphroditê was represented either in her higher aspect as Urania or as the popular goddess of love. In earlier art she was clothed. In later art she was unclothed and either rising out of the sea or a bath, or an object of feminine beauty.

Aphroditê had a number of cult titles. The following is a selection:

- ξ Ambologêra – posponer of old age
- ξ Apostrophia – averter of unlawful desires
- ξ Dôritis – bountiful
- ξ Epistrophia – she who turns to love
- ξ Morphô – of shapely form
- ξ Praxis – sexual action
- ξ Symmakhia – ally in love

Orphic Hymn LIV: To Aphroditê

Heavenly, illustrious, laughter-loving queen,
Sea-born, night-loving, of an awful mien;
Crafty, from whom necessity first came,
Producing, nightly, all-connecting dame:
It is yours the world with harmony to join,
For all things spring from you, O power divine.
The triple Fates are ruled by your decree,
And all productions yield alike to you:
Whatever the heavens, encircling all contain,
Earth fruit-producing, and the stormy main,
Your sway confesses, and obeys your nod,
Awful attendant of the brumal God:
Goddess of marriage, charming to the sight,
Mother of Loves, whom banquetings delight;
Source of persuasion, secret, savouring queen,
Illustrious born, apparent and unseen:
Spousal, lupercal, and to men inclined,
Prolific, most-desired, life-giving, kind:
Great sceptre-bearer of the Gods, it is yours,
Mortals in necessary bands to join;
And every tribe of savage monsters dire

In magic chains to bind, through mad desire.
Come, Cyprus-born, and to my prayer incline,
Whether exalted in the heavens you shine,
Or pleased in Syria's temple to preside,
Or over the Egyptian plains your car to guide,
Fashioned of gold; and near its sacred flood,
Fertile and famed to fix your blest abode;
Or if rejoicing in the azure shores,
Near where the sea with foaming billows roars,
The circling choirs of mortals, your delight,
Or beauteous nymphs, with eyes cerulean bright,
Pleased by the dusty banks renowned of old,
To drive your rapid, two-yoked car of gold;
Or if in Cyprus with your mother fair,
Where married females praise you every year,
And beauteous virgins in the chorus join,
Adônis pure to sing and you divine;
Come, all-attractive to my prayer inclined,
For you, I call, with holy, reverent mind.

[Selection from "*The Hymns of Orpheus*" Thomas Taylor, trans.]

Homeric Hymn VI: To Aphroditê

I will sing of stately Aphroditê, gold-crowned and beautiful,
whose dominion is the walled cities of all sea-set Cyprus.
There the moist breath of the western wind
wafted her over the waves of the loud-moaning sea in soft foam,
and there the gold-filleted Hours welcomed her joyously.
They clothed her with heavenly garments:
on her head they put a fine, well-wrought crown of gold,
and in her pierced ears they hung ornaments of orichalc and precious gold,
and adorned her with golden necklaces
over her soft neck and snow-white breasts,
jewels which the gold-filleted Hours wear themselves
whenever they go to their father's house
to join the lovely dances of the gods.
And when they had fully decked her, they brought her to the gods,
who welcomed her when they saw her, giving her their hands.

Each one of them prayed
that he might lead her home to be his wedded wife,
so greatly were they amazed at the beauty of violet-crowned Kythêrea..
Hail, sweetly-winning, coy-eyed goddess!
Grant that I may gain the victory in this contest,
and order you my song.
And now I will remember you and another song also.

[Selection from "*Hesiod, Homeric Hymns, Epic Cycle, Homerica*" Hugh G Evelyn-White, trans.]

Homeric Hymn X: To Aphroditê

Of Kythêrea, born in Cyprus, I will sing.
She gives kindly gifts to men: smiles are ever on her lovely face,
and lovely is the brightness that plays over it.
Hail, goddess, queens of well-built Salamis and sea-girt Cyprus;
grant me a cheerful song.
And now I will remember you and another song also.

[Selection from "*Hesiod, Homeric Hymns, Epic Cycle, Homerica*" Hugh G Evelyn-White, trans.]

Graeco-Egyptian Magick Invocation to Aphroditê

Either face East, or turn to face Venus if it is visible.
Burn powdered spikenard root, anoint your forehead with spikenard oil and chant "**ILAOUCH**."

PGM IV. 3209–3223 (Preliminary request for Aphroditê to manifest)

"**ÊIOCH CHIPHA ELAMPSÊR ZÊL A E Ê I O U Ô**"
"**TACHIÊL CHTHONIÊ DRAXÔ**."

Repeat the following three times:

"**IERMI PHILÔ Ô ERIKÔMA DERKÔ**
MALÔK GAULÊ APHRIÊL I ask."

"I call upon you, the mother and mistress of nymphs,
ILAOUCH OBRIÊ LOUCH TLOR;
[come] in, holy light, and give answer,
showing your lovely shape."

PGM IV. 3228–3246 (Additional request for Aphroditê to manifest)

"I call upon the **ILAOUCH** who has begotten Himeros,
the lovely Hôrai and you Graces;
I also call upon the Zeus-sprung Physis of all things,
two-formed, indivisible, straight, foam-beautiful Aphroditê.
Reveal to me your lovely light and your lovely face,
O mistress **ILAOUCH**.
I conjure you, giver of fire, [by] **ELGINAL**,
and [by the] great names
OBRIÊTUCH KERDUNOUCHILÊPSIN
NIOU NAUNIN IOUTHOU THRIGX TATIOUTH
GERTIATH GERGERIS GERGERIÊ THEITHI.
I also ask you [by] the all wonderful names,
OISIA EI EI AÔ ÊU AAÔ IÔIAIAIÔ SÔTHOU
BERBROI AKTEROBORE GERIÊ IÊOUA;
bring me light and your lovely face, you shining with fire,
bearing fire all around, stirring the land from afar,
IÔ IÔ PHTHAIÊ THOUTHOI PHAEPHI. Do it."

[*Tr.: J P Hershbell]

PGM IV. 1265–74

"I call on you Aphroditê by the name
which becomes known to no one quickly, **NEPHERIÊRI**."

[*Tr.: E N O'Neil]

PGM IV. 2916–2942 (Hymn of Compulsion)

"O foam-born Kythêreia,
mother of both gods and men, ethereal and chthonic,
All-Mother Nature, goddess unsubdued,
Who hold together things, who cause the great fire to revolve,
who keep the ever-moving **BARZA** in her unbroken course;
and you accomplish everything, from head to toes,
And by your will is holy water mixed,
When by your hands you'll move **RHOUZÔ** amid the stars,
the world's midpoint which you control.
You move holy desire into the souls of men and move women to man,

and you render woman desirable to man through all the days to come,
our Goddess Queen, come to these chants,
Mistress **ARRÔRIPHRASI GÔTHÊTINI**, Cyprus-born,
SOUI ÊS THNOBOCHOU THORITHE STHENEPIÔ,
Lady **SERTHENEBÊÊI**, and manifest before me.
But, blessed **RHOUZÔ**, grant this to me:
Just as into your chorus 'mid the stars
A man unwilling you attracted to your bed for intercourse,
and once he was attracted, he at once began to turn
Great **BARZA**, nor did he cease turning,
And while moving in his circuits, he's aroused:
Wherefore manifest before me,
But goddess Cyprus-born
Do you now to the full fulfil this chant."

PGM IV. 2901–2915 (Compulsion element of the rite)

"But, if as goddess you in slowness act,
You will not see Adônis rise from Hadês,
Straightway I'll run and bind him with steel chains;
As guard, I'll bind on him another wheel of Ixiôn;
no longer will he come to light,
and he'll be chastised and subdued.
Wherefore, O Lady, act, I beg: manifest before me – today
At once, quickly. For I adjure you, Kythêre,
NOUMILLON BIOMBILLON AKTIÔPHI ERESCHIGAL
NEBOUTOSOUALÊTH PHROURÊXIA THERMIDOCHÊ BAREÔ NÊ."

[*Tr.: E N O'Neil]

PGM IV. 3224–3227 (Greeting to Aphroditê)

"Hail very glorious goddess, **ILARA OUCH**.
And if you give me a response, extend your hand."

[*Tr.: J P Hershbell]

Meditation and Eucharist

See Ritual Performance and Ritual Preparation chapters for more information on Meditation and Eucharist.

Dismissal

I call on you Aphroditê
by the name which becomes known to no one quickly, **NEPHERIÊRI**.
I thank you for having come to me,
and may you always be a part of my life."

Commentary on Graeco-Egyptian Invocation

Anoint with spikenard oil and chant "**ILAOUCH**." This is one of the names of power for Aphroditê, as seen in the first spell.

The invocation of Aphroditê consists of three spells. The detailed explanations are supplied for information purposes only.

PGM IV. 3209–54 incorporating PGM IV. 3209–23 and PGM IV. 3228–46

This spell is a vessel divination. Preparation of the vessel is not necessary.

The original spell has four distinct sections. It starts with instructions and an initial invocation (*PGM* IV. 3209–23). Next is a greeting to be used if she manifests (*PGM* IV. 3224–27). This is followed by further requests for Aphroditê to manifest (*PGM* IV. 3228–46). It finishes with further preliminary instructions (*PGM* IV. 3247–54). In order to cover all contingencies I have assumed that the further requests will be necessary and have moved the greeting to the end of the ritual. However, if you intuit Aphroditê's presence at any stage, then the remainder of the ritual apart from the greeting can be omitted.

The instruction is to remain pure for seven days. After this a white saucer or a bronze drinking cup should be obtained. Using myrrh ink, write "**ÊIOCH CHIPHA ELAMPSÊR ZÊL A E Ê I O U Ô** (25 letters)" on the base. Beneath the base, on the underside, write "**TACHIEÊL CHTHONIÊ DRAXÔ** (18 letters)." On the outside of the rim at the top write "**IERMI PHILÔ Ô ERIKÔMA DERKÔ MALÔK GAULÊ APHRIÊL** I ask." ["**Ô**" in the translation actually appears as "6." I assumed this was an error.]

It was pointed out in the Closing Rite chapter that some scholars believe that the bracketed notes indicating the number of letters were a quick check for the scribe to confirm that the words of power had been transcribed correctly. In this case no other significance of the numbers 25 and 18 is readily apparent.

The saucer or drinking vessel should be sealed with white wax to make it waterproof and prevent the words of power from being washed away. The vessel should be filled with clean river water and pure olive oil. Place the vessel either on the floor or on your knees, and chant the words of power on the vessel. The words of power on the outside of the rim at the top should be repeated three times.

"I call upon you, the mother and mistress of nymphs, **ILAOUCH OBRIÊ LOUCH TLOR**; [come] in, holy light, and give answer, showing your lovely shape" summons Aphroditê. She is described as the mistress of nymphs, a reference to the Orphic Hymn above.

The name of power **ILAOUCH**, is repeated a number of times throughout the spell, and is even modified to **ILARA OUCH**.

One characteristic of Graeco-Egyptian vessel divinations and lamp divinations (where you stare into an oil lamp) is that deity manifests in light. Sometimes requests are made for the darkness to be dispelled in order that the light may manifest.

At this point, Aphroditê is referred to as holy light. Flattery is used when Aphroditê is described as having a lovely shape.

The original spell gives a greeting to Aphroditê at this point, to be used if she manifests (*PGM* IV. 3224–27). I have moved the greeting to the end of the ritual.

The spell then continues with further requests for Aphroditê to manifest (*PGM* IV. 3228–46). "I call upon the **ILAOUCH** who has begotten Himeros, the lovely Hôrai and you Graces; I also call upon the Zeus-sprung Physis of all things, two-formed, indivisible, straight, foam-beautiful Aphroditê."

Himeros is the personification of desire, and the companion of Erôs.

The Hôrai are followers of Aphroditê. They are a trinity of goddesses responsible for order in nature. They reputedly cause the seasons to change and bring all things into being in accordance with the seasons. The individual goddesses are Eunomia (Good Order), Dikê (Justice) and Eirênê (Peace).

The Graces (Kharites) were in Aphroditê's retinue and spread joy to the world and to the hearts of men. They were the personification of loveliness or grace. While there are differing accounts of their names and their number, the mostly widely accepted tradition has them as Aglaia (Aglaiê or Glory), Euphrosynê (Good Cheer) and Thalia (Thaliê or Festivity).

Physis refers to nature, and could be a reference to Aphroditê's original role as that of a fertility goddess whose domain encompassed all of nature. An alternative lies in considering that the Greeks classified everything as either nomos (order) or physis. Aphroditê's birth was a rebellion against the order of Ouranos, through Kronos castrating Ouranos and tossing his genitals into the Mediterranean Sea, and hence an aspect of physis (nature). Thus, "Zeus-sprung Physis" could be an acknowledgement of Zeus's supremacy over everything including nature. Alternatively, "Zeus-sprung" could be a reference to the early legend which asserts that Aphroditê was the daughter of Zeus and Diônê.

Foam-beautiful refers to how Aphroditê was born.

The spell returns to the theme of light with repeated requests for Aphroditê to reveal her lovely light, to bring light, while flattery is again used to tell her that she has a lovely face.

The reference to Aphroditê "shining with fire and bearing fire all around, stirring the land from afar" suggests a relationship with the sun. The sun after all is a ball of fire which stirs the land from afar. I shall be returning to this in the "Hymn of Compulsion" below.

Towards the end of the spell, Aphroditê is asked to bring "the true saucer divination..." This has been omitted, as the aim of the ritual is the manifestation of her presence.

PGM IV. 1265–74

This is a spell to win a woman who is beautiful.

The instruction is that the name of Aphroditê which "becomes known to no one quickly" is **NEPHERIÊRI**. The instruction is to remain pure for three days after which an offering of frankincense should be burnt and the name **NEPHERIÊRI** should be called over it. You should then approach the woman and say **NEPHERIÊRI** seven times in your soul. The procedure should be repeated for seven days.

NEPHERIÊRI in Egyptian means "the beautiful eye," which is a suitable epithet for Aphroditê/Hathor.

I am of the opinion that forcing your will upon another is wrong. While there is nothing wrong in using magick to make yourself more attractive to a potential partner, to specifically target the object of your desire is unethical.

PGM IV. 2891–2942 incorporating PGM IV. 2916–42 and PGM IV. 2891–2915

This spell is a love spell of attraction. It is titled "Offering to the star of Aphroditê," which refers to the planet Venus.

The spell is structured so that Aphroditê is compelled to manifest in verses 2901–2915, whereas she is politely asked in verses 2916–2942. I have rearranged the spell so that the request precedes the compulsion element.

The offering made to Aphroditê consists of a white dove's blood and fat, untreated myrrh and parched wormwood. These are made into pellets and burnt on vine wood or coals. If the words of compulsion are needed, an offering of the brains of a vulture should be made.

Interestingly, the instruction within the spell advises to make a protective charm consisting of a tooth from the upper right jawbone of a female ass or of a tawny sacrificial heifer, tied to the left arm with Anubian thread. Anubian thread is called upon in a couple of spells but is not fully explained. Given that Anubis presided over mummification, it is plausible that a thread used in the mummification process was meant. I feel that this protective charm is suggested because Aphroditê is compelled to fulfil the bidding in the spell.

While Aphroditê is currently thought of as a goddess of love, the Graeco-Egyptian magickians respected her ability to harm them. The Orphic Hymn above describes Aphroditê's ability to bind in magick chains through mad desire. Book 14 of Homer's Iliad describes Aphroditê's girdle as being the source of her charms – love, desire, and the sweet bewitching words that turn a wise man into a fool. The Graeco-Egyptian magickians clearly did not want to lose control of their emotions, hence the use of the protective charm detailed above.

Neither the offerings nor the protective charm are necessary for the success of the ritual so long as your motivation is pure. They have been included for information purposes only. I believe that the lesson here is to treat deities, and spiritual beings in general, with courtesy and respect.

PGM IV. 2916–2942

This portion of the spell is titled "Hymn of Compulsion" and uses flattery to coerce Aphroditê to perform your bidding.

"O foam-born Kythêreia" refers to Aphroditê's birth. Interestingly, within the spell, Aphroditê is twice described as Cyprus-born, but according to Hesiod, she was born in Kythêre (which had a temple for Aphroditê Urania), and first worshipped in Cyprus.

The theme of "Zeus-sprung Physis" is continued with "mother of both gods and men, ethereal and chthonic, All-Mother Nature," which suggests a very powerful goddess indeed.

Aphroditê is described as being the source of all things and of maintaining the order of the universe, including moving the stars around the "world's midpoint" which refers to the Pole Star. The function of moving the stars around the Pole Star properly belongs to the Bear, which will be experienced in the sequel to this book. However, in late antiquity, the Bear was sometimes associated with Aphroditê–Selênê. This can be seen in *PGM* VII. 862–918 which calls on Aphroditê Urania and Selênê in the "ritual of heaven and the north star over lunar offerings." It is clear that this particular spell is calling upon Aphroditê's highest octave, Aphroditê Urania.

The word of power, **BARZA**, is Persian and means "shining light" and here refers to the Sun. (The Persian influence in Graeco-

Egyptian magick will be discussed in the sequel to this book.) A very similar word, **BARZAN**, is also associated with the sun in *PDM* xiv. 104. Aphroditê Urania is here being credited with keeping the sun moving.

The word of power, **RHOUZÔ**, is used twice and refers to a celestial body. Given that Aphroditê is associated with Venus, I think it is a reasonable assumption that **RHOUZÔ** is a magickal name for the planet Venus. This is substantiated by the second usage of **RHOUZÔ**, where it is used as a magickal name for Aphroditê. The quote "the world's midpoint which you control," indicates that while Aphroditê is associated with Venus, as Urania, she is also assocated with the Pole Star. For the purpose of this book, it is important to focus on the link between Aphroditê and Venus. (The link between Aphroditê and the Pole Star will be explored in the sequel to this book.)

The spell then addresses the lower octaves of Aphroditê, as Aphroditê Pandêmos and Aphroditê Porne, where she is able to inflame desire between men and women. After a series of words of power, this theme is resumed with a "man unwilling" attracted to Aphroditê's bed for intercourse. The man is then revealed to be **BARZA**, the sun. The sun is thus seen to follow its daily course as an ongoing consequence of his amorous involvement with Aphroditê.

There is unfortunately no surviving legend of an amorous union between Aphroditê and the sun god, Hêlios. The only surving link between Aphroditê and Hêlios is actually one of hostility, as it was Hêlios who revealed Aphroditê's infidelity with Arês, the god of war, to her husband, Hêphaistos, the god of fire and metalworking.

This portion of the original spell concludes with a request that a woman be compelled to come. I have modified this to a request for Aphroditê to manifest.

PGM IV. 2891–2915

This portion of the spell is titled "Compulsion element of the rite" and coerces Aphroditê to perform that which is sought by making threats against her lover, Adônis. Mythology indicates that both Aphroditê and Persephonê became captivated by Adônis. Adônis spent a third of the year with Persephonê in the underworld and two-thirds of the year with Aphroditê. This went on till Adônis was fatally wounded while hunting. Hearing Adônis' death throes, Aphroditê rushed to his side. On the way, she pricked her foot on a white rose, which became stained red forever with her blood.

The name Adônis probably comes from the Semitic word "*adon*" meaning "lord" and is associated with Adonai, an epithet for the god of the Hebrews.

In the spell, threats are made to prevent Adônis resurrecting from Hadês and to "bind on him another wheel of Ixiôn." This refers to a popular myth in antiquity, where the King of Ixiôn was condemned by being fastened to an ever-turning wheel for attempting to make love to Hêra, the wife of Zeus.

This portion of the original spell also concludes with a request that a woman be compelled to come. I have modified this to a request for Aphroditê to manifest.

AKTIÔPHI is an epithet of Selênê.

ERESCHIGAL is the Babylonian underworld goddess.

NEBOUTOSOUALÊTH is referred to as "the light-bringing goddess" in *PDM* xiv. 104. In context, it appears to refer to a lunar goddess. This name is often used together with **AKTIÔPHI** and **ERESCHIGAL**. This trio is usually associated with the underworld.

PGM IV. 3224–3227 (Greeting to Aphroditê)

The greeting to Aphroditê has been extracted from *PGM* IV. 3209–54. If she manifests, you are instructed to say "Hail very glorious goddess, **ILARA OUCH**. And if you give me a response, extend your hand." When Aphroditê is seen to extend her hand, she will give answer to any enquiries.

Regarding the eucharist, it should be noted that apples are associated with Aphroditê. I normally use a slice of apple and glass of apple juice as sacraments. A red rose on the altar would be very appropriate given the references in one of the spells to the legend of Adônis.

Procedure for initiation

See "Bringing the planetary energies into everyday life" in the Ritual Performance chapter for a summary of these procedures.

Results

If you are reading this portion of the chapter, I assume that you have already invoked Aphroditê with the ritual above. If you haven't, stop reading and do so now!

Just as the Mercury Sphere was effective to invoke when studying, the Venus Sphere is effective to invoke when engaging in artistic pursuits. Venus leads to an appreciation of beauty in art. This appreciation should not be purely passive as participation is so much more rewarding. I think that everyone has a talent, or at least an enthusiasm, for some sort of artistic pursuit, be it craft, painting, sculpting, singing, playing an instrument, or writing poetry. The emphasis is on an expression of creativity rather than the creation of a masterpiece.

For some participants, the contact which was established with the life force in the Mercury Sphere takes on an empathic quality. Some participants have had vivid flashes of the animal (and its pain) from which the meat on their plate came, and then converted to vegetarianism.

Often past emotional experiences are revisited through flashbacks, ensuring that no lessons are missed.

Some participants find that their capacity for love increases and that their relationships strengthen.

A number of participants found themselves more sexually attractive after working with Aphroditê. One female was phoned almost immediately after a ritual by a male professing his love asking her to move in with him, while another began receiving numerous unwanted phone calls propositioning her for a week after a group ritual. One male had a number of females proposition him soon after a ritual, leading to claims of chronic exhaustion after a few weeks!

The challenges connected with the Venus Sphere involve the emotions becoming uncontrollable. There is the temptation of lust and depravity.

It is important to not pretend that negative emotions do not exist, but rather come to terms with them and attain mastery over them, rather than being mastered by them.

Specific results which have occurred in group rituals invoking Aphroditê include:

Presence of energy in ritual area

- The Aphroditê energy has often entered the ritual area as a gentle breeze. It has sometimes been felt moving around in a circle in the ritual area. Some participants have felt encompassed by it.
- Many participants felt warmth encompassing their whole body, whereas others felt warmth in specific areas, such as their arms and hands. This warmth typically lasted while Aphroditê was being experienced. A number of participants felt either warmth or a lot of activity in their solar plexus and heart chakras. Another felt her heart pounding throughout the ritual.
- Some participants saw the energy as having various colours.
- Some participants who had trouble visualising Aphroditê felt a tingling in their hands. Some felt touched on their hands, while others felt like they were lifted up by their hands.
- Some participants felt a heaviness in their lower body and a lightness in their upper body. Sometimes the heaviness was felt in all the limbs.
- Amongst those participants who stood during the ritual, there was often a gentle swaying. This took the form of being rocked from side to side, or back and forth, or spiralling. Some likened the feeling to being rocked like a baby.
- Many participants felt a need to sit down, crouch or lie down during the ritual. This was generally a gentle need which was not forced. Some participants, who resisted this need, either

felt weak at the knees or were strongly pushed backwards. This was clearly a gentle reminder to work with the energy and not against it.

Quality of energy

- ξ Contrary to the expectations of many participants, the Aphroditê energy was not erotic like that of Selênê. I am inclined to think that Aphroditê's embodiment of higher love (as Urania) and lower love (as Porne) were later developments that counterbalanced and polarised each other, and that her real nature lies in between, being that of a nature fertility goddess.
- ξ Many participants felt Aphroditê's energy as a motherly love – an understanding maternal energy.
- ξ Participants typically felt loved, accepted, at peace with everything, happy, calm and re-assured. They often experienced a subtle tender caressing feeling or pleasant tranquillity.
- ξ Some participants felt "spaced out," intoxicated, or peaceful and vague.
- ξ Other participants were less specific and described the experience as nice, wonderful, beautiful, pleasant or sweet.
- ξ Some participants experienced the energy as more intense, referring to gentle passive experiences of pure joy and ecstatic bliss.
- ξ Some participants had healing experiences for emotional traumas.

Experiences through physical senses

- ξ Vision was often enhanced, and participants appreciated the beauty of their surroundings, focusing on distant trees, shooting stars or seeing auras around other participants.
- ξ Lights often appeared more intense. This included the moon, the candles on the altar, and the stars.

ξ In a number of rituals a mist or haze was seen. During one such ritual there was a strong breeze blowing which under normal circumstances should have dispelled the mist.

Experiences through non-physical senses

ξ Many participants experienced flashbacks of their childhood. This took the form of either remembering the happiness of childhood or feelings of being nurtured.

ξ A few participants had visions of Aphroditê bathing in the ocean. Occasionally she was seen bathing in her temple.

ξ A few participants had visions of Aphroditê's temple, which included a castle-like building on a grassy hill; and a large white temple with pillars admitting a lot of light, above the clouds on a mountaintop in the Mediterranean.

ξ A number of female participants saw themselves going off on a journey accompanied by beasts of prey, including a wolf, a black panther and a tiger.

ξ A small number of participants also had experiences with white wings, either of seeing them or "growing" them. This appeared to be a connection with doves, which are sacred to Aphroditê.

Visions of Aphroditê

ξ The most frequently reported image of Aphroditê was that of Sandro Botticelli's painting "Birth of Venus." Typically she was seen as very pretty with strawberry blonde tresses and pale skin, despite preceding the rituals by studying ancient images (either carvings or vase paintings) of Aphroditê.

ξ Elements of Aphroditê seen include either red or blonde hair; flowing white or transparent robes; violet eyes; wearing gold jewellery; surrounded by golden light.

Messages received

ξ Many participants reported feeling a need to contact their mothers after this ritual.

- ξ Other messages were normally connected with emotions. These included being told to be patient, strong and embody love; to give in order to receive; to develop the courage to take action; to affirm self-worth; to not bottle up anger.

Astral experiences

- ξ While astral experiences are probably more in keeping with the Spheres of the Moon and Mercury, they were also experienced in the Sphere of Venus.
- ξ Some participants consciously left their physical bodies, while for others there was a non-specific feeling of being somewhere else. These "journeys" tended to be brief, and sometimes occurred in an attempt to flee the discomfort of the cold wind in outdoor rituals.

The influence of the Venus Sphere continues through the remaining Spheres with progressively more emotional depth and artistic appreciation being acquired.

Fourth Planetary Sphere – Sun

This is an extremely important Sphere which can have powerful and very effective results. This Sphere is the key to a number of the advanced rituals in the sequel to this book.

The Sphere of the Sun should only be undertaken after having mastered the previous Spheres. The lessons of the previous Spheres are built upon and come to fruition in this Sphere. You are potentially brought into a state of unity with your divine spark and then the cosmos.

For many, accessing the Sphere of the Sun will not come as easily as accessing the previous Spheres. In fact in some magickal traditions, there is reference to an obstacle or a veil preventing access to the Sphere of the Sun.

It is important to surrender totally to the solar energy in order to effectively link with it. While a state of passive receptivity is necessary for all the Spheres, it is absolutely crucial to the Sphere of the Sun. To access the divine spark, a true understanding of self must be acquired. This process requires brutal honesty. The degree of access to the divine spark increases in the Spheres of Mars and Jupiter.

God Invoked	Hêlios
Key properties	The Ego, harmony, divination and fertility; pride in achieving mastery over life.
(+)	Justice, sensing and imagining, success and honour.
(–)	Domineering arrogance.
Fragrance	Frankincense
Colour	Gold
Gemstone	Gold

Mythology

While the Greeks considered Apollô to be the god of solar light, the sun itself was personified by a special divinity, Hêlios. The cult of Hêlios was very ancient and practised in many parts of Greece, especially in the island of Rhodes where a colossal statue of Hêlios stood 30 metres high, and ships in full sail could pass between the god's legs. The statue was completed by Chares of Lindos in 292 BCE after twelve years of work. Hêlios was represented with a crown of sun-rays, a spear in his left hand and a flaming torch held aloft in his right. In 224 BCE an earthquake destroyed the statue and it was sold for scrap in 653 CE.

Legend has it that Hêlios was the son of the Titans Hyperiôn and Theia; and brother of Selênê and Êôs (Dawn). He was drowned in the ocean by his uncles, then raised to the sky where he became the luminous sun. Every morning Hêlios emerged from the East, dressed in sparkling gauze and wearing a golden helmet from which issued a crown of rays, riding in a golden chariot drawn by winged steeds which were dazzling white and breathed forth flame from their nostrils. Although nine names are given for the steeds of Hêlios, he is traditionally shown in a chariot drawn by only four horses – Eous, Aethiops, Bronte and Sterope. He was portrayed as a youthful, strong and beautiful god, with gleaming eyes and wavy locks, wearing a golden helmet, drawn in his swift chariot, shedding light on gods and men alike.

When swearing an oath Greeks would often call upon Hêlios as a witness, as they believed he "observes all things ands hears all things" (Homer's Iliad 3.277). He saw the entire world by day and the underworld by night. He was the All-seer because his rays penetrated everywhere, and he knew everything. Hence, he was associated with divination.

Hêlios was also associated with fertility due to the sun's role in agriculture.

Hêlios's wrath was evident when Odysseus and his men slaughtered and feasted on some of Hêlios' beloved cattle. Hêlios complained to Zeus, whereupon Zeus struck their ship with a thunderbolt. Hêlios' pride led him to punish boasts. When Arge, a huntress, boasted that she was faster than Hêlios, he transformed her into a doe. Similarly, the young sea god Nêritês, who was the lover of Poseidôn was transformed into a spiral shellfish by Hêlios, as Hêlios resented Nêritês' speed at swimming.

White things were particularly sacred to him, especially white horses, white roosters and white poplars.

Hêlios had two main cult centres, however, none of his cult titles have been preserved.

Orphic Hymn VII: To The Sun

Hear golden Titan, whose eternal eye
With broad survey, illumines all the sky:
Self-born, unwearied in diffusing light,
And to all eyes the mirror of delight:
Lord of the seasons, with your fiery car
And leaping coursers, beaming light from far:
With your right hand the source of morning light,
And with your left the father of the night.
Agile and vigorous, venerable Sun,
Fiery and bright around the heavens you run.
Foe to the wicked, but the good man's guide,
Over all his steps propitious you preside:
With various-sounding, golden lyre, it is yours
To fill the world with harmony divine.
Father of ages, guide of prosperous deeds,
The world's commander, borne by lucid steeds,
Immortal Zeus, all searching bearing light,
Source of existence, pure and fiery bright:
Bearer of fruit, almighty lord of years,
Agile and warm, whom every power reveres.
Great eye of Nature and the starry skies,
Doomed with immortal flames to set and rise:
Dispensing justice, lover of the stream,
The world's great despot, and over all supreme.
Faithful defender, and the eye of right,
Of steeds the ruler, and of life the light:
With sounding whip four fiery steeds you guide,
When in the car of day you glorious ride.
Propitious on these mystic labours shine,
And bless your suppliants with a life divine.

[Selection from "*The Hymns of Orpheus*" Thomas Taylor, trans.]

Homeric Hymn XXXI: To Hêlios

And now, O Muse Calliopê, daughter of Zeus,

begin to sing of glowing Hêlios whom mild-eyed Euryphaëssa,
the far-shining one, bare to the Son of Earth and starry Heaven.
For Hyperiôn wedded glorious Euryphaëssa,
his own sister, who bare him lovely children,
rosy-armed Êôs and rich-tressed Selênê
and tireless Hêlios who is like the deathless gods.
As he rides in his chariot, he shines upon men and deathless gods,
and piercingly he gazes with his eyes from his golden helmet.
Bright rays beam dazzlingly from him,
and his bright locks streaming from the temples of his head
gracefully enclose his far-seen face:
a rich, fine-spun garment glows upon his body
and flutters in the wind: and stallions carry him.
Then, when he has stayed his golden-yoked chariot and horses,
he rests there upon the highest point of heaven,
until he marvellously drives them down again through heaven to Ocean.
Hail to you, lord!
Freely bestow on me substance that cheers the heart.
And now that I have begun with you,
I will celebrate the race of mortal men half-divine
whose deeds the Muses have showed to mankind.

[Selection from "*Hesiod, Homeric Hymns, Epic Cycle, Homerica*" Hugh G Evelyn-White, trans.]

Graeco-Egyptian Magick Invocation to Hêlios

Face East if performing this ritual at night, or turn to face the Sun if performing this ritual during the day.

Burn frankincense resin, anoint your forehead with frankincense oil and chant "**ACHEBUKRÔM**."

PGM VIII. 73–80

"Borne on the breezes of the wand'ring winds,
Golden-haired Hêlios who wield the flame's untiring light,
Who drive in lofty turns around the great pole;
Who create all things yourself which you again reduce to nothing.
For from you come the elements

arranged by your own laws which cause the whole world
to rotate through its four yearly turning points."
[*Tr.: E N O'Neil]

PGM IV. 1596–1715

"I invoke you, the greatest god, eternal lord, world ruler,
who are over the world and under the world,
mighty ruler of the sea, rising at dawn, shining from the East
for the whole world, setting in the West.
Come to me, thou who risest from the four winds,
joyous Agathos Daimôn,
for whom heaven has become the processional way.
I call upon your holy and great and hidden names
which you rejoice to hear.
The earth flourished when you shone forth,
and the plants became fruitful when you laughed;
the animals begat their young when you permitted.
Give glory and honour and favour and fortune and power to me.
I invoke you, the greatest in heaven,
ÊI LANCHUCH AKARÊN BAL
MISTHRÊN MARTA MATHATH
LAILAM MOUSOUTHI SIETHÔ BATHABATHI
IATMÔN ALEI
IABATH ABAÔTH SABAÔTH ADÔNAI,
the great god, **ORSENOPHRÊ ORGEATÊS TOTHORNATÊSA KRITHI BIÔTHI IADMÔ IATMÔMI METHIÊI LONCHOÔ AKARÊ BAL MINTHRÊ BANE BAI(N)CHCHUCHCH OUPHRI NOTHEOUSI THRAI ARSIOUTH ERÔNERTHER**,
the shining Hêlios, giving light throughout the whole world.
You are the great Serpent, leader of all the gods,
who control the beginning of Egypt
and the end of the whole inhabited world,
who mate in the ocean, **PSOI PHNOUTHI NINTHÊR**.
You are he who becomes visible each day
and sets in the Northwest of heaven,
and rises in the Southeast.

In the 1st hour you have the form of a cat;
your name is **PHARAKOUNÊTH**.
Give glory and favour to me.

In the 2nd hour you have the form of a dog;
your name is **SOUPHI**.
Give strength and honour to me.

In the 3rd hour you have the form of a serpent;
your name is **AMEKRANEBECHEO THÔUTH**.
Give honour to me.

In the 4th hour you have the form of a scarab;
your name is **SENTHENIPS**.
Mightily strengthen me, for the work I undertake.

In the 5th hour you have the form of a donkey;
your name is **ENPHANCHOUPH**.
Give strength and courage and power to me.

In the 6th hour you have the form of a lion;
your name is **BAI SOLBAI**, the ruler of time.
Give success to me and glorious victory.

In the 7th hour you have the form of a goat;
your name is **OUMESTHÔTH**.
Give sexual charm to me.

In the 8th hour you have the form of a bull;
your name is **DIATIPHÊ**, who becomes visible everywhere.
Let all things [done] by me be accomplished.

In the 9th hour you have the form of a falcon;
your name is **PHÊOUS PHÔOUTH**,
the lotus emerged from the abyss.
Give success [and] good luck to me.

In the 10th hour you have the form of a baboon;
your name is **BESBUKI**.

In the 11th hour you have the form of an ibis;
your name is **MOU RÔPH**.
Protect me and give me luck, from this present day for all time.

In the 12th hour you have the form of a crocodile;
your name is **AERTHOÊ**.

You have set at evening as an old man,
who are over the world and [under] the world,
mighty ruler of the sea,
hear my voice in this night, in these holy hours,
and let [all things done] by me, be brought to fulfilment.
Please, lord **KMÊPH LOUTHEOUTH ORPHOICHE ORTILIBECHOUCH IERCHE ROUM IPERITAÔ UAI**.
I conjure earth and heaven and light and darkness
and the great god who created all,
SAROUSIN, you Agathon Daimônion the helper,
to help me accomplish everything [done] by myself."
When you complete this spell say: "The one Zeus is Sarapis."
[*Tr.: Morton Smith]

PGM XXXVI. 211–30

Anoint your hand with oil and wipe it on your head and face. Repeat the following prayer seven times:
"Rejoice with me,
you who are set over the East wind and the world,
for whom all the gods serve as bodyguards
at your good hour and on your good day,
you who are the Good Daimôn of the world,
the crown of the inhabited world,
you who rise from the abyss,
you who each day, rise a young man and set an old man,
HARPENKNOUPHI BRINTANTÊNÔPHRI BRISSKULMAS AROURZORBOROBA MESINTRIPHI,

NIPTOUMI CHMOUMMAÔPHI.
I beg you, lord, do not allow me to be overthrown,
to be plotted against, to receive dangerous drugs,
to go into exile, to fall upon hard times.
Rather, I ask to obtain and receive from you
life, health, reputation, wealth, influence, strength,
success, charm, favour with all men and all women,
victory over all men and all women.
Yes, lord, **ABLANATHANALBA AKRAMMACHAMARI**
PEPHNA PHÔZA PHNEBENNOUNI
NAACHTHIP ... OUNORBA,
accomplish the matter which I want, by means of your power."
[*Tr.: R F Hock]

PGM I. 222–31

"Hêlios, I adjure you by your great name,
BORKÊ PHOIOUR IÔ ZIZIA
APARXEOUCH THUTHE LAILAM
AAAAAA IIIII OOOO
IEÔ IEÔ IEÔ IEÔ IEÔ IEÔ IEÔ
NAUNAX AI AI AEÔ AEÔ ÊAÔ."
[*Tr.: E N O'Neil]

PGM VII. 528–39

"Hêlios, Hêlios, hear me, Hêlios, lord, Great God,
you who maintain all things and who give life
and who rule the world, toward whom all things go,
from whom they also came, untiring,
ÊIE ELÊIE IEÔA
ROUBA ANAMAÔ MERMAÔ
CHADAMATHA ARDAMATHA PEPHRE ANAMALAZÔ
PHÊCHEIDEU ENEDEREU SIMATOI MERMEREÔ
AMALAXIPHIA MERSIPHIA EREME THASTEU
PAPIE PHEREDÔNAX ANAIE GELEÔ AMARA
MATÔR MÔRMARÊSIO NEOUTHÔN
ALAÔ AGELAÔ AMAR AMATÔR
MÔRMASI SOUTHÔN ANAMAÔ GALAMARARMA.
Hear me, lord Hêlios."

[*Tr.: R F Hock]

PGM Va. 1–3

"O Hêlios, **BERBELÔCH CHTHÔTHÔMI ACH SANDOUM ECHNIN ZAGOUÊL**, bring me into union with you."

[*Tr.: Hubert Martin, Jr]

Meditation and Eucharist

See Ritual Performance and Ritual Preparation chapters for more information on Meditation and Eucharist.

Dismissal

"O Hêlios, **BERBELÔCH CHTHÔTHÔMI**
ACH SANDOUM ECHNIN ZAGOUÊL,
I thank you for having come to me,
and may you always be a part of my life."

[*Tr.: Hubert Martin, Jr]

Commentary on Graeco-Egyptian Invocation to Hêlios

The word to be chanted while anointing your forehead with frankincense oil is "**ACHEBUKRÔM**." This "signifies the flame and radiance of the disc" of the sun (*PGM* XIII. 446-8). [*Tr.: Morton Smith]

PGM VIII. 73–80

This prayer is extracted from a spell which invokes the Headless God, or Akephalos, who was called upon for dream oracles and exorcisms. (He will be met in the sequel to this book.) The spell calls on Hêlios with a prayer and beseeches him to compel the Headless God to bring a dream oracle.

This same prayer occurs in a portion of *PGM* IV. 296–466, where Hêlios is called upon to compel a daimôn, called the god of the dead, to carry out the instructions given within the spell.

Hêlios is portrayed as driving the sun around "the great pole." He is also portrayed as a god who creates, orders, and then destroys all things. The "four yearly turning points" are the solstices and equinoxes.

PGM IV. 1596–1715

This spell calls on Hêlios to consecrate a ring, phylactery, stone, or engraving. A phylactery, or *phylaktêrion*, in the PGM refers to a stone, material, papyrus amulet, or lamella which may or may not be engraved with a spell, that is worn for protection; it should not be confused with the Jewish technical term spelled the same way. I have adapted the spell so that the consecration falls upon the person performing it, rather than on a magickal object.

In the spell, Hêlios is equated with the serpent god, Agathos Daimôn, who was mentioned in the invocation of Hermês. This is an example of flattery, as Agathos Daimôn is a superior god to Hêlios. (Agathos Daimôn will be encountered in the sequel to this book.)

Hêlios is portrayed, at dawn, as a young man who lights up the heavens, bringing fertility, and setting at evening as an old man (a reference to Atum, the form of the sun god at setting).

One of the words of power is **LAILAM**, which is either derived from the Greek "*lailaps*" (storm or hurricane) or the Hebrew "*leolam*" (forever).

ORGEATÊS may be **ORGIASTÊS**, or "participant in orgiastic rites," which were normally secret and connected with Dionysus.

PSOI PHNOUTHI NINTHÊR is equivalent to the Egyptian "Agathodaimôn, the god (of) the gods."

Hêlios passes through the twelve hours of the day. Each hour has associated with the vision of an animal. The exception to this is the ninth hour which has the vision of an animal and the "lotus emerged from the abyss." The visions for the sixth and eighth hours are qualified with additional information; and so the lion who rules the middle of the day is the ruler of time, while the bull who rules the eighth hour is visible everywhere.

Each of the twelve hours has one or two words of power associated with it. Most of the hours each have a property to confer. The properties appear to have been omitted for the tenth and twelfth hours.

The procedure is to visualise the animal associated with the hour, chant the word(s) of power and then request that the property be conferred.

As Hêlios lit up the sky and then travelled into the underworld, he was seen as a mighty ruler "over the world" and "under the world."

In the ending of the spell, the scribe is affirming the equivalence of Zeus, the supreme god of Mount Olympus, with that of Sarapis (or Serapis), who was considered by some to be the supreme god of Alexandria. (For information on Serapis, see Appendix 1: Background to Graeco-Egyptian Magick.) Curiously, neither Zeus nor Sarapis are mentioned previously in the spell. It appears that either the scribe added this line to further potentiate the consecration, or it was interpolated subsequently by a devotee of Sarapis.

PGM XXXVI. 211–30

This prayer to Hêlios is described as a charm to restrain anger, for victory and for securing favour.

The instruction is to anoint your hand with oil and wipe it on your head and face. The oil is not specified, and so I recommend frankincense oil to maintain consistency with the remainder of the ritual.

The instruction with this prayer is that it is to be repeated seven times. I would recommend this the first few times the spell is performed. Eventually just saying the spell once should be sufficient. Let your intuition guide you.

Hêlios is referred to as the Good Daimôn, which is the same as Agathos Daimôn or Agathodaimôn, of the previous spell. He is again described as rising from the abyss as a young man and setting as an old man.

MESINTRIPHI is an Egyptian term meaning "born of Triphis," and is an epithet of Isis.

ABLANATHANALBA AKRAMMACHAMARI, were discussed in the invocation of Hermês. There however, the second of these words of power was spelt **AKRAMMACHAMAREI**.

Substituting **PEPHTHA** for **PEPHNA**, it is found that **PEPHTHA PHÔZA PHNEBENNOUNI** is an Egyptian expression meaning "he is Ptah the healthy, the lord of the Abyss." Ptah is an Egyptian creator god.

PGM I. 222–31

This prayer to Hêlios is taken from an invisibility spell. These instructions are provided for information purposes only.

The spell instructs that the fat or eye of a nightowl and a ball of dung rolled by a beetle should be mixed with the oil of an unripe olive and ground until smooth. The beetle mentioned is probably the scarab beetle, which was sacred to the sun god, Ra. The mixture should be applied to the whole body, after which Hêlios is called on by his "great name." This is then followed by a request for invisibility until sunset.

PGM VII. 528–39

This spell is actually a victory charm. These instructions are provided for information purposes only.

The spell instructs that an offering should be made over oak charcoal of sacred incense with which has been mixed the brain of a wholly black ram and the wheat meal of a certain plant. The sacred incense is quite possibly a reference to Kyphi, the Egyptian temple incense, for which a number of recipes have been preserved. The certain plant from which the wheat meal is obtained is also not identified.

In the spell, Hêlios is described as "Great God, you who maintain all things and who give life and who rule the world, toward whom all things go, from whom they also came, untiring." This is another example of flattery where Hêlios is assigned roles beyond his station.

This is followed by words of power, including **PAPIE**, which could be related to **PIPI**, a permutation of YHWH – the Hebrew Tetragrammaton.

The original spell ends with "Hear me, lord Hêlios, and let the NN matter take place on time." I have abbreviated this to "Hear me, lord Hêlios," as only his manifestation is being requested.

PGM Va. 1–3

This spell seeks to bring about a direct union with Hêlios. I have used the spell in its entirety.

The instructions are that you should anoint yourself to have a direct vision. The spell does not specify an oil, so I recommend frankincense oil.

I have used the words of this spell in the dismissal.

Procedure for initiation

See "Bringing the planetary energies into everyday life" in the Ritual Performance chapter for a summary of these procedures.

Results

If you are reading this portion of the chapter, I assume that you have already invoked Hêlios with the ritual above. If you haven't, stop reading and do so!

This Sphere is linked with the heart centre and if there are any unresolved emotional issues that have not been dealt with, they could well up to the surface. (Emotional issues should have been dealt with in the Sphere of Venus.)

Many magickal traditions highlight the difficulty of accessing the Sphere of the Sun. It is important to maintain proper focus by overcoming distractions in life such as problems with work, relationships and friendships. It is only with focus that the lessons of the previous Spheres are built upon and you begin to access the divine spark.

The beginnings of access to the divine spark manifest as an increase in the flow of information from the divine realms. Messages are transmitted through the intuition. There is an understanding of that which must be accomplished in life and a sense of joy as steps are taken to its fruition.

As the energy of the Sphere of the Sun increases in daily life, it is often experienced as a knowing that magick is in us and around us, and that it is the heart that really matters. Some participants realise the unimportance of external trappings such as magickal looking clothing and gaudy jewellery.

The need for submission intensifies to the extent that you begin to relinquish the need for control, and embrace the world, magick, and deities. You are brought into a state of unity with the cosmos, state where the distinction between your self and your world starts to blur. This state is variously referred to as cosmic consciousness, Christ consciousness, and enlightenment.

Access to the divine spark and the sense of unity with the cosmos will increase progressively while working with the Spheres of Mars and Jupiter.

Having attained the Solar Sphere, you have a large degree of empowerment as a result of harmonising with the cosmos.

There may be an understandable sense of pride which could turn into domineering arrogance. This is the primary challenge to be overcome.

Specific results which have occurred in group rituals invoking Hêlios include:

Presence of energy in ritual area

- Many participants felt great warmth throughout the ritual. Sometimes the whole body seemed warm, while at other times it was only the feet.
- Sometimes a lot of activity was felt in the chakras or the aura.
- Many participants swayed during the ritual or moved around in circles. Sometimes the movement took the form of erratic circular movements, a rocking motion, shaking, throbbing, or pulsing.
- A number of participants wanted to either lie down or sit down. For some this was gentle. Others were forced down by either becoming unsteady on their feet and almost falling over, or feeling tugged.

Quality of energy

- Many participants described the energy as easy, relaxing, calm, peaceful, and tranquil.
- A number of participants felt very strong and empowered.
- A few participants described the energy as being very healing.

Experiences through physical senses

- One participant observed numerous shooting stars during a ritual.

Experiences through non-physical senses

- A number of participants had visions of nature or of being connected to nature. Sometimes there is a sense of clarity, centredness, or of being in the now. There was a strong sense of the heart chakra being open.
- For a few participants there was a feeling of being unable to differentiate between observed objects and themselves. This was the first stage of cosmic consciousness wherein you perceive yourself as being one with the universe.
- A number of participants had visions which indicated that they were experiencing the abyss. (This illusion can lead to the perception that attainment of this Sphere is the end of the spiritual journey.) While this is not the abyss as such, there is a veil that makes access to the solar sphere difficult. It is this veil that results in experiences perceived as the abyss.
- A number of participants reported the ritual as being a cleansing process for their emotions.

Visions of deity

- Elements of Hêlios seen include a golden figure; blonde hair; curly hair; flames coming out of his head; very tall; very manly; in a carriage with horses.

Messages received

- Participants received messages pertaining to justice; that wisdom is correctly defining what should be done with life; patience; encouragement; affirmations that Hêlios would always be there; that they should to be proud.
- A few participants had intensely personal and intimate messages.

Astral experiences

- In all the times I have run this ritual no-one has reported actually externalising, however a number of participants experienced the early stages. This included feelings of being about to lift out of the body; feeling extremely tall; feeling expanded.

Fears (and a Warning)

Working with solar deities should only be undertaken by those who have thoroughly integrated the energies of the previous rituals.

- I can cite two instances of negative experiences as a result of rushing into working with the Sphere of the Sun prematurely.
- One participant felt an incredible inrush of energy, had too many thoughts to process, raised his arms to release his energy to others in the group, and collapsed on the ground, shivering, cold, scared and lonely. This participant claimed to be an experienced ritualist, but had not done any of the previous rituals in this book.
- One participant was inexperienced magickally and had unresolved emotional issues. His martial arts skills were focused on his legs which were the strongest part of his body. When the Hêlios energy entered the ritual area, this participant had his legs immobilised – rendering him potentially physically vulnerable, and had his heart chakra wide open – rendering him emotionally vulnerable. He did not wait for the end of the ritual but fled the area.

The influence of the Solar Sphere continues through the remaining Spheres with progressively greater access to the divine spark being acquired.

Fifth Planetary Sphere – Mars

This Sphere marks acquiring will power and applying it to the lessons of the previous Spheres. The importance of will power to the effective practice of magick cannot be overstated.

The Sphere of the Sun was characterised by the beginning of access to the divine spark. The degree of access to the divine spark increases in this Sphere.

God Invoked	Arês
Key properties	Development of the will, ambition, drive, determination, focus and willpower.
(+)	Courage, ruling diversity, ardent vehemence.
(–)	War, wrathfulness, unholy daring, rashness of audacity.
Fragrance	Costus
Colour	Red
Gemstone	Yellow-green onyx (or garnet or ruby)

Mythology

Arês was pre-eminently the Greek god of war from the Homeric period onwards. He was honoured throughout Greece and his cult was particularly well developed in Thrace and Scythia; he had a temple in Athens; and a spring was consecrated to him near Thebes, beneath the temple of Apollô.

Legend has it that Arês was the son of Zeus and Hêra and was one of the twelve Olympian deities. He was very tall, uttered terrible cries and normally fought on foot, although he could sometimes be found on a chariot. His sister, Eris, goddess of discord, and his two sons, Deimos (Fear) and Phobos (Terror) accompanied him. Terror was also the name of one of his chariot horses; the others were Fire, Flame, and Trouble.

Arês lived in Thrace, traditionally the home of the Amazons, who were his daughters. Most myths regard Arês as a bloodthirsty god of battles. There are also legends about Arês' love affairs, the most famous being with Aphroditê.

In Greek sculpture, Arês did not appear to have a fixed representation. In vase paintings he was at first depicted as a bearded warrior wearing a helmet with a tall crest, dressed in heavy armour, carrying a shield, spear and sword. Later depictions showed him as a young man, almost nude, who retained little of his warlike attributes except the spear and helmet.

His symbols were the spear and the burning torch.

Arês only had a few cult titles:

- Aphneios – abundant
- Gynaikothoinasea – feasted by women
- Hippios – of the horses
- Thêritas – beastly, brutish

Orphic Hymn LXIV: To Arês

Magnanimous, unconquered, boisterous Arês,
In darts rejoicing, and in bloody wars:
Fierce and untamed, whose mighty power can make
The strongest walls from their foundations shake:
Mortal destroying king, defiled with gore,
Pleased with war's dreadful and tumultuous roar:
You, human blood, and swords, and spears delight,
And the dire ruin of mad savage fight.
Stay, furious contests and avenging strife,
Whose works with woe, embitter human life;
To lovely Aphroditê, and to Dionysus yield,
To Dêmêtêr give the weapons of the field;
Encourage peace, to gentle works inclined,
And give us abundance, with benignant mind.

[Selection from "*The Hymns of Orpheus*" Thomas Taylor, trans.]

Homeric Hymn VIII: To Arês

Arês, exceeding in strength, chariot-rider, golden-helmed,
doughty in heart, shield-bearer, Saviour of cities,
harnessed in bronze, strong of arm, unwearying,
mighty with the spear,
O defence of Olympus, father of warlike Victory,
ally of Themis, stern governor of the rebellious,
leader of righteous men, sceptred King of manliness,

who whirl your fiery sphere among the planets
in their sevenfold courses through the aether
wherein your blazing steeds ever bear you
above the third firmament of heaven;
hear me, helper of men, giver of dauntless youth!
Shed down a kindly ray from above upon my life,
and strength of war,
that I may be able to drive away bitter cowardice from my head
and crush down the deceitful impulses of my soul.
Restrain also the keen fury of my heart which provokes me
to tread the ways of blood-curdling strife.
Rather, O blessed one, give you me boldness
to abide within the harmless laws of peace,
avoiding strife and hatred and the violent fiends of death.

[Selection from "*Hesiod, Homeric Hymns, Epic Cycle, Homerica*" Hugh G Evelyn-White, trans.]

Graeco-Egyptian Magick Invocation to Arês

Either face East, or turn to face Mars if it is visible.
Burn powdered costus root, anoint your forehead with costus oil and chant "**ORTHIARÊ**."

PGM IV. 296–466

"I entrust this spell to you, chthonic gods,
HUESEMIGADÔN and **KORÊ PERSEPHONE ERESCHIGAL** and **ADONIS** the **BARBARITHA**,
infernal **HERMES THÔOUTH PHÔKENTAZEPSEU AERCHTHATHOUMI SONKTAI KALBANACHAMBRÊ**
and to mighty **ANUBIS PSIRINTH**, who holds the keys to Hadês,
to infernal gods and daimôns,
to men and women who have died untimely deaths,
to youths and maidens,
from year to year, month to month, day to day, hour to hour.
I adjure all daimôns in this place
to stand as assistants beside this daimôn.
And arouse yourself for me, whoever you are,
whether male or female, and bring Arês to me."

"I adjure you by the name that causes fear and trembling,
the name at whose sound the earth opens,
the name at whose terrifying sound the daimôns are terrified,
the name at whose sound rivers and rocks burst asunder.
I adjure you, god of the dead, whether male or female,
by **BARBARITHA CHENMBRA BAROUCHAMBRA**
and by the **ABRAT ABRASAX**
SESENGEN BARPHARANGGÊS
and by the glorious **AÔIA MARI** and by the
MARMAREÔTH MARMARAUÔTH MARMARAÔTH
MARECHTHANA AMARZA MARIBEÔTH;
do not fail, god of the dead, to heed my commands and names,
but just arouse yourself from the repose which holds you,
whoever you are, whether male or female,
and bring Arês to me."

"If you accomplish this for me,
I will quickly allow you your repose.
For I am **BARBAR ADÔNAI** who hides the stars,
who controls the brightly shining heaven,
the lord of the world,
ATHTHOUIN IATHOUIN SELBIOUÔTH AÔTH
SARBATHIOUTH IATHTHIERATH ADÔNAI IA
ROURA BIA BI BIOTHÊ ATHÔTH SABAÔTH ÊA
NIAPHA AMARACHTHI SATAMA ZAUATHTHEIÊ
SERPHO IALADA IALÊ SBÊSI
IATHTHA MARADTHA
ACHILTHTHEE CHOÔÔ OÊ ÊACHÔ KANSAOSA
ALKMOURI THUR THAÔOS SIECHÊ.
I am **THOTH OSÔMAI**."

"Bring Arês to me, because I adjure you, god of the dead,
by the fearful, great **IAEÔ BAPH RENEMOUN**
OTHI LARIKRIPHIA EUEAI PHIRKIRALITHON
UOMEN ER PHABÔEAI, so that Arês may come to me."
[*Tr.: E N O'Neil]

PGM IV. 474 and PGM IV. 830

"...Arês endured, when Ôtos and mighty Ephialtês [bound] him."

[*Tr.: Hubert Martin, Jr]

Meditation and Eucharist

See Ritual Performance and Ritual Preparation chapters for more information on Meditation and Eucharist.

Dismissal

"I adjure you, god of the dead,
by the fearful, great **IAEÔ BAPH RENEMOUN OTHI LARIKRIPHIA EUEAI PHIRKIRALITHON UOMEN ER PHABÔEAI**,
so that Arês may go to his own places that the universe be maintained.
Arês, I thank you for having come to me,
and may you always be a part of my life."

[*Tr.: E N O'Neil]

Commentary on Graeco-Egyptian Invocation to Arês

Anoint your forehead with costus oil while chanting "**ORTHIARÊ**," which is derived from *Arês orthios* or "right-standing Arês." (See John Gager's "*Curse Tablets and Binding Spells from the Ancient World*," Tablet number 120.)

Powdered costus root, when burnt, has a subtle fragrance but is quite smoky, and so a well ventilated area is recommended.

PGM IV. 296–466

This spell is titled "Wondrous spell for binding a lover." I have included the performance instructions for information purposes only.

This spell clearly imposes a male magickian's will upon that of a female whom he desires. As such, I find it morally reprehensible. However, as this is the only spell that I have come across that invokes Arês and his power, I can only surmise that the Graeco-Egyptian magickians had an abhorrence towards Arês, and possibly war in general. I have adapted the spell so that it is an unadulterated invocation of Arês. I have used this spell successfully on numerous occasions with groups of participants to experience the energy of the Sphere of Mars in its purest form.

[The only other reference to the magickal use of Arês I have come across was of a statue depicting him bound in the "iron chains of Hermês" and supplicating the figure of Dikê, the Greek goddess of justice and revenge. The oracle of the Clarian Apollô advised this measure to the people of Syedra in the first century BCE, as part of their defence against attacks by pirates. This measure was clearly meant to bind the aggression of the pirates using sympathetic magick.]

The instructions begin with taking wax or clay from a potter's wheel and making two figures, a male and a female. The male is to be made in the form of Arês fully armed, holding a sword in his left hand and threatening to plunge it into the right side of female's neck. The female should be made with her arms behind her back and down on her knees. Magickal material should be fastened on the female's head or neck. Magickal material refers to anything that carries the vibrational energy of the woman to be attracted, namely hair, bodily fluids, or nail clippings. If these are unavailable, often worn jewellery or clothes may be substituted.

A number of words of power are supplied which are to be written on the figure of the woman being attracted. These are written on various body parts. The figure is then further personalised by writing on the figure of the woman, her name and that of her mother. (It was common in magickal writings of the period to give the identity of a person by describing them as the progeny of their mother. This was quite practical as while a father's identity may be in doubt, that of the mother was always known.)

Next, thirteen copper needles should be obtained and should be stuck in various body parts of the figure of the woman. As each needle is stuck, the magickian says "I am piercing your [such and such a member of her anatomy], NN, so that she may remember no one but me, NN, alone." (For the first NN, the woman's name is substituted, for the second, the magickian's name is substituted.)

Next, a binding spell is written on a lead tablet and recited. It is this spell which I have adapted into a pure invocation of Arês.

Obtain "thread from the loom" and tie 365 knots while saying "**ABRASAX**, hold her fast!" Abrasax or Abraxas, was encountered in the invocation of Hermês. Numerologically the value of his name is 365. The knotted thread is then used to tie the lead tablet to the figures.

It is pertinent to consider other magickal references to the number 365. A lead tablet from the third century CE has a spell that binds the "365 members" of the victim's body. A lead tablet from the fourth century CE has a spell that binds the "365 limbs and sinews" of athlete runners. (See John Gager's "*Curse Tablets and Binding Spells from the Ancient World*," Tablet numbers 4 and 8.) Thus 365 appears to be used to refer to the totality of the human body. The Apocryphon of John from Nag Hammadi outlines the creation of Man in the image of God by specifying the various parts of the body along with the divine authorities placed over them. The total number of angels involved is 365. The number 365 seems to be imbued with magickal properties.

The figures should then be placed as the sun is setting, beside the grave of one who has died untimely or violently, and placing seasonal flowers beside it. Energy emanating from those who had died untimely or violently was commonly used by the Graeco-Egyptian magickians. (This will be explored in the sequel to this text, in the chapter on the Daimôn of the Dead.)

The spell begins by addressing a number of familiar chthonic gods, namely, Persephonê (Korê), Ereschigal, Adônis, Hermês, Thoth and Anubis. "I entrust this spell to you, chthonic gods, **HUESEMIGADÔN** and **KORÊ PERSEPHONE ERESCHIGAL** and **ADONIS** the **BARBARITHA**, infernal **HERMES THÔOUTH PHÔKENTAZEPSEU AERCHTHATHOUMI SONKTAI KALBANACHAMBRÊ** and to mighty **ANUBIS PSIRINTH**, who holds the keys to Hadês..."

A very similar spell begins with "I entrust this binding spell to you, gods of the underworld, **PLUTÔN** and **KORÊ PERSEPHONÊ ERESCHIGAL** and **ADÔNIS** the **BARBARITHA** and **HERMES** of the underworld **THÔOTH PHÔKENSEPSEU EREKTATHOU MISONKTAIK** and to mighty **ANOUBIS PSÊRIPHTHA**, who holds the keys to (the gates of) Hadês..." (See John Gager's "*Curse*

Tablets and Binding Spells from the Ancient World," Tablet number 28.)

Comparing the two spells suggests equivalence between **HUESEMIGADÔN** and **PLUTÔN**. In the "Second Planetary Sphere – Mercury" I referred to a lead tablet from Alexandria in the third century CE, which sought to bind a man by appealing to a number of underworld gods (repeatedly using the same names of power). Apart from Hermês, the tablet calls on "Pluto **HUESEMMIGADÔN MAARCHAMA**" repeatedly. (See John Gager's "*Curse Tablets and Binding Spells from the Ancient World,*" Tablet number 110.) In addition, **HUESEMIGADÔN** appears a number of times in various magickal spells such as a dream oracle (*PGM* II. 1-64) where it is spelt **UESSEMMIGADÔN**.

I think it is safe to assume that **HUESEMIGADÔN** is a magickal name for Ploutôn. Ploutôn ("the Rich Man") is the most common epithet for Hadês, the god of the dead. He was originally the god of the fields, and the ground is the source of all wealth.

Adônis is referred to as "the **BARBARITHA**," which is of unknown meaning, but in other spells is sometimes spelt **BARBARATHAM**.

The spell also calls on those mortals who have died untimely deaths, who together with the chthonic gods are to compel a daimôn (referred to as god of the dead), to assist. This daimôn is of uncertain gender, as it is referred to as "whoever you are, whether male or female." Egyptian lists of daimôns were careful to distinguish between male and female. Daimôn means "spirit" and has no connotation of being good or evil. Its corruption into "demon" was the result of Christian prejudices against everything contrary to their world view. (Thoth and Anubis will be experienced in the sequel to this book.)

The daimôn is asked to seek out, attract and bind the woman whom the magickian desires. The daimôn is then further asked to ensure that the woman is unable to experience intimacy with anyone other than the magickian, and be unable to eat or drink, find contentment, strength, peace of mind, and sleep without the magickian.

The daimôn is compelled by "the name that causes fear and trembling, the name at whose sound the earth opens, the name at whose terrifying sound the daimôns are terrified, the name at whose sound rivers and rocks burst asunder." This name consists of a number of words of power, beginning with "**BARBARITHA CHENMBRA BAROUCHAMBRA** and by the **ABRAT ABRASAX SESENGEN BARPHARANGGÊS**..."

This is strikingly similar to some of the names of power involved in the invocation of "the cat-faced god." "**BARBARATHAM CHELOUBRAM BAROUCHAMBRA SESENGENBARPHARANGÊS**..." (*PGM* III. 109-10). (Bast, the cat-faced goddess will be experienced in the sequel to this book.)

BAROUCH is Hebrew for "blessed," and is used to address the God of the Hebrews and in prayers.

SESENGEN BARPHARANGGÊS is often written as **SESENGEN BARPHARANGÊS** or **SESENGENBARPHARANGÊS**. This is a very common term in Graeco-Egyptian Magickal writings. Coptic Christians interpreted the name as a group of angels. In Jewish circles the term was interpreted as a powerful demonic spirit called Sesengen, the son (*bar*) of Pharanges. According to Jewish angel lore, angels have no parents, whereas the Talmud teaches that demons propagate like humans. Another possibility for the derivation of **BARPHARANGGÊS** is that there was a well-known fig tree which produced powerful drugs near a place called Baaras in a ravine (tês pharangos).

These words of power are followed by "**MARMAREÔTH MARMARAUÔTH MARMARAÔTH**." Words of power based on "marmar" with various suffixes occur commonly and appear to derive from the Aramaic phrase "Lord of Lords."

The daimôn is again compelled to "heed my commands and names, but just arouse yourself from the repose which holds you" and bring the woman to the magickian who desires her. If this is accomplished, the magickian offers to "quickly allow you your repose." This time, the magickian identifies himself with a number of deities, in the hope of using their power to compel the daimôn.

The magickian then returns to the use of words of power to attract the woman to him for all eternity. The last words of power in the spell "**IAEÔ BAPH RENEMOUN OTHI LARIKRIPHIA EUEAI PHIRKIRALITHON UOMEN ER PHABÔEAI**" form a palindrome which occurs on the lead tablet mentioned above. Sections of this palindrome occur in other spells.

When I first began studying this spell, it dawned on me that not only was the daimôn, known as the god of the dead, compelled to bring a woman to a magickian who desired her, but that Arês was being compelled to bind the woman. I then replaced all references to a woman being compelled to come, with requests that Arês be summoned. The result is a spell that effectively invokes the pure energy of Arês.

It should be noted that the Louvre Museum has a statuette, found in Egypt, of a bound kneeling female with thirteen nails driven into her and with very similar names of power to those recommended in this spell written on her limbs. The statuette however, was found on its own, sealed in a ceramic jug. Variations of the spell have been found on a number of metal tablets from various locations in Egypt. This proves that the spell was employed frequently.

PGM IV. 474 and PGM IV. 830

This verse (which appears twice in the PGM) is taken from Homer's Iliad 5. 385, where the twin giants, Ôtos and Ephialtês, who were known as the Alôadai, imprisoned Arês in a bronze jar for thirteen months until Hermês released him. (Perhaps the sealing of the Louvre Museum statuette in a jar implied the presence of Arês, negating the need for his statuette.) Ephialtês was also the name of the daimôn of nightmare among the Greeks.

The Graeco-Egyptian Magickians considered the verses of Homer magickal. There are no instructions included for the use of this verse, but it appears to have the form of a victory charm to help triumph over adversity.

Dismissal

The dismissal is adapted from the last portion of the invocation of Arês.

Procedure for initiation

See "Bringing the planetary energies into everyday life" in the Ritual Performance chapter for a summary of these procedures.

Results

If you are reading this portion of the chapter, I assume that you have already invoked Arês with the ritual above. If you haven't, stop reading and do so!

The Mars Sphere represents acquiring will power and focus, and applying them to magickal ability. With improved will power and focus, your rituals become much more potent and the degree of harmonisation with the cosmos increases.

The Mars Sphere often results in a consolidation of direction in life. Doubts regarding ventures are clarified and resolve is intensified.

The challenge associated with the Sphere of Mars is that the improved will power can potentially spiral out of control into aggression.

Specific results which have occurred in group rituals invoking Arês include:

Presence of energy in ritual area

- Many participants experienced body movement. Some moved backwards and forwards, others moved in circles, still others moved in figure eights. Some had a sense of being taller.
- A couple of participants had their arms come up and stay in a raised position for the duration of the ritual.
- Many participants felt heat of various intensities. Sometimes the heat was over the whole body, but in others it was specific to particular regions, usually the top of the body or the hands.
- Some participants reported an incredible surge of energy while one saw it as a bright white light. Some felt a tingling

sensation at the base of their spine or felt activity in their chakras.
- Two participants reported dilated pupils.

Quality of energy

- Many participants felt strength, vitality and empowerment.
- For some participants, the energy was gentle and they felt centred, grounded, calm, relaxed, peaceful, and reassured.
- For other participants, the energy was more powerful and they felt invulnerable and that there was nothing that they could not overcome. Many felt that they would be able to call upon this power in the future when it was needed.
- Contrary to the expectations of some participants, no-one felt anything aggressive whatsoever in the energy of Arês.

Experiences through physical senses

- A number of rituals were timed to coincide with close approaches of Mars to the earth and participants would stare at the planet. Numerous participants noted that Mars appeared to become brighter during the rituals.
- Many participants found themselves intensely aware of sounds and everything around them. Some said that noises, including those of birds, cats and dogs, appeared magnified.
- One interesting application of the energy of the Sphere of Mars was by a participant who suffered chronic backache as a result of years of driving taxis. He felt incredibly empowered in the ritual and demanded that his pain leave him. He is reportedly still pain free. This is a surprising example of the creative use to which empowerment can be put.

Experiences through non-physical senses

- A number of participants had visions in which they were given weaponry – helmets, swords or spears, suggestive of empowerment. Many of the visions experienced by participants had similar themes of empowerment and encouragement.

- Some participants had rapid flashes of images.
- One participant had a Nirvana experience with no concept of self, which started with seeing her skeletal structure and the atoms within herself. This experience effectively pre-empted the Sphere of Saturn.
- One participant felt a lot of energy at her crown and her arms reached upwards in a gesture of receiving. She did not receive any visions, possibly because she had fought against her tendency to sway throughout the ritual.

Visions of Arês

- Elements of Arês seen include wearing armour, which was sometimes red or silver/white; an armoured mask; a full helmet which obscured his face or a gold helmet.
- Participants have described his facial features as a grim stern warrior face, flaming red eyes, bearded, and a "gorgeous" manly face. He was sometimes described as tall.
- He was occasionally seen in a chariot. One participant described the chariot as being shiny bronze coloured and drawn by flaming horses.

Messages received

- Participants were typically told about the nature of strength and how it could be used for peace; defending the weak; and the importance of keeping emotions in check in a confrontational situation. Some were given words of encouragement and others were told to know themselves. One was encouraged to heal rather than defend.

Astral experiences

- A couple of participants reported feeling that something was trying to lift them out of their bodies. Another actually felt that she was hovering above her body.

Fears

- ξ Two participants felt their hearts racing to the extent that they thought they would have heart attacks. One was so tired that she felt as if she had run a marathon at the end of the ritual. These experiences highlight the need for fitness in the practice of Graeco-Egyptian Magick.

The influence of the Mars Sphere continues through the remaining Spheres with will power being progressively strengthened.

Sixth Planetary Sphere – Jupiter

This Sphere marks building upon the harmonisation of the Sun and the will power of Mars to acquire power and wealth. Spiritual abilities are honed to the extent that the mantle of a magickian may deservedly be worn. Potentially anything can be manifested.

The Spheres of the Sun and Mars led to a significant degree of access to the divine spark. This Sphere results in even greater access to the divine spark.

God Invoked	Zeus
Key properties	Development of power. Means to bring power about. Archetypal father, justice, leadership, popularity, charisma and acquisition of wealth.
(+)	Creation, royalty, prudent ruling, practical intellect.
(–)	Lust for power, striving for wealth.
Fragrance	Indian Bay Leaf
Colour	Purple/White
Gemstone	Amethyst

Mythology

Originally Zeus was the god of the sky and of atmospheric phenomena. He was lord of the winds, of the clouds, of rain both destructive and beneficial, of the thunder. He resided in the ether, the upper part of the air, and on mountain tops. He was literally the All-high. He was worshipped in elevated spots all over the Hellenic Empire.

Later Zeus took on a moral personality and became the supreme god uniting in himself all the attributes of divinity. He was omnipotent, all-seeing and all-knowing. He was the source of all divination. As a wise sovereign, he ordained all according to the law of Fate with which his own will was merged, and watched over justice and truth. To mortals he dispensed good and evil, but was kind and compassionate. While he chastised the wicked, he was capable of pity. He averted threatened dangers; he protected the weak, the indigent, the fugitive and all suppliants. His solicitude extended to the family, marriage, friendship, and peoples' assemblies. Homer called him "the father of gods and men." Finally, he was the protector-god of all Greece – Panhellenic Zeus.

In various legends Zeus was represented as being the consort of a number of goddesses and mortal women. He was however, generally portrayed as having one legitimate spouse, Hêra.

Even the gods feared the wrath of Zeus when his decrees were defied. Zeus was known to hurl his dreaded thunderbolts to earth, and leave death and destruction in his wake.

Zeus was normally depicted as a mature man, with a muscular body, thick wavy hair, broad forehead, deeply set eyes, finely curled beard and a serious expression. Except in primitive images he was rarely nude. He usually wore a long mantle which left his chest and right arm free. His attributes were the sceptre in his left hand, in his right hand the thunderbolt and at his feet the eagle. The eagle and the oak were sacred to him. On his brow he wore a crown of oak leaves or a wreath of olive leaves, which were the victor's prize in the Olympic games that were put on in his honour.

Zeus had numerous cult titles. The following is a selection of titles:

- Astrapaios – of the lightning
- Basileus – king, chief, ruler
- Keraunios – of the thunderbolt
- Ktêsios – of gain
- Moiragetês – leader of the Moirai (Fates)
- Panellênios – of all the Greeks
- Plousios – of wealth
- Theos Agathos - the good god

Orphic Hymn XIV: To Zeus

O Zeus much-honoured, Zeus supremely great,
To you our holy rites we consecrate,
Our prayers and expiations, king divine,
For all things round your head exalted shine.
The earth is yours, and mountains swelling high,
The sea profound, and all within the sky.
Kronos king, descending from above,
Magnanimous, commanding, sceptred Zeus;

All-parent, principle and end of all,
Whose power almighty, shakes this earthly ball;
Even Nature trembles at your mighty nod,
Loud-sounding, armed with lightning, thundering God.
Source of abundance, purifying king,
O various-formed from whom all natures spring;
Propitious hear my prayer, give blameless health,
With peace divine, and necessary wealth.

[Selection from "*The Hymns of Orpheus*" Thomas Taylor, trans.]

Homeric Hymn XXIII: To The Son of Kronos, Most High (Zeus)

I will sing of Zeus, chiefest among the gods and greatest,
all-seeing, the lord of all, the fulfiller who whispers
words of wisdom to Themis as she sits leaning towards him.
Be gracious, all-seeing Son of Kronos, most excellent and great!

[Selection from "*Hesiod, Homeric Hymns, Epic Cycle, Homerica*" Hugh G Evelyn-White, trans.]

Graeco-Egyptian Magick Invocation to Zeus

Either face East, or turn to face Jupiter if it is visible.
Burn powdered Indian Bay leaves, anoint your forehead with Indian Bay Leaf oil and chant "**ZAS**."

PGM V. 459–89

"I call upon you who created earth and bones and all flesh and all spirit
and who established the sea and suspended (?) the heavens,
who separated the light from the darkness,
the Supreme Intelligence who lawfully administrates all things.
Eternal Eye, Daimôn of daimôns, god of gods,
the lord of the spirits,
the invariable **AIÔN IAÔ OUÊI**, hear my voice.
I call upon you, master of the gods, high-thundering Zeus,
sovereign Zeus, **ADÔNAI**, lord **IAÔ OUÊE**;
I am he who calls upon you, great god,
in Syrian: '**ZAALAÊRIPHPHOU**,'
and you must not ignore my voice

(in Hebrew: '**ABLANATHANALBA ABRASILÔA**');
for I am **SILTHACHÔOUCH LAILAM BLASALÔTH**
IAÔ IEÔ NEBOUTH SABIOTH
ARBÔTH ARBATHIAÔ IAÔTH SABAÔTH
PATOURÊ ZAGOURÊ BAROUCH
ADÔNAI ELÔAI ABRAAM BARBARAUÔ NAUSIPH,
high-minded one, immortal,
who possess the crown of the whole [world],
SIEPÊ SAKTIETÊ BIOU BIOU SPHÊ SPHÊ
NOUSI NOUSI SIETHO SIETHO CHTHETHÔNI
RIGCH ÔÊA Ê ÊÔA AÔÊ IAÔ ASIAL SARAPI
OLSÔ ETHMOURÊSINI SEM LAU LOU LOURIGCH."
[*Tr.: D E Aune]

PGM IV. 467–468, PGM IV. 824 and PGM IV. 831–32

"Will you dare to raise your mighty spear against Zeus?"
[*Tr.: R F Hock and M W Meyer]

PGM XIII. 759

"I call on the name of Zeus, **CHONAI IEMOI CHO ENI KA ABIA SKIBA PHOROUOM EPIERTHAT**
manifest in my midst."
[*Tr.: Morton Smith]

Meditation and Eucharist

See Ritual Performance and Ritual Preparation chapters for more information on Meditation and Eucharist.

Dismissal

"I call on the name of Zeus, **CHONAI IEMOI CHO ENI KA ABIA SKIBA PHOROUOM EPIERTHAT.**
I thank you for having come to me,
and may you always be a part of my life."
[*Tr.: Morton Smith]

Commentary on Graeco-Egyptian Invocation to Zeus

To understand this invocation, it is important to remember that while the classical Greeks considered Zeus the supreme god of Mount Olympus, the Graeco-Egyptian magickians of Alexandria were far removed, in terms of geography, time in history, and religious belief. Many functions that in Greece would normally have been attributed to Zeus were in Alexandria taken over by other gods, notably Hêlios, Sarapis and Aiôn.

In the entire corpus of PGM writings there is only one full spell for working with Zeus (*PGM* V. 459–89). Apart from this there is a charm which is a verse from Homer, and a reference to the name of Zeus in an invocation of Ogdoas.

Anoint with Indian Bay Leaf oil while chanting an old name for Zeus, "**ZAS**" (*PGM* II. 117 and *PGM* XIXa. 44). Take care to not get the oil in contact with your eyes. Enter the ritual area, and burn Indian Bay leaves. A well ventilated area is recommended as Indian Bay Leaves may smoke a little.

PGM V. 459–89

This spell is claimed to loosen shackles, induce invisibility, send dreams to another; and enable you to gain favour.

The spell indicates that the magickian who composed it saw strong parallels between Zeus and YHWH, the god of the Hebrews. Remembering that Jupiter was the Roman equivalent of Zeus, it is interesting to consider the words of Augustine in "*The Harmony of the Evangelists*:"

> *"But their own Varro, than whom they can point to no man of greater learning among them, thought that the God of the Jews was Jupiter, and he judged that it mattered not what name was employed, provided the same subject was understood under it; in which, I believe, we see how he was subdued by His supremacy. For, inasmuch as the Romans are not accustomed to worship any more exalted object than Jupiter, of which fact their Capitol is the open and sufficient attestation, and deem him to be the king of all gods; when he observed that the Jews worshipped the*

supreme God, he could not think of any object under that title other than Jupiter himself."
[Selection from "*St. Augustine The Harmony Of The Gospels*" Rev. S. D. F. Salmond, trans.]

The Capitolium was a temple to Jupiter, Juno and Minera.

The opening line in the spell, "I call upon you who created earth and bones...", is reminiscent of Job 10:9–11:

"Remember, please, that You moulded me like clay, and that You will return me to the dust. Behold, You poured me out like milk, and curdled me like cheese. You clothed me with skin and flesh; You covered me with bones and sinews."

[Selection from "*The Stone Edition Tanach*" Rabbi Nosson Scherman, ed.]

Zeus is described as he "...who separated the light from the darkness..." This is similar to a number of biblical verses:

"God saw that the light was good, and God separated between the light and the darkness. God called to the light: 'Day,' and to the darkness He called: 'Night.'"

Genesis 1:4–5

"God said, "Let there be luminaries in the firmament of heaven to separate between the day and the night; and they shall serve as signs, and for festivals, and for days and years;"

Genesis 1:14

"And God set them in the firmament of heaven to give light upon the earth, to dominate by day and by night, and to separate between the light and the darkness."

Genesis 1:17–18

[Selections from "*The Stone Edition Tanach*" Rabbi Nosson Scherman, ed.]

Zeus is described as "...the Supreme Intelligence..." which is a reference to the divine Nous (Mind) concept in Greek philosophy. It is reminiscent of a biblical verse:

"She is indeed more beautiful than the sun, and surpasses all the constellations. She outrivals light, for light gives way to night, but evil cannot prevail against wisdom."
Wisdom of Solomon. 7:29–30
[Selection from "*The Stone Edition Tanach*" Rabbi Nosson Scherman, ed.]

Zeus is described as he "...who lawfully administrates all things..." which indicates a philosophical influence. This is similar to a biblical verse:

"Wisdom displays her strength from one end of the earth to the other ordering all things rightly."
Wisdom of Solomon. 8:1
[Selection from "*The Stone Edition Tanach*" Rabbi Nosson Scherman, ed.]

Zeus's description as "Eternal Eye" appears to refer to him as the source of all divination. Hêlios is similarly described in the Orphic Hymn dedicated to him. Zeus was thought of as conferring the power of divination upon Hêlios.

"Daimôn of daimôns, god of gods, the lord of the spirits" further reinforces the idea of Zeus being the supreme god.

Zeus is described as "the invariable **AIÔN IAÔ OUÊI**," which is a comparison with Aiôn, and an example of the magickal use of flattering gods. It should be remembered in the Opening Rite that Hêlios was compared to Aiôn.

"I call upon you, master of the gods, high-thundering Zeus, sovereign Zeus..." is a reference to the popular conception of Zeus as the supreme god on Mount Olympus.

Thundering also alludes to Zeus' function of a rain god, as can be seen in an inscription from Phrygia in 175 CE "... wet the earth, that she becomes heavy with fruit and flowers with ears of corn. This I, Metrodoros, beg you, Zeus son of Kronos..."

The words "**BAROUCH ADÔNAI ELÔAI ABRAAM**" correspond to the Jewish blessing "Blessed be YHWH, ... god of Abraham." "**ADÔNAI**" was normally substituted for YHWH (the tetragrammaton), as the pronunciation of YHWH was forbidden to Jews.

The words "high-minded one, immortal, who possess the crown of the whole world" continue with the theme of Zeus being the supreme god.

PGM IV. 467–468, PGM IV. 824 and PGM IV. 831–32

The verse "Will you dare to raise your mighty spear against Zeus?" appears in the PGM writings three times. Twice it is a standalone verse preceded by the title "Charm to restrain anger." The verse is taken from Homer's Iliad, Book 8, verse 424. As has been stated previously, Homeric verses were often used with charms and amulets.

PGM XIII. 759

The invocation of Ogdoas, who was encountered in the Opening Rite, lists a number of names of power, including "... the name of Zeus, **CHONAI IEMOI CHO ENI KA ABIA SKIBA PHOROUOM EPIERTHAT**." I have incorporated this, adding "...manifest in my midst." I have used this same excerpt for the dismissal.

Procedure for initiation

See "Bringing the planetary energies into everyday life" in the Ritual Performance chapter for a summary of these procedures.

In the commentary above, the connection between Zeus and YHWH was established. Developing this idea further, it should be noted that Homer referred to Zeus as "the father of gods and men" in The Iliad Book 8 and The Odyssey: Book 12.

I believe that one of the important keys to effectively experiencing the energy of Zeus lays in the words of Jesus Christ. According to the King James version of the bible, in Luke 17:21, Jesus says "The Kingdom of Heaven is within you." Most modern bibles however, assume that the translation of *entos* as "within" is a grammatical error and substitute "among" or "in the midst of." In John 10:30, Jesus says, "I and the Father are one." The sense was that for Jesus, at least, the Father was within.

More so than any of the other gods, Zeus as the cosmic father should be visualised within. This concept will take on great importance in the Integrating Graeco-Egyptian Magick into Everyday Life chapter.

Results

If you are reading this portion of the chapter, I assume that you have already invoked Zeus with the ritual above. If you haven't, stop reading and do so!

In the Jupiter Sphere, power, leadership and wealth are all within your grasp. With such power comes great temptation, where power and wealth become ends in themselves rather than the means to further spiritual development.

The Sphere is normally thought of as being benevolent and pleasant to experience. However, a number of participants have found that in order to take advantage of its transformative effects a strong focus is required, which precludes attempting the invocation whilst tired. Participants have reported a greatly strengthened commitment to their spiritual path as a result of their experiences with the Sphere of Jupiter.

Specific results which have occurred in group rituals invoking Zeus include:

Presence of energy in ritual area

- Many participants reported the now familiar swaying. For many it was a circular motion but occasionally figure eights (or infinity signs) are reported. One reported swaying more in this ritual than in any other.
- Many participants reported various degrees of heat ranging from mild to fiery.
- A number of participants reported a feeling of strong energy which manifested as tingling or pulsing. For some it was a sensation throughout the whole body, while for others it was

localised in the chakras (especially in the third eye area), hands, arms, feet or legs.

- A number of participants found difficulty in remaining upright and were forced to either sit or kneel. The sensation of being forced was either due to the feeling of being pushed down; the legs becoming wobbly; or the body becoming heavy.
- Other participants however, had no problems in remaining upright. One felt expanded out, one felt like his body had expanded outwards, and another who had a sore foot was able to stand without pain throughout the entire ritual.

Quality of energy

- This is the only planetary ritual in this book that had some gender specific effects. For a number of females there was a strong sensual component that was lacking for the males. A number of females reported the energy as embracing and loving.
- Just as the Aphroditê energy had a maternal feel, the Zeus energy often had a paternal feel.
- Many participants reported feelings of incredible euphoria, benevolence, wisdom, gentle power, relaxing and compassion. For a few participants there were feelings of being strong, empowered, and even invincible.

Experiences through physical senses

- A number of participants found that their senses were intensified. Some were very aware of noises around them, one reported hearing birds which sounded like harpsichords. A number reported various smells. One reported seeing lightning in the distance and another saw numerous bats overhead.

Experiences through non-physical senses

- ξ Two participants reported coming face to face with their true selves which indicates a high degree of access to the divine spark.
- ξ Some participants had visions of their fathers or saw themselves as children.
- ξ One participant had a vision of an amazing place with Middle Eastern type buildings which she believed was paradise. I am inclined to believe that this was an illusory vision suggesting that the spiritual journey was over and there was no reason to advance further.
- ξ A number of female participants felt either caressed or stroked, or touched on the tops of their heads or faces. One described the feeling as being smothered in thousands of kisses like soft warm rain.

Visions of Zeus

- ξ Elements of Zeus seen include seeing either his face or his whole figure in the clouds; fine facial features; a wizened old man; holding a lightning bolt; seated on a throne in a white marble palace; a general with a breast plate and toga.

Messages received

- ξ One participant felt that Zeus was a teacher of the soul in preparation for its next incarnation.
- ξ One participant was told to trust and relax and accept responsibility without tension.
- ξ One participant asked for the answer to life and strength and was given a purple seed in one hand and a bolt of lightning in the other hand.

Astral experiences

- ξ One participant had a sense of being lifted but did not separate from his physical body.

- One participant had her eyes closed but could clearly see the fence and the building near the ritual area, which indicated that she was engaging her astral senses. She did not separate from her physical body.

Fears

- One participant's vision ended with a feeling of having been slapped in her face. She realised afterwards that this was a wake-up call, as would be expected from a father.

The influence of the Jupiter Sphere continues through the Saturn Sphere with a greater understanding of the ethical issues involved in acquiring power and wealth.

Seventh Planetary Sphere – Saturn

Saturn marks the end of the spiritual journey in this book. The Saturn Sphere presents an opportunity to refine existing magickal abilities by bringing negative traits to an end. As such it leads to great wisdom. It is an important Sphere and should not be rushed.

Accessing the Sphere of Saturn can present difficulties as it involves overcoming the illusion of personality and duality. These illusions are the product of the experiences of an entire lifetime. It takes courage to shatter these illusions and embrace uncertainty in order to face that which has remained hidden. The reward is unimpeded access to the divine spark. (In Qabalistic magick, an obstacle is perceived as preventing access to the Sphere of the Saturn that is referred to as the Abyss.)

In order to facilitate the process of overcoming the illusion of duality, a Gnostic text called "The Thunder, Perfect Mind" has been included for study – see Appendix 4: Integration of the Divine Spark.

God Invoked	Kronos
Key properties	End of the journey. Gateway to next incarnation, through greater consciousness and fulfilment.
(+)	Philosophy, supreme intellect, reason and theorising.
(–)	Gloom, tears, torpor, ensnaring falsehood, pain, restriction, discipline, destruction and even death.
Fragrance	Storax
Colour	Black
Gemstone	Obsidian

Mythology

Kronos was originally a harvest god. His name was sometimes confused with Chronos (Time) resulting in him being thought of as a god of time.

In Hesiod's "Theogony," the world emerged from chaos, followed by the birth of the twelve Titans, whose parents were Ouranos (the Sky) and Gaia (the Earth). The Titans were honoured in Greece as the ancestors of men, and were attributed with inventing the arts and magick.

Unprepared for fatherhood, Ouranos hid his offspring inside Gaia's body. Gaia disapproved of the rejection of her offspring and planned a terrible vengeance against Ouranos. From adamantine she fashioned a sharp sickle and told her children of her plan. All were horrified except Kronos, the youngest, who agreed to castrate Ouranos by night, and then threw his genitals into the Mediterranean Sea.

When Ouranos was made impotent, Kronos liberated his brothers (with some exceptions) and became chief of the new dynasty. Under the reign of Kronos, the work of creation continued and the Golden Age of civilization ensued. Of this Golden Age, Hesiod in Works and Days, wrote of the men:

> *"And they lived like gods without sorrow of heart, remote and free from toil and grief: miserable age rested not on them; but with legs and arms never failing they made merry with feasting beyond the reach of all evils. When they died, it was as though they were overcome with sleep, and they had all good things; for the fruitful earth unforced bare them fruit abundantly and without stint. They dwelt in ease and peace upon their lands with many good things, rich in flocks and loved by the blessed gods.*
>
> *But after the earth had covered this generation – they are called pure spirits dwelling on the earth, and are kindly, delivering from harm, and guardians of mortal men; for they roam everywhere over the earth, clothed in mist and keep watch on judgements and cruel deeds, givers of wealth; for this royal right also they received..."*

[Selection from "*Hesiod, Homeric Hymns, Epic Cycle, Homerica*" Hugh G Evelyn-White, trans.]

Hesiod implies that the men of the Golden Age (a time associated with the rule of Kronos) lived as peaceful vegetarians, and upon death became benevolent guardian spirits and protectors of the living.

There was, however, a prophecy that Kronos would be supplanted by one of his children, and so Kronos swallowed each of his children as it was born.

Kronos' wife, Rhêa, was overwhelmed with boundless grief at the loss of her progeny. When the time approached for her to give birth to Zeus, she beseeched her own parents, Ouranos and Gaia, for help. Gaia took the newborn baby and agreed to raise him. Meanwhile Rhêa wrapped an enormous stone in swaddling clothes and presented it to the unsuspecting Kronos, who swallowed it up at once.

When Zeus reached adulthood he planned to punish his father. He summoned to his aid Mêtis, daughter of Okeanos (or Oceanus, another Titan). Mêtis gave Kronos a drug that made him vomit up the stone and the gods (his own children), whom he had swallowed.

Zeus then led the Olympians in a ten year war against Kronos and his Titans, who were eventually bound in chains and imprisoned beneath the earth in Tartaros (the lowest region of the world, as far below earth as earth is below heaven).

Zeus eventually released Kronos from his bonds and gave him dominion over the Islands of the Blessed, where the dead heroes live untouched by sorrow.

It is interesting to note that in a parallel myth, the Orphics saw the cosmic egg of creation encircled by a serpent identified with Kronos. This ties in with the concept of the universe used by the Gnostic group known as Ophians (Ophites) which portrayed the spheres of the seven planets being encircled by a serpent biting its own tail, known variously as Leviathan and Ouroboros.

In works of art, Kronos was represented as an old man with a mantle drawn over the back of his head, holding a sickle.

There were four temples dedicated to Kronos, however, none of his cult titles have been preserved.

Orphic Hymn XII: To Kronos

Etherial father, mighty Titan, hear,
Great sire of Gods and men, whom all revere:
Endued with various council, pure and strong,
To whom perfection and decrease belong.
Consumed by you all forms that hourly die,
By you restored, their former place supply;
The world immense in everlasting chains,

Strong and ineffable your power contains;
Father of vast eternity, divine,
O mighty Kronos, various speech is thine:
Blossom of earth and of the starry skies,
Husband of Rhêa, and Promêtheus wise.
Obstetric Nature, venerable root,
From which the various forms of being shoot;
No parts peculiar can your power enclose,
Diffused through all, from which the world arose.
O, best of beings, of a subtle mind,
Propitious hear to holy prayers inclined;
The sacred rites benevolent attend,
And grant a blameless life, a blessed end.

[Selection from "*The Hymns of Orpheus*" Thomas Taylor, trans.]

Homeric Hymn

There is no Homeric Hymn for Kronos.

Graeco-Egyptian Magick Invocation to Kronos

Either face East, or turn to face Saturn (if it is visible).
Burn storax resin, anoint your forehead with storax oil and chant: "**KRONOS.**"

PGM IV. 3086– 3124

Grind two handfuls of salt in a handmill (salt grinder) while repeating the following spell numerous times until Kronos is sensed.

"I call you, the great, holy,
the one who created the whole inhabited world,
against whom the transgression was committed by your own son,
you whom Hêlios bound with adamantine fetters
lest the universe be mixed together,
you hermaphrodite, father of the thunderbolt,
you who hold down those under the earth,
AIE OI PAIDALIS PHRENOTEICHEIDÔ
STUGARDÊS SANKLEON GENECHRONA

KOIRAPSAI KÊRIDEU THALAMNIA OCHOTA ANEDEI;
come, master, god,
for I am the one who revolted against you,
PAIDOLIS MAINOLIS MAINOLIEUS."

To compel Kronos if he appears threateningly, say:
"**KUDOBRIS KODÊRIEUS ANKURIEUS XANTOMOULIS.**"
Add: "**CHTHOUMILON.**"
[*Tr.: W C Grese]

Meditation and Eucharist

See Ritual Performance and Ritual Preparation chapters for more information on Meditation and Eucharist.

Dismissal

"**ANAEA OCHETA THALAMNIA KÊRIDEU**
KOIRAPSIA GENECHRONA SANÊLON STUGARDÊS
CHLEIDÔ PHRAINOLE PAIDOLIS IAEI,
go away, master of the world, forefather;
go to your own places in order that the universe be maintained.
Be gracious to us, lord."
[*Tr.: W C Grese]

Commentary on Graeco-Egyptian Invocation

PGM IV. 3086–3124

Anoint your forehead with storax oil while chanting "**KRONOS**," as there is no obvious name of power. Take care to not get the oil in contact with your eyes.

The original spell is actually an oracle called "Little Mill," where Kronos is compelled to appear and answer questions. The instructions in the spell are presented for information purposes only.

The instruction is to prepare a phylactery (defined in Fourth Planetary Sphere – Sun chapter) made out of either the rib of a young pig or the rib of a black, scaly, castrated boar. On the rib, Zeus holding a sickle is to be carved. Next to this should be carved the name "**CHTHOUMILON**."

The phylactery draws on the power of Zeus to control Kronos, based on the mythological defeat of Kronos. The portrayal of the sickle in the hands of Zeus appears to be an implicit threat to inflict, on Kronos, the same act that Kronos inflicted on Ouranos with the sickle. Zeus was thought of as a benevolent god and so the magickian writing the spell had no concerns about beseeching his assistance. This is an example of the Graeco-Egyptian magickians' use of compulsion in forcing deities to do their bidding. (See Structure of Graeco-Egyptian Magick rituals in Ritual Performance chapter.)

I feel that this protective charm was advised because Kronos was compelled to perform the magickian's bidding within the spell. This was also the case in one of the spells to invoke Aphroditê.

The threat perceived in Kronos' power is demonstrated in his usage in binding spells. In one example he was described as "Kronos who restrains the anger/passion of mankind..." (See John Gager's "*Curse Tablets and Binding Spells from the Ancient World*," Tablet number 111.) In another example, Selênê is told:

> *"As everlasting band round your temples you wear great Kronos' chains, unbreakable and unremovable, and you hold in your hands a golden scepter. Letters 'round your scepter Kronos wrote himself and gave to you to wear that all things stay steadfast."*
> *PGM* IV. 2840-6 [*Tr.: E N O'Neil]

This illustrates that Kronos is able to empower another deity but simultaneously restrict the deity's usage of that power.

The next instruction is to be clothed with "clean linen in the garb of a priest of Isis," which shows that having a clean robe, preferably of linen, is an appropriate sign of respect for any deity being invoked.

The spell instructs to carry the phylactery to "a place where grass grows" at night. Two measures of salt should be ground with a handmill while repeating the spell many times until the god appears. (According to David Talbot in "*The Saturn Myth*, " the tradition of a cosmic mill is found in cultures from Iceland to Finland to India to Greece, and is identified with either the Pole Star or Saturn.)

The final instruction is that while speaking, the sound of the heavy step of someone and a clatter of iron will be heard, implying that Kronos is coming bound with chains, holding a sickle. The magickian will be safe as long as protected by the phylactery. An offering of sage, the heart of a cat and horse manure should be made to Kronos before questioning him.

The first few times I performed this invocation I used a piece of pig leather from a wallet as a substitute for a pig rib, and cat hair as a substitute for the heart of a cat. I have since performed the invocation without the phylactery and without the offering. I have performed the invocation outdoors on grass and indoors. There is no discernible difference. The invocation derives its effectiveness from the words of power and intent. The phylactery and offering are unnecessary. As Saturn is the seventh Sphere, in group workings I normally repeat the spell seven times.

"The great, holy, the one who created the whole inhabited world" is a reference to Kronos' contribution to creation as one of the Titans and also as a snake wrapped around the Orphic egg. His ongoing function in creation is alluded to in a spell for picking a plant, where the plant selected is addressed as

> *"...you who were sown by Kronos..."*
> *PGM* IV. 2980 [*Tr.: E N O'Neil]

"The transgression was committed by your own son" is a reference to Kronos being emasculated and driven from his throne by his son, Zeus.

Kronos is described as he "whom Hêlios bound with adamantine fetters." Adamantine is a legendary material which nothing can break (see *PGM* XIII. 1002 for an example of the usage of adamant).

Kronos is also described as a hermaphrodite. The creator gods of many cultures were reputed to be hermaphrodites.

"Father of the thunderbolt," refers to Kronos being the father of Zeus, who was normally associated with thunder and lightning.

"You who hold down those under the earth," is possibly a reference to Kronos' dominion over the Islands of the Blessed and its dead heroes.

This is followed by a string of words of power which in the original text are followed by "come, master, god, and tell me by necessity concerning the NN matter, for I am the one who revolted against you." I have omitted "and tell me by necessity concerning the NN matter" to keep the spell a pure invocation.

The magickian by saying "for I am the one who revolted against you," is identifying with Zeus so as to have power over Kronos. This ties in with the carving of Zeus holding a sickle on the phylactery.

When Kronos is sensed, the formula of compulsion is chanted "**KUDOBRIS KODÊRIEUS ANKURIEUS XANTOMOULIS**." The spell advises that if Kronos appears threateningly, this formula may be used in order that he might be subdued and speak about that which was asked.

In order to dismiss Kronos, almost the same words of power are used as in the invocation but they are reversed. Whether the differences are deliberate or an error on the part of the scribe will possibly never be known unless another copy of the spell is found for the sake of comparison. I have not attempted to change any of the words of power to make them consistent, as the spell is effective as written.

It is interesting that the spell used indicates that Kronos was invoked by a single magickian, as it starts with "I call you..." In the dismissal, Kronos is urged to "be gracious to us, lord." This suggests that the spell was to be recited by a single magickian with one or more people in attendance.

Procedure for initiation

See "Bringing the planetary energies into everyday life" in the Ritual Performance chapter for a summary of these procedures.

Results

If you are reading this portion of the chapter, I assume that you have already invoked Kronos with the ritual above. If you haven't, stop reading and do so!

This Sphere marks the last of the planets known to the ancients. At the Jupiter Sphere, the apex of magickal power in the material world is attained. With the prospect of no further major gain in magickal abilities and a loss of the personality, a few magickians will choose to cease their development at the Jupiter Sphere. These magickians are sometimes called "Black Brothers," as they have no interest harmonising with the cosmos, but rather endeavour to have dominion over it.

Magickally, the Saturn energy can be used to end impediments to progress in the previous Spheres, such as bad habits, addictions and afflictions. As such it can be used to finetune spiritual progress and enhance the degree of harmonisation with the Spheres already worked, leading to greater consciousness and fulfilment.

In the Saturn Sphere the distinction between magick and mysticism begins to blur. You can look forward to wisdom through an augmented understanding of the lessons of the previous Spheres.

In order to fully realise the Saturn energy, Qabalists teach that the Abyss must be crossed. This process involves the "death" of the personality. This is extremely difficult as everything that has been taken for granted has to be abandoned. The sheer uncertainty of the task can lead to gloom. For the person who is equal to the challenge of "destroying" their personality, only the divine spark remains. Accessing the divine spark directly gives an understanding of the true self, an appreciation of your divinity.

Accessing Saturn is a very transformative experience. It is important that once the illusory personality is destroyed in the crucible of Saturn, the reintegration process excludes the dross and only pure gold remains. The gold was always there, laying hidden, occasionally betraying its presence with a glint of light.

There are challenges here greater than those associated with any other planetary Sphere. Saturn is representative of pain, restriction, discipline, destruction and even death. This translates to tests as to attachment to the material plane and commitment to a spiritual path.

Specific results which have occurred in group rituals invoking Kronos include:

Presence of energy in ritual area

- The Kronos energy was sometimes seen as entering the ritual area as a dark grey mist; or felt as a dampness in the atmosphere.
- A number of participants reported various degrees of warmth. For some participants the energy came very quickly. Some felt energy in their hands.
- There was the usual swaying, with some participants feeling either being pushed backwards or forwards, with one moving in a squashed figure eight pattern.
- Most participants reported a heaviness. A number were forced down to either sit or kneel.
- One participant reported a strong constriction around her heart during the ritual.

Quality of energy

- Most participants felt power in the energy and did not find it threatening.
- Some participants perceived the energy as being there to help, teach, discipline or to take their burdens.
- Some felt the energy as a cleansing process as they were able to target things in their life that they wanted to end.

Experiences through physical senses

- During one outdoor ritual, the clouds cleared up halfway through.
- During another ritual one participant observed lightning in the distance.

- ξ During another ritual a number of participants were distracted by a barking dog which prevented them from having vivid visions. It is quite possible that these participants were not ready to experience the energy of Kronos.
- ξ One participant heard rattling chains.

Experiences through non-physical senses

- ξ A number of participants had experiences which are in keeping with crossing the Abyss. For some, a black hole was perceived as a doorway to the Abyss. These participants sometimes felt death beckoning to them. All returned safely.
- ξ Some participants felt their souls disintegrating into atoms, dissolving into the universe, and then coming back together in a distinctly different form. Sometimes the route taken by the soul to return to the body was different from the path taken to leave the body.
- ξ Some participants had experiences of themselves as old.
- ξ A number of participants used the ritual to bring undesirable elements in their lives to an end. Sometimes the ties to these elements were seen to be cut by Kronos' sickle.
- ξ A number of participants had visions of snakes, either on their own or in association with Kronos.

Visions of deity

- ξ Elements of Kronos seen included an old man; the Grim Reaper; a benevolent old man like Father Christmas; and Francisco Goya's painting "Saturn Devouring One of His Sons."
- ξ Less specific visions have included an old man's face with numerous lines, a laughing face coming through in flames, a man on a throne, a face in the darkness, a dark figure in a black hole, and a dark robed hooded figure in his sixties or seventies with a beard and piercing eyes.

Messages received

- ξ The wisdom of Saturn prepares for the journey beyond the cosmos as it is the result of contemplating the lessons of the previous Spheres. With old age comes the debilitation of the physical body and only wisdom remains.
- ξ Humility, discipline, and taking things slowly are necessary.
- ξ The end is not the end, but a new beginning.
- ξ To have a wish granted or to cross the Abyss, something must be given in return.

Astral experiences

- ξ Only one participant reported what was almost an astral experience. He stated that he started to externalise but the experience stopped suddenly.

Revisiting the Spheres after having experienced the Saturn Sphere results in a renewed appreciation for their intrinsic natural properties.

Integrating Graeco-Egyptian Magick into Daily Life

By this stage, you have experienced each of the seven planetary deities, their energies, and their correspondences in sequence. The more diligently you have strived, the more profound will be the results obtained from the practices outlined below.

It is now time to integrate all seven of these energies into everyday life. Understanding and harmonising with the various energies that permeate the universe is the secret to enriching everyday life.

Weekly harmonisation with planetary energies

The energies corresponding to the seven planetary deities can be integrated into everyday life on a weekly basis.

Always aim to be in harmony with the universe. This means harmonising with the predominant planetary energies wherever possible.

The predominant planetary energy of each day can be greatly intensified by means of repeating the process of initiation for each planetary Sphere during its corresponding day. (The planetary days were listed in the Ritual Preliminaries chapter.)

Thus for each day of the week, you should be aware of the planetary day and its corresponding energy, and adhere to at least some of the following:

- ξ study and meditate on the planetary Sphere
- ξ select some items of clothing in the aspected colour
- ξ burn the aspected incense or essential oil
- ξ dab on a small quantity of the aspected essential oil (take care with these)
- ξ wear the aspected gemstone or metal as a ring or other piece of jewellery

- ξ recite the Orphic and Homeric Hymns
- ξ perform the Graeco-Egyptian Magick invocation
- ξ perform tasks whose nature is in keeping with the predominant planetary energy

The last point indicates that, if possible, you should try to structure your week so that tasks can be performed in accordance with the predominant planetary energies of the day. For example, Thursday is the optimum day for wealth creation schemes, while affairs of the heart should be pursued on Friday.

Now for a bit of perspective. It will not always be possible to strictly adhere to the principles above. The events of a day may necessitate tapping into one or more planetary energies other than the predominant one. It may not always be possible to find the time or inclination to harmonise with the predominant planetary energies. The advice here is simple. If you fall off a horse, you climb back on. If you break a diet and binge, you resume the diet. So it is with a spiritual path. If you stray off the path, resume it when it feels appropriate.

One of the mundane joys of this system is that indecision regarding clothing colour, fragrance and jewellery choices becomes a thing of the past. On a deeper level however, harmonisation with the predominant planetary energies is taking place ensuring that your life proceeds far more smoothly than it would otherwise.

Daily harmonisation with planetary energies

While the planetary energies certainly lend themselves to weekly harmonisation, they can also be experienced in their totality through a meditation based on the Sevenths in the Opening Rite. Experiencing the energies in their totality gives you a true understanding of self, and is incredibly empowering.

Up until this point the Sevenths have been used solely within the Opening Rite as a preliminary to magickal invocations. They can however, be applied to form a powerful meditation suitable for use on a daily basis.

As mentioned previously, the Opening Rite used by the Graeco-Egyptian magickians utilises a seven direction system that ties in with the seven vowels of the Greek alphabet, and the seven planets. We now have to determine which vowel ties in with which planet.

Plutarch of Chaeronea, a priest at the temple of Apollô at Delphi explained the attribution of Epsilon (E) to Apollô in ancient times:

> *"There are seven vowels in the alphabet and seven stars that have an independent and unconstrained motion; E is the second in order of the vowels from the beginning, and the Sun the second planet after the moon, and practically all Greeks identify Apollô with the Sun."*
> [Selection from "*The Greek Qabalah*" Kieren Barry]

Plato, Aristotle and other early Greek philosophers believed that the order of the planets was the Moon, Sun, Mercury, Venus, Mars, Jupiter and Saturn. This was known as the Platonic order of the planets. This order was corrected in the time of Archimedes (287-212 BCE) to what became known as the Ptolemaic order of the planets (which has been used throughout this book).

According to Iranaeus of Lyons (125-203 CE), one of the Gnostic schools connected the vowels to the heavens as follows:

> *"And the first heaven indeed pronounces Alpha, the next to Epsilon, the third Eta, the fourth, which is in the midst of the seven, utters the sound of Iota, the fifth Omicron, the sixth Upsilon, the seventh, which is also fourth from the middle, utters the element Omega."*
> [Selection from "*The Greek Qabalah*" Kieren Barry]

It is thus evident that attribution of the vowels to the planets was corrected in the changeover from the Platonic to the Ptolemaic order of the planets. In the analysis of the Opening Rite, the attribution of vowels to the directions in the Sevenths was discussed. Combining this information, with the attribution of the vowels to the planets, we find that each direction corresponds to a different planetary energy:

Table 22: Attribution of planetary energies to directions

Direction	Vowel	Planet	Deity
East	A	Moon	Selênê (Mênê)
North	E	Mercury	Hermês
West	Ê	Venus	Aphroditê
South	I	Sun	Hêlios
Earth	O	Mars	Arês
Centre	U	Jupiter	Zeus
Cosmos	Ô	Saturn	Kronos

This set of planetary attributions is very apt:

- A full Moon appears bigger and more spectacular as it rises in the East due to the diffraction of the Earth's atmosphere.
- In the Northern Hemisphere, the planets follow the ecliptic, which is an arc starting in the East, trending towards the South, and ending in the West. If one of the planets was to find its way to the North, which better than the messenger planet, Mercury?
- Venus is known as the Evening Star, and is often seen dominating the Western sky just after sunset.
- The Sun is at its most powerful at its apex in the South.
- Mars is the only planet with an underworld connection, as Arês would supply Hadês with souls in a mutually beneficial arrangement.
- Jupiter is the cosmic father (see Sixth Planetary Sphere – Jupiter chapter).
- Saturn, being the last of the planets known to the ancients, is the gateway to the Cosmos.

Meditation exercise

Sit comfortably facing the East and contemplate the seven directions in sequence. Each direction corresponds to a planetary Sphere and its numerous properties. Straight ahead is the Moon, to the left is Mercury, behind is Venus, to the right is the Sun, below is Mars, within is Jupiter, and above is Saturn. With practice, you will be able to visualise the seven planetary Spheres and their properties in all seven directions simultaneously.

As stated previously, the energies corresponding to these seven Spheres make up the totality of your spiritual, intellectual, emotional and physical existence. The person who has diligently worked with all seven planetary energies will find this exercise incredibly powerful as it enables the perception of the totality of their existence in seven neat compartments. If however, any part of your existence appears to lie beyond these seven planetary energies then further introspection is required.

This meditation exercise opens the doors to self-knowledge, and ultimately, empowerment.

Final thoughts

The process in this book may appear deceptively simple, but if followed diligently is incredibly profound. Once the seven planetary energies have been integrated into everyday life, the distinction between the spiritual and the mundane blurs. You will be able to harmonise with the subtle energies permeating your world everyday, as well as understand and embrace who you truly are. You will become fully empowered and self-reliant, reclaiming your birthright of being the very best that you can be.

Is this the end of the spiritual path?

Just as successive weeks cycle repeatedly throughout life, so too does the cycle of birth and rebirth repeat leading to plural lives. The Gnostics and Hermeticists wrote of their sublime experiences in the eighth and ninth Spheres that exist beyond the planets. The eighth and ninth Spheres are the key to transcending the cycle of birth and rebirth in order to reunite with the all-pervading God force, thereby achieving immortality.

Graeco-Egyptian Magick can be used to attain to the eighth and ninth Spheres and this will be the subject of the sequel to this book. However, before this journey can be undertaken, you must fully integrate the seven planetary energies into their psyche on a daily basis. This means diligent regular magickal work. And thus ends this book, with the promise of a new beginning...

Appendix 1
Background to Graeco-Egyptian Magick

The knowledge that we have of Graeco-Egyptian Magick comes from deliberately hidden writings discovered in recent times. The primary references in this book are from a large cache of magical papyri obtained from Egyptian tombs in the early nineteenth century and auctioned off to museums in Europe. These writings are collectively referred to as the Greek Magickal Papyri (PGM) and the Demotic Magickal Papyri (PDM). The spells therein were written in the Greek, Demotic Egyptian, and Coptic alphabets. They were penned by a number of magickians in Egypt from the second century BCE to the fifth century CE. Sometimes more than one alphabet was used in a single spell. In general, Greek was used in pagan and cosmopolitan writings, Demotic was mostly Egyptian, and Coptic was a Hermetic/Christian synthesis.

The PGM and PDM writings were translated piece by piece. The first English translation of a portion of these papyri was published by Charles Wycliffe Goodwin in 1853. It was not until 1986 that a complete version of these magickal writings was available in English.

Apart from the PGM and PDM writings, the unadulterated remnants of the Graeco-Egyptian Magickal tradition are to be found in various artefacts including inscriptions on gemstones, clay bowls and statues, tablets made of various metals including gold, silver, lead and tin. The lead tablets were generally reserved for curses. These curse tablets are the secondary references used in this book, and were produced during the period from the fifth century BCE to the fifth century CE in an area spanning northern Africa and Europe.

The eclectic remnants of the Graeco-Egyptian Magickal tradition represent a synthesis of the magick practised by the Sumerians, Babylonians, Egyptians, Greeks, Hebrews and Christians, along with miscellaneous religious references. Let us now consider the threads composing the rich tapestry of Graeco-Egyptian Magick.

Sumerian thread

Most modern scholars think of the cradle of civilisation as lying in southern Mesopotamia, the fertile crescent of the Middle East near the Persian Gulf. There seems to be no consensus among academics as to when the Sumerians first came to this region, however, the earliest Sumerian writings date back to roughly 3400 BCE.

The Sumerians lived in agricultural communities supporting a priestly caste which provided organised practices of their sciences and the worship of the gods. Indeed it is to Sumeria that the origins of astronomy and astrology are often traced. Astrology is of particular relevance to the system of magick presented in this book as it provides a model for celestial influences on mankind.

Possibly all agricultural societies, including the Sumerians, were aware of the celestial drama played by the Sun. Complex mythologies were woven around the natural personalities involved in this drama. These mythologies were connected with fertility, sowing, reaping and harvesting. The Sun was seen as being born at the spring equinox, reaching its zenith at the summer solstice, weakening and aging at the autumn equinox, and dying at the winter solstice. The dead Sun would go into the underworld in preparation for being reborn at the spring equinox.

Babylonian thread

Babylon was a city state within the Sumerian empire. As the Sumerian empire waned, that of Babylon came into being in 1950 BCE. The history of this part of the world documents various nomadic peoples infiltrating Mesopotamia.

The land in this region was flat, necessitating the building of towers, called ziggurats, to scan the horizon. Babylonian priests lived in seclusion in monasteries near these ziggurats. They developed a lunar calendar to measure time. The lunar calendar, however, consisted of thirteen lunar months, each of which was twenty-eight days long – a total of 364 days. Hence every year, one and a quarter days were lost. Over time this discrepancy would become quite significant.

The Babylonian priests observed the skies overhead for many generations and determined that apart from the Moon and the Sun, there were five wandering stars or planets – Mercury, Venus, Mars, Jupiter and Saturn. Initially the stars and the planets were regarded as actual gods. However, over time the Babylonian priests realised that the gods were separate from, and in fact ruled, the celestial bodies.

We have records of the Babylonian priests observing earthly phenomena such as floods, wars and rebellions, and correlating these phenomena to simultaneous celestial events. They eventually came to the conclusion that the laws governing movements of celestial bodies also governed events on earth.

The Babylonian priests ascribed one of their deities to each of the planets:

- Sin (Suen or Nanna), the Lord of Wisdom, was identified with the Moon and with measuring time.
- The fastest moving of the remaining planets was Mercury, which became identified with Nabu (Nabium). Nabu was the messenger of the gods and the divine scribe.
- Venus was prominent in the morning, giving birth to day, and was hence seen as possessing the female qualities of love, gentleness and procreation. Venus thus became identified with Ishtar (Inana).
- Shamash (Utu), the illuminating bestower of knowledge through divination and omniscient dispenser of justice, was seen as travelling across the heavens brandishing his pruning saw, and was identified with the Sun.
- Red Mars was identified with Nergal (Erra), the fiery god of war, forest fires, fevers and plagues.
- Marduk, became king of the gods contemporaneously with the rise of Babylon from city state to empire capital, and was identified with Jupiter.
- Ninurta (Ningirsu), the champion of the celestial gods, destroying the enemy, became identified with Saturn, the slowest moving of all the planets.

The Assyrians preserved these astrological writings after their conquest of the entire fertile crescent area. The Assyrio-Babylonian astrologers came to be known as the Chaldeans. This name will be very familiar to readers of the Bible. Babylon eventually fell to the Medo-Persians in 539 BCE.

Egyptian thread

The Egyptian culture is truly ancient. Before 4000 BCE, the Egyptians were already trading in copper, building dams and canals, and irrigating their lands.

In Egypt, the earliest astronomical texts appeared on coffin lids of the Middle Period (2100–1800 BCE) and were partly religious, and partly practical. The Egyptians developed a simple agricultural calendar based on the flooding of the Nile. It consisted of three four-month periods called Inundation, Planting and Harvest. The Egyptian year was divided into thirty-six ten-day periods, with a further five days of feasting. This made a total of 365 days. This was only a quarter day shorter than the calendar year currently used.

The Egyptians measured time with a day divided into twelve parts from sunrise to sunset, and a night divided into twelve parts from sunset to sunrise. It is interesting to note that magickians still use this system of measuring time when determining optimal times for casting spells, referring to them as "Planetary Hours."

Egypt was renowned as having the most powerful magickians in the ancient world. Magick was an everyday fact of life for all in Egypt. The Pharaoh was the master magickian in Egypt, responsible for the welfare of Egypt as a whole. He ensured that the Nile flooded by just the right amount – too little and the people starved, too much and the land was inundated. (There are accounts of Nectanebus, the last native Pharaoh of Egypt, in 358 BCE making wax models of enemy ships which he would conquer magickally in order to pave the way for a victory in the physical world.) Lesser magickal tasks were delegated to the plethora of priests throughout the land.

The Persians conquered Egypt in the sixth century BCE and brought with them the astrology of Babylon. The Egyptians at this time, however, were still xenophobic and resistant to change from without.

Egypt fell to a number of invaders in the first millennium BCE, all of whom left their mark. One of the most notable was Alexander the Great, who conquered Egypt in 332 BCE. Upon his death, Egypt was seized by his general, Ptolemy, who established a ruling dynasty. Many scholars from the Hellenic Empire were drawn to the Great Library in Alexandria, paving the way for this region to become the epicentre of Graeco-Egyptian spirituality and philosophy. Eventually in 31 BCE, Egypt was conquered by the Romans and became a mere province.

It should be noted that Egypt always exerted a certain fascination to everyone in the ancient world. The Egyptians had a reputation as master magickians, and at the time of the Roman occupation still had functioning temples. Many were drawn to Egypt seeking spiritual advancement, including Orpheus, Pythagoras and Apollonius of Tyana. Some early opponents of Christianity claimed that Jesus Christ had also trained as a magickian in Egypt.

Greek thread

Until the reign of Philip of Macedon, Greece was a collection of distinct city states. Philip united these states and created an empire stretching up to the Danube. Philip's son, Alexander the Great came to the throne in 336 BCE at twenty years of age. He initially consolidated his inherited empire by quelling unrest and introducing a common language throughout all of the Greek city states. He conquered the east from 334–323 BCE, extending his dominion – the Hellenic empire – as far as India.

Alexander respected the religions and cultures of the conquered countries. One of the most radical characteristics of the Hellenic empire was that an individual was classed as a Hellene not by birth, but by education. The residents of the conquered countries were allowed to keep their belief systems so long as they expressed themselves in Greek. This led to large scale cross-cultural mixing between all the countries that had been absorbed into the Hellenic empire. Politically, the Hellenic empire came to an end with

Alexander's death, but the cross-cultural mixing of the Hellenistic period continued for 600 years from 325 BCE to 313 CE.

The Ptolemaic world view of the Greeks came into standard use in the second century BCE. It portrayed the earth surrounded by seven concentric planetary spheres, which moving outwards were Moon, Mercury, Venus, Sun, Mars, Jupiter and Saturn.

The Greek planets were named descriptively as follows:

Table 23: The Greek planets

Planet	*Greek name*
Mercury	Twinkling Star
Venus	Herald of the Dawn, Herald of Light, Vespertine, Star of the Evening
Mars	Fiery Star
Jupiter	Luminous Star
Saturn	Brilliant Star, Indicator

As early as the seventh century BCE, citizens of the Greek city states were resident in Babylon, where they observed the association of certain Babylonian deities with each of the planets. The Greeks also noticed great similarities between the Babylonian deities and their own. After the fourth century BCE the Greek deities that closely resembled Babylonian deities began to be associated with the planets. Hence:

Table 24: Babylonian and Greek planetary deities

Planet	*Babylonian Deity*	*Greek Deity*
Moon	Sin	Selênê (Mênê)
Mercury	Nabu	Hermês
Venus	Ishtar	Aphroditê
Sun	Shamash	Hêlios
Mars	Nergal	Arês
Jupiter	Marduk	Zeus
Saturn	Ninib	Kronos

The Chaldeans had categorised the attributions of the planets to metals, gems, plants, animals, and so on. The Greeks then extended these attributions. These attributions were the predecessors of those widely used by esotericists in the Middle Ages and are still used by magickians today.

Whilst magick was acceptable to the Greeks, there was harsh legislation against black magick everywhere except Athens. Examples of black magick included moving crops from a neighbour's field to your own, or cursing your neighbour's crops.

A major contribution of the Greeks to magick and divination was isopsephy, where each letter was assigned a numerical value. This led to links between words and combinations of worlds, through the sum of their numerical values, which could then be analysed. Isopsephy flourished during the Hellenistic Age, and tradition held that Pythagoras had used it for divination. It was greatly expanded by the Gnostics in the second century CE. It was around this time that isopsephy was incorporated by the Jews into their system of mysticism, the Qabala, where it became known as *gematria*.

Isopsephy did not however, begin with the Greeks. One tantalising inscription remains to show that it existed amongst the Babylonians. It is along a wall at Khorsabad built during the reign of Sargon II (727-707 BCE) which states that the length of the wall was:

> *"... equivalent to the value of his name."*
> [Selection from "*The Greek Qabalah*" Kieren Barry]

It was from the ziggurat of the palace at Khorsabad that the colours used in this book were derived. It is quite fitting that we should revisit Khorsabad to investigate the origins of isopsephy. The Babylonians were also known to have attributed numbers to certain gods.

Many names of power in the PGM were constructed using isopsephy. Those readers hungry for a greater understanding of some of the names of power used in this book, would do well to study Kieren Barry's "*The Greek Qabalah*."

Hebrew thread

The Hebrews differed religiously from most other peoples, as they were monotheists. (Egypt briefly experimented with monotheism during the reign of Akhenaten, but reverted to polytheism after his death.) Many magickians reasoned that if the Hebrews had need of but one God, then this God had to be incredibly powerful.

The Bible is riddled with references to magick. A study of biblical writings indicates that the greatest of the Hebrew magickians was Moses. It should be remembered that Moses was raised as an Egyptian in the palace of the Pharaoh. As the adopted son of the Pharaoh's daughter, he may well have been groomed for the throne. At the very least, Moses would have received an education of the highest order. As mentioned previously, Egypt had numerous magickians, with the most powerful being the Pharaoh. It would be folly to believe that Moses was not exposed to Egyptian magick everyday of his life, and as a denizen of the palace, it would have been the powerful magick reserved for the Pharaohs.

Magick is not performed spontaneously, but is practised and perfected. When Moses engaged the Pharaoh's magickians in a magickal battle, they all performed the same acts of magick. This implies that Moses would have practised the same magick as Pharaoh's magickians. It is little wonder that Pharaoh was initially unimpressed and refused to take Moses' demands seriously.

The Bible tells that when the Hebrews finally escaped servitude in Egypt, Moses protected them from snakebite with a bronze serpent that he raised. For the following reasons it is logical that the bronze serpent raised by Moses was in fact a bronze cobra and it is highly likely that it would have doubled as Moses' magick wand:

- ξ Egypt has two venomous snakes – the horned viper and the cobra, which is by far the more venomous. Cobras held to the chests of convicted criminals were actually used as an effective form of execution in ancient Egypt. It stands to reason that the Egyptians would have been far more worried about the bite of the cobra than that of the horned viper.
- ξ Egyptian magick is based on sympathetic principles; for example, a representation of Sobek, the crocodile god, would be used for protection against crocodile attack. Similarly, a representation of a cobra could be used as part of a spell to protect against cobra bite.
- ξ The Egyptian god of magick was Heka, who was portrayed as holding two magick wands in the form of bronze cobras. Egyptian magickians would most certainly copy this and use a bronze cobra as a magick wand.

Moses also carried a staff, which he used to cause water to gush from a rock and to part the Sea of Reeds. An Egyptian magickian would normally carry a staff as a symbol of his authority over magickal forces. It seems that Moses was still availing himself of the magickal training of his youth when leading the Hebrews through the desert.

Moses' superiority as a magickian, presumably, came about as he incorporated the name of the Hebrew God into his spells. This would effectively make Moses the forerunner of the Graeco-Egyptian Magickians, as they employed a syncretistic approach to constructing their spells, mixing pantheons and ideas to maximise effectiveness.

Another great magickian of the Bible was Solomon. His magick, however, was based on the submission and control of spiritual forces. This approach to magick was the basis of the spiritual evocations performed throughout medieval Europe. A medieval evocation involves the magickian being protected inside a magick circle and calling upon a spiritual entity which is constrained within a triangle of manifestation to the east of the circle. The magickian would then interrogate or manipulate the entity. The lengthy lists of words of power spoken during these evocations are very reminiscent of those used in Graeco-Egyptian Magick suggesting common influences.

Also worthy of note was Daniel, whose ability to interpret dreams and visions exceeded that of the Babylonian sages and wizards, and resulted in his promotion to a privileged rank in Babylon.

Christian thread

Christianity crept into the pagan world surreptitiously. The Christians were initially a small cult seeking acceptance and recognition. While there is evidence of some persecution, by and large most pagans were unperturbed by this new faith which flourished amongst the downtrodden, referring to it as a slave cult.

The Egyptian pantheon featured many gods that formed trinities, the best known being Osiris, Isis and Horus. When the Christians introduced their trinity of God the Father, Jesus and the Holy Spirit, it was readily accepted by the Egyptians as just another trinity.

Christianity became the state religion of the Roman Empire in 312 CE. At this point a religious vocation in the Christian Church became a means of acquiring political clout. Every powerful family aspired to have a relative high within the Church. With its ranks burgeoning with individuals harbouring political aspirations, the Christian Church began to consolidate its power base by ruthlessly quashing all opposition. In 391 CE, an edict was passed in Rome that all Egyptian temples be closed. The well-educated pagans and their magickal practices were seen as a threat as they could not be easily manipulated.

Rather than humbly preach the good news as Christ had instructed, the Church forced Christianity upon the world. Huge amounts of invaluable material were destroyed. Undoubtedly some pagans willingly burnt their magickal texts on converting to Christianity, as in the Ephesus episode described in the Acts of the Apostles (Acts 19:19). However, most of the book burnings were forced. (On occasions the owners of the books were burnt along with their books.)

Magick did not die, but was forced underground. The Egyptians who had traditionally resorted to magick for millennia now looked to the Coptic priests. The Coptic Church as a whole was hostile to the practise of magick. However, some of the Coptic priests practised a Christianised form of Graeco-Egyptian Magick, where instead of sundry spirits, angels were called upon, and instead of a plethora of deities, there was only one. Essentially the names of power that characterise Graeco-Egyptian Magick were removed, rendering it greatly disempowered.

Miscellaneous religious thread

Apart from the mythology and magickal practises of the nations mentioned above various other religious ideas were incorporated into the Graeco-Egyptian Magickal writings. These religious ideas, which transcended national borders, included Zoroastrianism, Mithraism, Gnosticism, Neo-Platonism, Hermeticism and Serapism. Particularly noteworthy are the Orphic and Homeric Hymns that have been incorporated into the body of the text of this book.

Zoroastrianism

In the sixth and seventh century BCE, a vast reformation of the ancient Iranian religion was undertaken by Zarathustra (Zoroaster). Zarathustra taught that Ahura Mazda ("sovereign knowledge") was the sole creator and lord of the world, and the only god to be worshipped. This institution of a supreme deity was to influence the monotheistic religions Judaism, Christianity, and Islam.

Zarathustra retained the pantheon of the hundreds of Persian deities, assembling and dividing them into a complex dualistic system so that they came under the rule of either Ahura Mazda (the supreme god of goodness) or Ahriman (the ultimate embodiment of evil). The apparent contradiction of dualism and monotheism was resolved in the predicted ultimate triumph of Ahura Mazda at the end of time.

In the Near Eastern and Mediterranean world during the Hellenistic Age, Zoroaster came to represent mysterious Eastern occult knowledge. Many esoteric texts were written in his name, and Mithraism, an offshoot of Zoroastrianism, spread to the west.

Mithraism

Mithras was a Greek form of the name of an Indo-European god, Mithra or Mitra. In the original Persian pantheon, Mithra was an angel lower than Ahura Mazda, but higher than the Sun. In Zarathustra's system, Mithra became the "Judger of Souls" and the divine representative of Ahura Mazda on earth, protecting the righteous from the evil of Ahriman.

According to Plutarch, Mithraism began to be absorbed by the Romans during Pompey's campaign against Cilician pirates around 70 BCE. Mithraism became a soldier religion offering salvation based not just on faith and compassion, but fidelity, honesty, high moral standards, manliness and bravery. It appears to have been a mystery cult only practised by males and was in many respects the forerunner of freemasonry. The initiations in Mithraism were very severe and involved ascending through seven grades, each aligned with a planet.

Mithraism became an almost universal religion throughout the male population of the entire Roman Empire. Mithraism was the leading rival of Christianity in Rome, and was more successful in the first four centuries CE. When Christianity consolidated its power base, Mithraism was forcibly wiped out at the beginning of the fifth century CE. All Mithraic literature was destroyed and temples were desecrated with rubbish and cemetery dirt. In at least one case, a Mithraic priest was murdered and his body was left on his altar.

Christianity copied many details of Mithraism. The founding fathers of Christianity initially claimed that the worshippers of Mithras had copied Christian theology. In the face of opposition from learned pagans, the resemblance was later explained that the devil had anticipated their true faith by creating a counterfeit before Christ's birth.

Gnosticism

Gnosticism is an umbrella term for numerous ideological and mythological systems espoused by a number of teachers and their communities. The word Gnosticism comes from the Greek "gnosis" meaning "knowledge." Cross-cultural mixing throughout the entire

Hellenic empire continued for centuries allowing the various Gnostic communities to fuse religious ideas from Greek, Jewish, Iranian, Christian, Indian and Far East sources.

Gnosticism rejected the Christian Church's teaching that only faith would bring salvation. The Gnostics taught that each person had within a divine spark, which had fallen from the divine realm beyond the cosmos ruled over by the "unknown God," into this world created and ruled by the evil Demiurge, fettered with destiny, birth and death. The recurring theme of alienation results from this dualistic separation of the divine spark from the divine realm.

The idea of initiation being a preparation for death is very evident in Gnosticism. For the divine spark to ascend back to the divine realm it must pass through the prison walls of the planetary spheres. Initiations would equip the Gnostic with necessary magickal tools to penetrate through the planetary Spheres.

Neo-Platonism

The Neo-Platonists aptly and succinctly identified the aim of their spirituality as a re-union with the all-pervading God force. Some Neo-Platonists recommended that this aim be attained through contemplation. Iamblichus (255–330 CE) however, recommended the use of an exalted form of magick termed Theurgy. Theurgy is the invocation of divine forces so as to effect spiritual transformation in the magickian. Contemplation is a slow passive process, whilst invocation is a rapid active process.

The system of magick taught in this book is essentially Theurgy based on Graeco-Egyptian Magick. The writings of Iamblichus and Apuleius of Madauros suggest that philosophy and magickal practice were complementary in the pursuit of spiritual development.

Hermeticism

Alexandria in the Nile delta was a thriving city, a cosmopolitan centre for trade, and the main grain supply for the Imperial Roman armies. In fact, many soldiers from all over the Roman Empire retired there. It was also populated by a large Jewish community. Numerous religious movements flourished there. Elements of all the philosophical systems known at the time, especially Gnosticism and Neo-Platonism, were blended into a harmonious whole laying the foundations for Hermeticism as an eclectic cult during the first four or five centuries CE.

Hermeticism refers to a philosophical body of writings popularly attributed to Hermês Trismegistus (or "Thrice Great Hermês"), a deity resulting from the fusion of the Greek Hermês and the Egyptian Thoth. Hermês was associated with knowledge, commerce, travel, healing and magick. Thoth was the spokesman and scribe of the gods; and invented all the arts and sciences, soothsaying, magick, medicine, surgery, music, musical instruments, drawing and writing (without which his discoveries would have been lost). Thoth was thought of by the Greeks as the Egyptian Hermês and the exemplary model of the magickian.

Probably the best known collections of Hermetic philosophical writings are the Greek "Corpus Hermeticum" and Latin "Asclepius." The idea of an ascension process, after death, through the planetary Spheres occurs in Hermetic writings. The Hermetic writings were the basis of the medieval Hermetic magick practised in Europe, and ultimately modern ceremonial magick.

Serapism

In ancient Egypt there existed a cult of a combination god, named Osirapis (or Userhapi, Asar-Hapi), which was a fusion of Osiris and the bull Apishad, and represented the sacred bull of Memphis after its death. This fusion was enabled by one of the common epithets of Osiris being "Bull of the West," while Apis was believed to be animated by the soul of Osiris, and to be Osiris incarnate.

The founder of the Greek Ptolemaic dynasty, Ptolemy I, wished to unite the native Egyptians and the Greeks under a supreme god, resulting in the creation of Serapis (Sarapis, Zaparrus). Serapis was a composite of Osirapis and a number of Hellenistic deities, including Zeus (divine majesty), Hêlios (the sun), Dionysus (fertility), Poseidon (god of the sea), Hadês (the underworld and afterlife) and Asklepius (healing). His main attributes concerned the afterlife and fertility.

Temples and sanctuaries to Serapis were built in Alexandria and throughout the Mediterranean world. The destruction of the Alexandrian Serapeum in 391 CE by the Christians marked the end of his cult. The Christians however, adopted numerous trappings of the Serapis cult including chants, lights, bells, vestments, processions and music.

Orphic Hymns

Orpheus was the first legendary Greek magus. All that remains of Orpheus are myths indicating that he was the son of the muse Calliopê, and he was one of Jason's Argonauts. Orpheus was supposed to have learnt his magick in Egypt. His music could charm animals and move trees and rocks. Rivers paused in mid-flow and mountains moved when he sang. Orpheus travelled to the underworld in search of his wife, Eurydice, where he charmed the rulers of the dead. He had almost succeeded in rescuing her, but at the last minute he looked back at her (against the instructions issued) and was torn to pieces by Maenads who threw his head into the river, Hebrus. His head then became an oracle.

Orphism was a mystery cult in the ancient Greek world around 600 BCE and was believed to have been based on the writings of Orpheus. The Orphics believed that the physical body was the prison of true essence (divine spark) which was caught up in an endless cycle of rebirth until it was released through initiatic processes.

The Orphic Hymns were found on gold lamellae that were placed on corpses to protect the spirits of the dead in the afterlife and on their journey in the rebirth cycle. The earliest of these lamellae date back to the sixth century BCE, the most recent have been dated to the fourth century CE, indicating that Orphism as a cult endured for at least a thousand years.

In the PGM writings there are a few references to the tenets of Orphism and even a spell claimed to come from Orpheus (*PGM* XIII. 934–946). It is evident that Orpheus was held in high regard by the Graeco-Egyptian Magickians.

Homeric Hymns

Amongst the greatest texts of Western culture are the two epic poems of Homer: the Iliad (about the siege of Troy) and the Odyssey (the tale of Ulysses' wanderings). Also credited to Homer were the Homeric Hymns, the comic Batrachomyomachia and the Margites.

History has it that Homer was an Asiatic Greek, born probably in Smyrna (now Izmir in Turkey). He was believed to have been blind and probably lived and worked in Ionia (now the West coast of Turkey) around 850 BCE.

Debates over whether Homer authored the works attributed to him and whether he actually existed have raged since antiquity. Some scholars believe that Homer was a female. Many modern scholars now appear to believe that the Homeric Hymns, the Margites and the Batrachomyomachia were later derivative works, whereas the Iliad and the Odyssey were written by different people. It has also been claimed that in the eighth century BCE, the Homeric poems recited by bards who came to Athens were recorded and collated to form the Iliad and the Odyssey.

Whatever the truth about Homer, to the Graeco-Egyptian magickians, the Homeric writings were imbued with magickal power. Some verses were used magickally, for example as a charm to restrain anger (*PGM* IV. 467–68) and a charm to obtain friends (*PGM* IV. 833–34). There is even a complex spell using three Homeric verses that can be used for necromancy, to confer victory, invulnerability and protection (*PGM* IV. 2145–2240). A Homeric Oracle was in use wherein three dice or knucklebones were rolled to select one of 216 Homeric verses extracted from the Iliad and the Odyssey (see *PGM* VII. 1–48).

Remainder thread

The PGM and PDM spells contain words of power. These words are often familiar as the names or epithets of the deities of various cultures. However, some of the words of power are unrecognisable. The unrecognisable words are often referred to by scholars as "gibberish" or "nonsensical words" designed to impress the magickian's client. I have referred to these words as the remainder thread.

As mentioned above, the earliest writings of the Sumerians date back to roughly 3400 BCE. However, there is controversial evidence suggesting that far more ancient advanced civilisations existed. These pre-Sumerian civilisations left no written records, so their spiritual beliefs and practices were transmitted orally (as was the wisdom of the Hebrews before the texts of the Bible were written). The tantalising question begging to be asked is: Just how long were the traditions transmitted, or did they die with the civilisations which spawned them?

By way of answer, it is interesting to note that Freemasons claim that their tradition came from ancient Egypt. Following the discovery of the Rosetta Stone in 1799 CE, Champollion translated the ancient Egyptian hieroglyphs. Some early Masonic rituals were found to be very similar to newly translated hieroglyphic texts, somewhat substantiating this claim.

History is full of tales of secret societies and zealous individuals dedicated to the preservation of ancient wisdom in repressive times. A Gnostic sect called the Mandeans survives to this day in parts of the Middle East, whilst families of Egyptian snake charmers still practise the wisdom of the ancient magickians. Is it so impossible that ancient systems of magick were preserved as oral transmissions by dedicated individuals and incorporated into the PGM and PDM writings?

It is incredibly arrogant of scholars to criticise PGM and PDM writings given that their knowledge of ancient pantheons is far from complete. If no Cuneiform writings had survived we would be ignorant of most of the Mesopotamian deities, and so their names when they appear would also be referred to as "gibberish." Future archaeological discoveries may unearth hitherto unknown deities (such as those of the pre-Sumerian civilisations) and further expand our knowledge.

Actually practising Graeco-Egyptian magick shows that the sublime beauty of many magick spells is greatly enhanced by the hypnotic sound of the mysterious unrecognisable words of power, giving credence to the supposition that they are god names from ancient systems of magick that have been lost in the mists of time. In addition, certain unidentifiable words of power appear repeatedly in numerous spells indicating a now lost magickal vocabulary shared by at least some of the Graeco-Egyptian magickians.

Magick is an art, where different words of power have been found to work well in certain combinations in given situations. Fine tuning of words of power by individual magickians, or possibly regional dialects, may well account for minor spelling differences.

Apart from the words of power, vowels were chanted. This technique was used by the ancient Egyptian priests, and is still utilised by shamans in certain parts of the world to open portals into other dimensions.

Regarding vowel chanting, Demetrius in De Eloutione, writes:

> *"...in Egypt the priests, when singing hymns in praise of the gods, employ the 7 vowels which they utter in due succession and the sound of these letters is so euphonious that men listen to it in place of the flute and lyre."*
> [Selection from "*The Egyptian Hermes: A Historical Approach to the Late Pagan Mind*" Garth Fowden]

The importance of not changing the words of power was unequivocally spelt out in the Chaldean Oracles, considered by many Neo-Platonic Theurgists to be divine:

> *"Never change the Barbarous Names;*
> *For there are Names in every Nation given from God,*
> *which have an unspeakable power in Rites."*
> [Selection from "*Chaldean Oracles: As set down by Julianus*" Stanley Thomas, trans.]

Weaving the threads into the rich Graeco-Egyptian tapestry

Over the course of the first five centuries CE, while Egypt was under Roman occupation, Egyptian culture eventually became absorbed into the Hellenic stream. This absorption took a great deal of time, and involved fundamental changes to the written scripts used by the higher classes in Egypt, as the Egyptians were traditionally mistrustful of anything that was not Egyptian.

Hieroglyphs, reputedly from the god Thoth in ancient times, were used purely for religious purposes. Hieroglyphs were greatly expanded around 500 BCE with hundreds of new signs being introduced. They were last used at the end of the fourth century CE.

Demotic script – introduced about 660 BCE as a simplified and widely used alternative to the cumbersome hieroglyphs – was initially used for business and literary purposes. During the fourth century CE it was gradually replaced by Greek and the Greek-derived Coptic alphabet. Demotic was last used at the beginning of the fifth century CE.

The wholesale adoption of Greek and Demotic scripts led to the spiritual knowledge previously jealously guarded by the Egyptian priests becoming accessible to a much wider audience.

The Graeco-Egyptian magickians did not limit themselves to influences from areas in close geographical proximity to Alexandria. Ancient trade routes ensured that there was much cultural exchange between distant locations. Some of the incenses used by the Graeco-Egyptian magickians were from the Himalayas and China. It is interesting to note that the feats attributed to the ancient Greek shamans were very similar to those of the Indian fakirs and yogis of today. A close inspection of the performance techniques of Graeco-Egyptian Magick reveals elements that are at variance with those of other western magickal systems, such as those of the Sumerians, suggesting an exotic influence.

Much Graeco-Egyptian Magick was practised to satisfy the desires of clients for love, wealth, health, fame, knowledge of the future, control over other persons, and so on. A study of Graeco-Egyptian Magick texts reveals that some spells are mere folk magick (commonly termed low magick) while others are sublimely beautiful (high magick).

Low magick is preoccupied with worldly things. Examples in the Graeco-Egyptian Magical writings include spells to keep bugs out of the house (sprinkle a mixture of goat bile and water); keep fleas out of the house (wet rosebay with salt water, grind and spread); eat garlic and not stink (eat baked beetroots); drink a lot without inebriation (eat a baked pig's lung); improve luck in gambling; love spells; revenge spells; and divination.

In high magick the magickian invokes divine energies, thereby accelerating spiritual development. This book deals solely with high magick.

An important difference between low magick and high magick is that when a low magick spell is cast, the magickian remains the same whereas there is an effect on the magickian's environment. When a high magick spell is cast, there is no immediate effect on the magickian's environment, but the magickian undergoes a degree of transformation. As the magickian is transformed, the magickian's immediate environment also undergoes transformation, but it is an indirect process.

In the Graeco-Egyptian source texts, the delineation is not as clearly cut. High magick spells occasionally have low magick influences, as can be seen in those spells involving animal sacrifice. I am firmly of the opinion animal sacrifice has no place in magick. The Graeco-Egyptian magickians lived in a different world, where your larder would be stocked by butchering your own animals. Butchery was a fact of life. I have found that no animal sacrifice is necessary for these spells to be effective. By way of comparison, it is interesting to note that towards the end of the Old Testament, the God of the Hebrews announced that he was interested in the hearts of his followers and not their sacrifices.

The presence of low and high magick suggests two different classes of magickians. So, who were the Graeco-Egyptian magickians?

The first class of magickians were priests sojourning from temple duty. In Egypt, very few priests worked full-time in the temples devoted to Egyptian and Greek deities. Most would work just three times a year. They would work for one month and then spend three months in the community. This would effectively put them in harmony with the three seasons of the Egyptian calendar. These highly trained priests would be in need of employment during their times away from the temple, and would presumably offer their magickal services to rich patrons. I believe that they incorporated large amounts of the temple liturgy of the time into their spells. The extensive use of vowel chants and a detailed knowledge of mythology and words of power in their spells are all indicative of very advanced magickal training.

The second class of magickians were like the beggar priests and diviners coming to rich men's doors offering services as described in Plato's Republic. These magickians were purveyors of folk magick.

Graeco-Egyptian magick as an initiatic system

The Gnostics, Mithraists and Hermeticists used systems of spiritual development based upon working with planetary energies. The exact techniques used however, are not known.

Some Neo-Platonic Theurgists practised spiritual development through invoking divine energies. This indicates that the invocation of planetary energies could lead to a comprehensive initiatic system. However, apart from a few fragments there are no extant Neo-Platonic Theurgical rituals.

Graeco-Egyptian Magick amalgamates the magickal practices of the ancient Sumerians, Babylonians, Egyptians, Greeks, Hebrews and Christians. It provides numerous spells involving all of the planetary deities.

This book effectively utilises invocations extracted from authentic Graeco-Egyptian Magick spells and combines the ideology of the Neo-Platonic Theurgists as well as the Gnostics, Mithraists and Hermeticists to form a complete system of planetary initiation.

Appendix 2
Pronunciation

All of the words of power in the spells in this book are transliterated from Greek. The convention adopted and correct pronunciation is as set out below. The pronunciation is taken from F Kinchin Smith and T W Melluish's "*Ancient Greek: A foundation course*" and Professor Donald J Mastronarde's "*Ancient Greek Tutorials: Pronunciation Guide.*"

The bolded letters are those used through the rituals. In brackets are the names of each of the letters, the corresponding Greek capital and Greek small letter.

Vowels

A (Alpha, A, α) .... Long as in f*a*ther, or short as in *a*ha.
E (Epsilon, Δ, ε) .... As in fr*e*t or p*e*t.
Ê (Eta, H, η)................. As in French p*e*re or t*ê*te.
I (Iota, I, ι) .... Long as in f*ee*d, or short as in p*i*t.
O (Omicron, O, o) .... As in n*o*t.
U (Upsilon, Y, υ).......... Long as in French r*u*e, short as in French d*u* pain.
Ô (Omega, Ω, ω)........... As in h*o*me or g*o*, but can be 'aw' as in s*aw*.

Diphthongs

Diphthongs are pairs of vowels which are slurred together when pronounced.

AI (AI, αι)...................... As in 'ai' in Is*ai*ah.
AU (AY, αυ) .... As in 'ow' in g*ow*n.
EI (ΔI, εi)....................... As in 'ey' in gr*ey* or 'ei' in *ei*ght.
EU (ΔY, ευ) .... As in 'ew' in f*ew* or 'eu' in f*eu*d.

ÊU (HY, ηυ)................. As in 'ew' in f*ew* or 'eu' in f*eu*d *(extending pronunciation).*
OI (OI, οι) .... As in 'oi' in b*oi*l or c*oi*n.
OU (OY, ου) .... As in 'oo' in m*oo*n or p*oo*l.
UI (YI, υι) .... As in 'ui' in French l*ui*.

Consonants

The pronunciation of **G** and **S** may vary depending on the consonant following it.

B (Beta, B, β) .... As in *b*ad.
G (Gamma, Γ, γ) .... As in *g*et.
  GG (ΓΓ, γγ)............ As in 'ng' in a*ng*er.
  GK (ΓΚ, γκ)........... As in 'ngk' in Chu*ngk*ing.
  GCH (ΓΚ, γκ)........ As in 'nkh' in mo*nkh*ood.
  GX (ΓΧ, γχ)............ As in 'nx' in ly*nx*.
D (Delta, Δ, δ) .... As in *d*oes.
Z (Zeta Z, ζ).................. As 'zd' in Ma*zd*a or 'sd' in wi*sd*om, in classical Attic pronunciation.
Like 'z' in do*z*e or 's' in ro*s*e after 350 BCE.
TH (Theta, Θ, θ) .... Aspirated T as 'th' in po*th*ook, in classical Attic pronunciation.
Like 'th' in *th*in in late ancient pronunciation.
K (Kappa, K, κ)............ As in *k*ing.
L (Lambda, Λ, λ).......... As in *l*yre.
M (Mu, M, μ)................ As in *m*use.
N (Nu, N, ν) .... As in *n*ow or *n*et.
X (Xi, Ξ, ξ) .... As in wa*x* or fo*x*.
P (Pi, Π, π) .... As in *p*ush.
R (Rho, P, ρ)................. As in *r*ich (trilled).
S (Sigma, Σ, σ) .... As in mou*s*e.
  SB (ΣΒ, σβ) .... As in ha*s* *b*een.
  SG (ΣΓ, σγ) .... As in ha*s* *g*one.
  SD (ΣΔ, σδ) .... As in ha*s* *d*one.
  SM (ΣΜ, σμ) .... As in ha*s* *m*ade.

T (Tau, Τ, τ) .... As in *t*ap.
PH (Phi, Φ, φ) .... Aspirated P as 'ph' in ha*ph*azard, in classical Attic pronunciation.
Like 'f' in *f*oot in late ancient pronunciation.
CH (Chi, Χ, χ) .... As in lo*ch*.
PS (Psi, Ψ, ψ) .... As in la*ps*e.

Given that virtually all the source texts in this book are from late antiquity, use the later pronunciation for Zeta (Z), Theta (TH) and Phi (PH).

Further Vowel Hints

Further pronunciation hints are provided in *PGM* V. 24-30 [*Tr.: W C Grese]. This spell is a vessel divination which calls on Zeus, Hêlios, Mithras, Sarapis and Bainchôôôch. (Mithras and Bainchôôôch will be encountered in the sequel to this book.)

A is pronounced "with an open mouth, undulating like a wave."
E is pronounced "with enjoyment, aspirating it."
Ê is pronounced "like a baboon."
O is pronounced "succinctly, as a breathed threat."
U is pronounced "like a shepherd, drawing out the pronunciation."

Still having trouble?

While some readers will have no trouble at all pronouncing all the Greek names of power in this book, I realise that some will be challenged. I have a recording of all of the rituals in this book available through my website (www.hermeticmagick.com). Readers will be able to progressively improve their proficieny in pronouncing the words of power, by following them in the book and chanting along.

Appendix 3
Rotation and Counter-Rotation

This appendix is not meant to be a collection of rituals, but rather an illustration of a principle permeating much of Graeco-Egyptian magick.

A perusal of the PGM and PDM spells indicates that there is no evidence of the Graeco-Egyptian magickians tracing a 360° circle for protection, as they were already protected by powerful deities. In the case of Egyptian priests, this protection sometimes took the form of magickal tattoos.

In the Opening and Closing Rites we saw that there was a balancing of clockwise and anti-clockwise movements when working with the four cardinal directions. With the exception of the Opening Rite, this balancing involves a rotation of 270° followed by a counter-rotation of 270°. This need for rotational balance is a recurring theme in Graeco-Egyptian Magick, as the following quotes indicate.

Rotation and Counter-Rotation principles illustrated

PDM Suppl. 130–135

"O Isis, O Nephthys, O noble soul of Osiris Wennefer,
come to me!
I am your beloved son, Horus.
O gods who are in heaven,
O gods who are in the earth,
O gods who are in the primeval waters,
O gods who are in the South, O gods who are in the North,
O gods who are in the West, O gods who are in the East,
come to me tonight!
Teach me about such and such a thing about which I am asking;
quickly, quickly; hurry, hurry."
[*Tr.: Janet H Johnson]

This spell comes from the Demotic Magickal Papyri (PDM) which is different to the PGM in that it is the last flowering of pure Egyptian magick. The PGM, as discussed previously is a fusion of many magickal streams. This ritual is actually a dream oracle. Its very structure however, because it employs the now familiar seven direction system, lends itself to an Opening Rite.

Performance instructions

Start by facing the East.

Cosmos:	*Look up and say* "O gods who are in Heaven"
Earth:	*Look down and say* "O gods who are in the Earth"
Centre:	*Visualise within and say* "O gods who are in the primeval waters"
South:	*Turn clockwise to South and say* "O gods who are in the South"
North:	*Turn clockwise to North and say "O gods who are in the North"*
West:	*Turn anti-clockwise to West and say "O gods who are in the West"*
East:	*Turn anti-clockwise to East and say* "O gods who are in the East"

Face East and look upwards to open a portal to the cosmos. Then look down to open a portal to the depths of the earth. Looking ahead, visualise the centre of your being and the present moment. Then turn 90° clockwise to face South and then a further 180° clockwise to face North, making a total of 270°. Then turn anti-clockwise 90° to face West and then a further 180° to face East, making a total of 270°.

A comparison between this ritual and the Closing Rite shows a remarkable similarity with respect to the way the cardinal points are called. In both, you face East and turn 270° clockwise to the North (stopping at South on the way) and then turning 270° anti-clockwise to the East (stopping at West on the way). Both rituals preserve the same balance between clockwise and anti-clockwise rotation. In both rituals there is no need for a circle and so a 360° rotation is not required.

In the Opening Rite, rotational balance is preserved by moving anti-clockwise in a full circle and then clockwise in a full circle. In the Opening Rite, you ask for Aiôn's protection, whereas in this ritual you identify yourself with Horus. What need of protection would Aiôn or Horus have?

At the risk of being pedantic, the exciting thing about this comparison is that two apparently separate magickal traditions employ a ritual structure that is conceptually identical.

PGM IV. 3172–3186

Dream-producing charm using three reeds:
The picking of the three reeds is to be before sunrise.
After sunset raise the first,
look to the East and say three times:
"MASKELLI MASKELLÔ PHNOUKENTABAÔ
OREOBAZAGRA RÊXICHTHÔN HIPPOCHTHÔN
PURIPÊGANUX AEÊIOUÔ LEPETAN
AZARACHTHARÔ,
I am picking you up in order that you might give me a dream."
Raise the second to the South
*and say again the **"MASKELLI"** formula,*
*the vowels and **"THRÔBEIA"**;*
hold the reed and spin around;
look toward the North and the West
and say three times the same names, those of the second reed.
Raise the third and say the same names and these things:
*"**IÊ IÊ**, I am picking you for such-and-such a rite."*
[*Tr.: W C Grese]

Performance instructions

East: *Say* "**MASKELLI**" *formula, vowels,* "**LEPETAN AZARACHTHARÔ**"
South: *Turn clockwise to South and say* "**MASKELLI**" *formula, vowels,* "**THRÔBEIA**"
North: *Turn clockwise to North and say* "**MASKELLI**" *formula, vowels,* "**THRÔBEIA**"

West:	*Turn anti-clockwise to West and say* "**MASKELLI**" *formula, vowels,* "**THRÔBEIA**"
East:	*Turn anti-clockwise to East and say* "**MASKELLI**" *formula, vowels,* "**IÊ IÊ**"

Again start by facing East. This is followed by turning 90° clockwise to face South and then a further 180° clockwise to face North, making a total of 270°. Turn anti-clockwise 90° to face West and then a further 180° to face East, making a total of 270°. Again there is the same balance between clockwise and anti-clockwise rotations.

The so-called "**MASKELLI**" formula is **MASKELLI MASKELLÔ PHNOUKENTABAÔ OREOBAZAGRA RÊXICHTHÔN HIPPOCHTHÔN PURIPÊGANUX**. It occurs repeatedly in Graeco-Egyptian Magickal spells. It is thought that **OREOBAZAGRA** is possibly an epithet for Hekatê or another lunar goddess, **RÊXICHTHÔN** possibly means "bursting forth from the earth," **HIPPOCHTHÔN** means "horse plus earth" and, **PURIPÊGANUX** possibly means "lord of the fount of fire." The meaning of the remaining word is unknown.

PGM VIII. 1–63

On lines 9 to 11 of this invocation to Hermês we find:

"I also know what your forms are:
in the East you have the form of an ibis,
in the West you have the form of a dog-faced baboon,
in the North you have the form of a serpent,
and in the South you have the form of a wolf."
[*Tr.: E N O'Neil]

Performance instructions

East:	*Visualise an ibis*
West	*Turn clockwise to West and visualise a dog-faced baboon*
North:	*Turn clockwise to North and visualise a serpent*
South:	*Turn anti-clockwise to South and visualise a wolf*
East:	*Turn anti-clockwise to return to East*

Again start by facing East. This is followed by turning 180° clockwise to face West and then a further 90° clockwise to face North, making a total of 270°. Then turn anti-clockwise 180° to face South and then a further 90° to face East, making a total of 270°. Again there is the same balance between clockwise and anti-clockwise rotations.

PGM II. 64–184

On lines 106 to 115 of this invocation to Apollô, we find:

"Who dwell throughout the whole inhabited world,
you [whose] bodyguard is the sixteen giants,
you who are seated upon the lotus
and who light up the whole inhabited world;
you who have designated the various living things upon the earth,
you who have the sacred bird upon your robe
in the eastern parts of the Red Sea,
even as you have upon the northern parts
the figure of an infant child seated upon a lotus,
O rising one, O you of many names,
SESENGENBARPHAMNGÊS;
on the southern parts you have the shape of the sacred falcon,
through which you send fiery heat into the air,
*which becomes **LERTHEXANAX;***
in the parts toward the West
you have the shape of a crocodile with the tail of a snake,
from which you send out rains and snows;
in the parts toward the East you have [the form of] a winged dragon,
a diadem fashioned of air, with which you quell all discords
beneath the heaven and on earth
for you have manifested yourself as god in truth,..."
[*Tr.: John Dillon]

Performance instructions

East: *Visualise the sacred bird*
North *Turn anti-clockwise to North and visualise an infant*

	child seated upon a lotus
South:	*Turn anti-clockwise to South and visualise a sacred falcon*
West:	*Turn clockwise to West and visualise a crocodile with the tail of a snake*
East:	*Turn clockwise to return to East and visualise a winged dragon, a diadem of air*

In this spell, the direction of rotation is reversed.

Again start by facing East. This is followed by turning 90° anti-clockwise to face North and then a further 180° clockwise to face South, making a total of 270°. Then turn clockwise 90° to face West and then a further 180° to face East, making a total of 270°. Again there is the same balance between clockwise and anti-clockwise rotations. (Apollô will be invoked in the sequel to this book.)

Conclusion

It is evident that when the Graeco-Egyptian magickians worked with the four cardinal directions, they rotated and counter-rotated through 270°, starting and finishing by facing East.

There are differences in the details, insofar as some spells call for a clockwise rotation followed by an anti-clockwise rotation, while others utilise the opposite. The order of calling the cardinal points was unimportant as was the initial direction of rotation. The commonality lies in facing each of the cardinal points while maintaining rotational balance.

Appendix 4
Integration of the Divine Spark

The process of spiritual development in this book involves gaining access to the divine spark in the Sphere of the Sun and enhancing this access in the Spheres of Mars and Jupiter. This is followed by the death of the personality to reveal the true self in the Sphere of Saturn. A necessary process to facilitate this is to transcend the illusion of duality.

We live in a dualistic world where opposite properties abound – good/evil, black/white, hot/cold, male/female, and so on. A material object can only be one of these properties at a time. For example, an object cannot be hot and cold, it has to be one or the other. The mind however, is capable of imagining an object having opposing properties simultaneously. This process, if pursued diligently, effectively enables the mind to transcend duality.

The Chaldean Oracles describe creation in terms of the Monad, which generates the Dyad, which in turn manifests the Triad to govern and order all things. To transcend duality is to perceive things as they are in an undifferentiated form.

To this end I would strongly recommend studying a Gnostic tractate (or text) called "The Thunder, Perfect Mind." This manuscript was found as part of the Nag Hammadi group of documents, and exists only in Coptic. It appears, however, to be based on a now lost Greek document possibly dating to second or third century CE Alexandria.

Scholars agree on the uniqueness among Gnostic literature of "The Thunder, Perfect Mind," but disgree on its finer points. It is clear that it is an amalgamation of various influences, amongst them Jewish and Christian Wisdom texts, Isis aretalogies (self-definition through multiple "I am" statements), Platonic dialogue, Stoicism, and various Gnostic schools.

"The Thunder, Perfect Mind" features a female voice, coming from a divine male figure who created her, to those who seek her. She describes herself through the juxtaposition of opposites. Her relentless intellectual paradoxes uniting polar opposites are reminiscent of Zen *koans*. She appears to be a saviour figure who offers to take those who understand her message to a place of restful immortality, where "they will live and they will not die again."

The text appears to be a revelatory text produced by a Gnostic who had reconciled opposites and transcended duality. Meditating upon this text with the heart and mind will go a long way to reproducing the achievement of the Gnostic who wrote it.

The Thunder, Perfect Mind

(Translated by Professor Anne McGuire)

I was sent from the Power
And I have come to those who think upon me.
And I was found among those who seek after me.

Look at me, you who think upon me;
And you hearers, hear me!
You who are waiting for me, take me to yourselves.
And do not pursue me from your vision.
And do not make your sound hate me, nor your hearing.
Do not be ignorant of me at any place or any time.
Be on guard!
Do not be ignorant of me.

For I am the first and the last.
I am the honored and the scorned,
I am the harlot and the holy one.
I am the wife and the virgin.
I am the m[oth]er and the daughter.
I am the members of my mother.

I am the barren one and the one with many children.
I am she whose marriage is multiple, and I have not taken a husband.
I am the midwife and she who does not give birth.
I am the comforting of my labor pains.

I am the bride and the bridegroom.
It is my husband who begot me.
I am the mother of my father and the sister of my husband.
And he is my offspring.
I am the servant of him who prepared me and I am the lord of my offspring.
But he is the one who be[got me] before time on a day of birth and he is my offspring in time, and my power is from him.
I am the staff of his power in his youth and he is the rod of my old age.
And whatever he wills happens to me.

I am the incomprehensible silence and the much-remembered thought.
I am the voice of many sounds and the utterance (logos) of many forms.
I am the utterance of my name.

Why, you who hate me, do you love me
And hate those who love me?
You who deny me, confess me,
And you who confess me, deny me.
You who speak the truth about me, tell lies about me,
And you who have told lies about me, speak the truth about me.
You who know me, become ignorant of me; and may those who have been ignorant of me come to know me.

For I am knowledge and ignorance.
I am shame and boldness.
I am unashamed, I am ashamed.
I am strength and I am fear.
I am war and peace.

Give heed to me.

I am the disgraced and the exalted one.

Give heed to my poverty and my wealth.
Do not be haughty to me when I am discarded upon the earth,

And you will find me among [those] that are to come.

And do not look upon me on the garbage-heap and go and leave me discarded.

And you will find me in the kingdoms.

And do not look upon me when I am discarded among those who are disgraced and in the least places,
And then laugh at me.
And do not cast me down among those who are slain in severity.

But as for me, I am merciful and I am cruel.

Be on guard!
Do not hate my obedience,
And do not love my self-control in my weakness.
Do not forsake me,
And do not be afraid of my power.

Why then do you despise my fear
And curse my pride?.

I am she who exists in all fears and boldness in trembling.
I am she who is weak, and I am well in pleasure of place.
I am foolish and I am wise.

Why have you hated me in your counsels?

(Is it) because I shall be silent among those who are silent,
And I shall appear and speak?

Why then have you hated me, you Greeks?
Because I am a non-Greek among non-Greeks?.

For I am the Wisdom of Greeks
And the Gnosis of non-Greeks.
I am judgment for Greeks and non-Greeks.
I am the one whose image is multiple in Egypt.
And the one who has no image among non-Greeks.

I am she who has been hated everywhere and who has been
loved everywhere.

I am she who is called Life and you have called Death.
I am she who is called Law and you have called Lawlessness.

I am the one you have pursued, and I am the one you have
restrained.
I am the one you have scattered and you have gathered me
together.
Before me you have been ashamed and you have been
unashamed with me.

I am she who observes no festival and I am she whose
festivals are many.
I, I am godless and I am she whose God is multiple.

I am the one upon whom you have thought and whom you
have scorned.
I am unlearned, and it is from me they learn.

I am she whom you have despised and upon whom you think.
I am the one from whom you have hidden and to whom you
are manifest.
But whenever you hide yourselves, I myself will be manifest.
For whenever you are manifest, I myself [will hide f]rom you.

Those who have [...]
[...]
[...] senselessly

Take me [...] [underst]anding out of pain,
and receive me to yourselves out of understanding [and] pain.
Receive me to yourselves out of disgraceful places and contrition.
And seize me from those which are good even though in disgrace.
Out of shame, receive me to yourselves in shamelessness.
And out of shamelessness and shame, blame my members among yourselves.
And come forward to me, you who know me and who know my members.
Establish the great ones among the small first creatures.

Come forward to childhood and do not despise it because it is little and small.
And do not bring back some greatnesses in parts from smallnesses,
for the smallnesses are known from the greatnesses.

Why do you curse me and honor me?
You have wounded and you have had mercy.

Do not separate me from the first ones whom you have k[nown.
And] do not cast anyone [out
and do not] bring anyone back [...]
...brought you back
and ... [kno]w him not.

[I...] what is mine
[...] I know the fi[rst ones] and those after them know me.
But I am the [perfect] mind and the repose of the [...]
I am the gnosis of my seeking, and the finding of those who

seek after me.
And the command of those who ask of me.

And the power of the powers by my gnosis
of the angels who have been sent by my logos,
And the gods in their seasons by my command,
And it is with me that the spirits of all humans exist,
and it is within me that women exist.

I am she who is honored and praised and who is despised scornfully.
I am peace and because of me war has come to be.
And I am an alien and a citizen.
I am substance and she who has no substance.
Those who come into being from my synousia are ignorant of me,
And those who are in my substance know me.

Those who are close to me have been ignorant of me
And those who are far from me have known me.

On the day when I am close to [you, you] are far away [from me
And] on the day when I [am far away] from you, [I am] [close] to you.
I [am] [....] within.
[I..] ..... of the natures.
I am [......] of the creation of spirits ....request of the souls.

[I am} restraint and unrestraint.
I am union and dissolution.
I am the abiding and I am the loosing.
I am descent and they come up to me.
I am the judgment and the acquittal.
I, I am sinless and the root of sin is from me.
I am desire in appearance and self-control of the heart exists within me.

I am the hearing which is attainable to everyone and the ungraspable utterance.
I am a non-speaking mute and great is my multitude of utterances.

Hear me in softness and learn from me in harshness.

I am she who cries out,
And I am cast out upon the face of the earth.
I prepare the bread and my mind within.
I am the gnosis of my name.
I am she who cries out and I am the one who listens.

I appear an[d...] walk in [...]
seal of my [...]...[sign] of the
I am [...] the defense.
I am she who is cal[led] Truth. And violence [...].

You honor me [...] and you whisper against [me].
You who are defeated,
judge them before they pass judgment against you.
For the judge and partiality exist within you.
If you are condemned by this, who will acquit you?
Or if you are acquitted by him, who will be able to restrain you?

For what is inside of you is what is outside of you.
And the one who molded you on the outside has made an impression of it inside of you.
And that which you see outside of you,
you see inside of you.
It is manifest and it is your garment.

Hear me, listeners, and be taught my utterances, you who know me!

I am the hearing that is acceptable in every matter;
I am the utterance that cannot be restrained.

I am the name of the voice and the voice of the name.
I am the sign of writing and the manifestation of difference.

And I ...
[3 lines missing]
[...] light [...] and [...]
[...] listeners [...] you.

[...] the great power.
And [...] will not move the name.
[...] the one who created me.
But I shall speak his name.

Behold, then, his utterances and all the writings that have been completed.
Give heed, then, listeners, and you also, angels,
And those who have been sent,
And you spirits who have arisen from the dead,

For I am the one who alone exists,
And I have no one who will judge me.

For many are the sweet forms that exist in numerous sins
And unrestrained acts and disgraceful passions, and temporal pleasures,
Which are restrained until they become sober
And run up to their place of rest.
And they will find me there,
And they will live and they will not die again.
[Selection from "*Diotima*" Anne McGuire, trans.]

Bibliography

Allen, Richard Hinckley. *Star Names: Their Lore and Meaning.* New York: Dover Publications Inc, 1963.

Angus, S. *The Mystery Religions: A Study in the Religious Background of Early Christianity.* New York: Dover Publications, 1975.

Assman, Jan. *The Search for God in Ancient Egypt.* Ithaca: Cornell University Press, 2001.

Athanassakis, Apostolos N (trans.). *The Homeric Hymns: Translation, Introduction, and Notes.* Baltimore: The John Hopkins University Press, 1976.

Atsma, Aaron. *Theoi Project: Guide to Greek Mythology.* ©2000-2006. [http://www.theoi.com/]

Baerg, Harry J. *Bible Plants and Animals: Volume 3 Plants.* Washington: Review and Herald Publishing Association, 1989.

Baigent, Michael. *From the Omens of Babylon: Astrology and Ancient Mesopotamia.* London: Arkana Penguin Books, 1994.

Babelon, Ernest. *Manual of Oriental Antiquities: Including the Architecture, Sculpture, and Industrial Arts of Chaldea, Assyria, Persia, Syria, Judaea, Phoenicia, and Carthage.* London: H Grevel and Co., 1889. [Translated and enlarged by B T A Evetts, MA]

Barry, Kieren. *The Greek Qabalah.* York Beach: Samuel Weiser, 1999.

Beard, Mary & North, John. *Pagan Priests.* London: Duckworth, 1990.

Beard, Mary, North, John and Price, Simon. *Religions of Rome: Volume 2 A Sourcebook.* Cambridge: Cambridge University Press, 1999.

Bell, H Idris. *Cults & Creeds in Graeco-Roman Egypt.* Chicago: Ares Publishers Inc, 1957.

Betz, Hans Dieter (ed.). *The Greek Magical Papyri in Translation.* Chicago: The University of Chicago Press, 1986.

Bittleston, Adam. *The Seven Planets.* Edinburgh: Floris Books, 1985.

Black, Jeremy and Green, Anthony. *Gods, Demons and Symbols of Ancient Mesopotamia: An Illustrated Dictionary.* London: British Museum Press, 1992.

Bokser, Ben Zion. *The Jewish Mystical Tradition.* New York: The Pilgrim Press, 1981.

Bottero, Jean. *Religion in Ancient Mesopotamia.* Chicago: The University of Chicago Press, 2001.

Boylan, Patrick. *Thoth: The Hermes of Egypt.* Chicago: Ares Publishers Inc, 1987.

Breasted, James Henry, PhD. *Development of Religion and Thought in Ancient Egypt.* New York: Charles Scribner's Sons, 1912.

Bremmer, Jan N. *The Early Greek Concept of the Soul.* Princeton: Princeton University Press, 1993.

Brier, Bob. *Ancient Egyptian Magic: Spells, Incantations, Potions, Stories, and Rituals.* New York: Quill, 1980.

Bromage, Bernard, MA. *The Occult Arts of Ancient Egypt.* London: The Aquarian Press, 1960.

Brown, Brian. *The Wisdom of the Egyptians.* New York: Brentano's, 1923.

Budge, E A Wallis. *The Gods of the Egyptians or Studies in Egyptian Mythology: Volume 1.* New York: Dover Publications Inc, 1969.

Budge, E A Wallis. *The Gods of the Egyptians or Studies in Egyptian Mythology: Volume 2.* New York: Dover Publications Inc, 1969.

Budge, E A Wallis. *Egyptian Magic.* New York: Dover Publications Inc, 1971.

Burkert, Walter. *Greek Religion.* Oxford: Blackwell Publishers Ltd, 2000.

Butler, E M. *Ritual Magic.* Cambridge: Cambridge University Press, 1949.

Cavendish, Richard. *A History of Magic.* London: Weidenfeld & Nicolson, 1977.

Cavendish, Richard. *The Black Arts.* New York: G P Putnam's Sons, 1967.

Churton, Tobias. *The Gnostics.* London: Weidenfeld & Nicolson, 1987.

Chuvin, Pierre. *A Chronicle of the Last Pagans.* Cambridge: Harvard University Press, 1990.

Collins, Andrew. *From the Ashes of Angels: The Forbidden Legacy of a Fallen Race.* London: Michael Joseph Ltd, 1996.

Conybeare, F C (trans). *Philostratus: The Life of Apollonius of Tyana.* London. Harvard University Press, 2000.

Cooper, D Jason. *Mithras: Mysteries and Initiation Rediscovered.* York Beach: Samuel Weiser, 1996.

Copenhaver, Brian P. *Hermetica: The Greek Corpus Hermeticum and the Latin Asclepius in a new English translation with notes and introduction.* Cambridge: Cambridge University Press, 2000.

Crow W B. *A Fascinating History of Witchcraft Magic & Occultism.* North Hollywood: Wilshire Book Company, 1968.

Crowley, Aleister. *Magick.* London: Routledge & Kegan Paul, 1973.

Crowley, Aleister. *Seven Seven Seven.* Hastings: Metaphysical Research Group, 1977.

Cryer, Frederick H & Thomsen, Marie-Louise. *Witchcraft and Magic in Europe: Biblical and Pagan Societies.* London: The Athlone Press, 2001.

Cumont, Franz. *The Mysteries of Mithra.* New York: Dover Publications Inc, 1956.

Daraul, Arkon. *Secret Societies: The Underground World of Initiation Rites and Rituals.* London: Tandem, 1965.

David, Rosalie. *Religion and Magic in Ancient Egypt.* London: Penguin Books Ltd, 2002.

De Laurence, L W (ed.). *The Lesser Key of Solomon Goetia: The Book of Evil Spirits.* Isle of Arran: The Banton Press, 1995.

De Laurence, L W (ed.). *The Sixth and Seventh Books of Moses.* Chicago: The De Laurence Company Inc.

De Lubicz, Isha Schwaller. *The Opening of the Way: A Practical Guide to the Wisdom of Ancient Egypt.* New York: Inner Traditions International, 1981.

Denning, Melita & Phillips, Osborne. *Planetary Magick - A Complete System for Knowledge and Attainment.* St Paul: Llewellyn Publications, 1989.

Dodds, E R. *The Greeks and the Irrational.* Berkeley: University of California Press, 1951.

Dreyer, Ronnie Gale. *Venus: The Evolution of the Goddess and Her Planet.* Hammersmith: Aquarian, 1994.

Eliade, Mircea. *Rites and Symbols of Initiation: The Mysteries of Birth and Rebirth.* New York: Harper Torchbooks, 1975.

Evelyn-White, Hugh G. *Hesiod, Homeric Hymns, Epic Cycle, Homerica.* Cambridge: Harvard University Press, 2000.

Evslin, Bernard. *Gods Demigods & Demons. An Encyclopedia of Greek Mythology.* New York: Scholastic Book Services, 1975.

Faraone, Christopher A. *Ancient Greek Love Magic.* Cambridge: Harvard University Press, 1999.

Faraone, Christopher A & Obbink, Dirk (ed.). *Magika Hiera: Ancient Greek Magic & Religion.* New York: Oxford University Press, 1997.

Flowers, Stephen Edred. *Hermetic Magic: The Postmodern Magical Papyrus of Abaris.* York Beach: Samuel Weiser, 1995.

Ford, Akkadia. *The Powers That Seek: Unlocking the Magick within Ancient Egyptian Creation Legends.* Chieveley: Capall Bann Publishing, 1998.

Fowden, Garth. *The Egyptian Hermes: A Historical Approach to the Late Pagan Mind.* Princeton: Princeton University Press, 1986.

Fox, Robin Lane. *Pagans and Christians: In the Mediterranean world from the second century AD to the conversion of Constantine.* London: Penguin Books, 1988.

Frankfort, Henri. *Kingship and the Gods: A Study of Ancient Near Eastern Religion as the Integration of Society and Nature.* Chicago: The University of Chicago Press, 1978.

Frankfurter, David. *Religion in Roman Egypt: Assimilation and Resistance.* Princeton: Princeton University Press, 1998.

Freke, Timothy & Gandy, Peter. *The Hermetica: The Lost Wisdom of the Pharoahs.* London: Judy Piatkus (Publishers) Ltd, 1997.

Gager, John G. *Curse Tablets and Binding Spells from the Ancient World.* New York: Oxford University Press, 1999.

Gaster, Moses, PhD. *The Sword of Moses: An Ancient Book of Magic.* New York: Samuel Weiser, 1970.

Godwin, David. *Light in Extension: Greek Magic from Homer to Modern Times.* St Paul: Llewellyn Publications, 1992.

Godwin, Joscelyn. *Mystery Religions in the Ancient World.* London: Thames and Hudson Ltd, 1981.

Godwin, Joscelyn. *The Mystery of the Seven Vowels: In Theory and Practice.* Grand Rapids: Phanes, 1991.

Graf, Fritz. *Magic in the Ancient World.* Cambridge: Harvard University Press, 1999.

Grant, Frederick C (ed.). *Hellenistic Religions.* Indianapolis: Bobbs-Merrill Company Inc, 1953.

Graves, Robert (trans.). *The Transformations of Lucius: Otherwise Known as The Golden Ass by Lucius Apuleius.* Harmondsworth: Penguin Books Ltd, 1972.

Grene, David. *Herodotus: The History.* Chicago: The University of Chicago Press, 1988.

Griffith, F Ll & Thompson, Herbert (ed.). *The Leyden Papyrus: An Egyptian Magical Book.* New York: Dover Publications Ltd, 1974.

Grigson, Geoffrey. *The Goddess of Love: The Birth, Triumph, Death and Return of Aphrodite.* London: Quartet Books Limited, 1978.

Guirand, Felix. *New Larouse Encyclopedia of Mythology.* Twickenham: Hamlyn Publishing, 1986.

Guthrie, Kenneth Sylvan (trans.). *The Pythagorean Sourcebook and Library.* Grand Rapids: Phanes Press, 1988.

Guthrie, W K C. *Orpheus and Greek Religion.* Princeton: Princeton University Press, 1993.

Hall, Manly P. *The Adepts in the Esoteric Classical Tradition.* Los Angeles: The Philosophical Research Society Inc, 1981.

Harris, Eleanor L. *Ancient Egyptian Divination and Magic.* York Beach, Samuel Weiser Inc, 1998.

Hart, George. *A Dictionary of Egyptian Gods and Goddesses.* London: Routledge & Kegan Paul Inc, 2000.

Harvey, Paul. *The Oxford Companion to Classical Literature.* Oxford: Oxford University Press, 1986.

Henson, Mitch (ed.). *Lemegeton: The Complete Lesser Key of Solomon.* Jacksonville: Metatron Books, 1999.

Hoeller, Stephan A. *Gnosticism: New Light on the Ancient Tradition of Inner Knowing.* Wheaton: Quest Books, 2002.

Hornung, Erik. *The Secret Lore of Egypt: It's Impact on the West.* Ithaca: Cornell University Press, 2001.

Hrozny, Bedrich, PhD. *Ancient History of Western Asia, India and Crete.* Prague: Artia, 1953.

Hyde, Walter Woodburn. *Greek Religion and its Survivals.* London: George G Harrap & Co Ltd.

Jacobsen, Thorkild. *The Treasures of Darkness: A History of Mesopotamian Religion.* London: Yale University Press, 1976.
Jacq, Christian. *Magic and Mystery in Ancient Egypt.* London: Souvenir Press, 1998.
Janowitz, Naomi. *Magic in the Roman World: Pagans, Jews and Christians.* London: Routledge, 2001.
Jayne, Walter Addison, M D. *The Healing Gods of Ancient Civilisations.* New Hyde Park: University Books Inc, 1962.
Johnson, Thomas M (trans.). *Iamblichus: The Exhortation to Philosophy.* Grand Rapids: Phanes Press, 1988.
Jonas, Hans. *The Gnostic Religion: The Message of the Alien God and the Beginnings of Christianity.* Boston: Beacon Press, 1963.
Kerenyi, C. *The Gods of the Greeks.* London: Thames and Hudson, 1979.
Kerenyi, Karl. *Hermes: Guide of Souls.* Putnam: Spring Publications, 1976.
King, Francis & Skinner, Stephen. *Techniques of High Magic: A Guide to Self-Empowerment.* Rochester: Destiny Books, 1991.
King, Karen L. *What is Gnosticism?* Cambridge: The Belknap Press of Harvard University Press, 2003.
Kirk, G S. *The Nature of Greek Myths.* Harmondsworth: Penguin Books Ltd, 1985.
Klimkeit, Hans-Joachim. *Gnosis on the Silk Road: Gnostic Parables, Hymns & Prayers from Central Asia.* San Francisco: Harper, 1993.
Kraig, Donald Michael. *Modern Magick: Eleven Lessons in the High Magickal Arts.* St Paul: Llewellyn Publications, 1988.
Kramer, Samuel Noah. *Sumerian Mythology: A Study of Spiritual and Literary Achievement in the Third Millennium BC.* Philadelphia: University of Pennsylvania Press, 1972.
Kramer, Samuel Noah. *The Sumerians: Their History, Culture, and Character.* Chicago: The University of Chicago Press, 1963.
Lamy, Lucie. *Egyptian Mysteries: New Light on Ancient Knowledge.* London: Thames and Hudson, 1986.
Lang, Andrew. *Myth, Ritual & Religion: Volume One.* London: Senate, 1995.
Lang, Andrew. *Myth, Ritual & Religion: Volume Two.* London: Senate, 1996.

Layton, Bentley. *The Gnostic Scriptures: Ancient Wisdom for the New Age.* New York: Doubleday, 1995.

Leadbeater, C W. *Ancient Mystic Rites.* Wheaton: A Quest Book, 1988.

Leick, Gwendolyn. *A Dictionary of Ancient Near Eastern Mythology.* London: Routledge, 1998.

Livingston, G Herbert. *The Pentateuch in its Cultural Environment.* Grand Rapids: Baker Book House, 1980.

Luck, Georg. *Ancient Pathways & Hidden Pursuits: Religion, Morals, and Magic in the Ancient World.* University of Michigan, 2000.

Luck, Georg. *Arcana Mundi: Magic and the Occult in the Greek and Roman Worlds.* Wellingborough: Crucible, 1987.

Lurker, Manfred. *The Gods and Symbols of Ancient Egypt.* London: Thames and Hudson Ltd, 1988.

McCarren, Vincent P (ed.). *Michigan Papyri.* Atlanta: Scholars Pr, 1981.

McGuire, Anne. *The Thunder, Perfect Mind.* Diotima: Materials for the Study of Women and Gender in the Ancient World, Translation ©2000. [http://www.stoa.org/diotima/anthology/thunder.shtml]

MacGregor-Mathers, S L. *The Book of the Sacred Magic of Abramelin, the Mage: As Delivered by Abraham the Jew Unto His Son Lamech.* Chicago: The De Laurence Company Inc, 1948.

MacGregor-Mathers, S Liddell. *The Key of Solomon the King (Clavicula Salomonis).* London: Routledge & Kegan Paul, 1972.

McIntosh, Christopher. *Astrology: The Stars and Human Life.* London: Macdonald Unit 75, 1970.

McIntosh, Christopher. *The Astrologers and their Creed.* London: Arrow Books Ltd, 1971.

Manniche, Lise. *An Ancient Egyptian Herbal.* London: British Museum Publications Limited, 1989.

March, Jenny. *Dictionary of Classical Mythology.* London: Cassell, 2000.

Mastronarde, Donald J. *Ancient Greek Tutorials: Pronunciation Guide* ©1999-2005. [http://socrates.berkeley.edu/~ancgreek/pronunchtml/omegaU.html]

Mead, G R S. *Fragments of a Faith Forgotten.* London: Theosophical Publishing Society, 1906.

Mead, G R S. *The Doctrine of the Subtle Body in the Western Tradition.* Dorset: Solos Press.

Mead, G R S. *Thrice Greatest Hermes: Studies in Hellenic Theosophy and Gnosis.* Montana: Kessinger Publishing Company.

Merkur, Dan. *Gnosis: An Esoteric Tradition of Mystical Visions and Unions.* Albany: State University of New York Press, 1993.

Meyer, Marvin W. *The Ancient Mysteries: A Sourcebook.* San Francisco: Harper & Row, 1987.

Meyer, Marvin & Smith, Richard. *Ancient Christian Magic: Coptic Texts of Ritual Power.* San Francisco: Harper, 1994.

Miller, Richard Alan and Miller, Iona. *The Magical and Ritual Use of Perfumes.* Rochester: Destiny Books, 1990.

Morenz, Siegfried. *Egyptian Religion.* Ithaca: Cornell University Press, 1973.

Naydler, Jeremy. *Temple of the Cosmos: The Ancient Egyptian Experience of the Sacred.* Rochester: Inner Traditions, 1996.

Nema. *Maat Magick: A Guide to Self-Initiation.* York Beach, Samuel Weiser Inc, 1995.

Nilsson, Martin P. *Greek Folk Religion.* New York: Harper Torchbooks, 1961.

Peters, F E. *The Harvest of Hellenism: A History of the Near East from Alexander the Great to the Triumph of Christianity.* London: George Allen & Unwin Ltd, 1972.

Peterson, Joseph H (ed.). *The Lesser Key of Solomon, Lemegeton Clavicula Salomonis: Detailing the Ceremonial Art of Commanding Spirits Both Good and Evil.* York Beach, Samuel Weiser Inc, 2001.

Petrie, W M Flinders. *Personal Religion in Egypt before Christianity.* London: Harper & Brothers, 1909.

Petrie, W M Flinders. *Religious Life in Ancient Egypt.* London: Constable & Company Ltd, 1932.

Petrie, W M Flinders. *The Religion of Ancient Egypt.* London: Archibald Constable & Co Ltd, 1908.

Pinch, Geraldine. *Magic in Ancient Egypt.* London: British Museum Press, 1994.

Rabinowitz, Jacob. *The Rotting Goddess: The Origin of the Witch in Classical Antiquity.* Brooklyn: Autonomedia, 1998.

Regardie, Israel. *Ceremonial Magic.* Wellingborough: The Aquarian Press, 1985.

Regardie, Israel. *The Golden Dawn.* St Paul: Llewellyn Publications, 1982.

Regardie, Israel. *The Tree of Life: A Study in Magic.* New York: Samuel Weiser, 1980.

Rice, David G and Stambaugh, John E. *Sources for the Study of Greek Religion.* Atlanta: The Society of Biblical Literature, 1979.

Ringgren, Helmer. *Religions of the Ancient Near East.* London: SPCK, 1973.

Robbins, F E (trans). *Ptolemy Tetrabiblos.* Cambridge: Harvard University Press, 1980.

Robinson, James M (ed.). *The Nag Hammadi Library, revised edition.* San Francisco: HarperCollins, 1990.

Rogers, Robert William. *The Religion of Babylonia and Assyria: Especially in its Relations to Israel.* New York: Eaton & Mains, 1908.

Romano, James F. *Death, Burial, and Afterlife in Ancient Egypt.* Pittsburgh: The Carnegie Museum of Natural History, 1990.

Rony, Jerome-Antoine. *A History of Magic.* New York: Walker and Company, 1962.

Roux, Georges. *Ancient Iraq.* Harmondsworth: Penguin Books, 1980.

Rudolph, Kurt. *Gnosis: The Nature & History of Gnosticism.* New York: HarperCollins Publishers, 1987.

Salmond, Rev S D F (trans.). *St. Augustine The Harmony Of The Gospels, Book I,* taken from *The Early Church Fathers and Other Works.* Edinburgh: Wm. B. Eerdmans Pub. Co., 1867. [The digital version is by The Electronic Bible Society, http://www.ewtn.com/library/PATRISTC/PNI6-2.TXT]

Sauneron, Serge. *The Priests of Ancient Egypt.* New York: Grove Press Inc, 1960.

Scherman, Rabbi Nosson (ed.). *The Stone Edition Tanach: The Torah / Prophets / Writings, The Twenty-Four Books of the Bible Newly Translated and Annotated.* Brooklyn: Mesorah Publications Ltd, 1996.

Scholem, Gershom G. *Jewish Gnosticism, Merkabah Mysticism, and Talmudic Tradition.* New York: The Jewish Theological Seminary of America, 1965.

Schure, Edouard. *Pythagoras and the Delphic Mysteries.* London: William Rider & Son, Limited, 1923.

Seyffert, Oskar. *Dictionary of Classical Antiquities.* New York: Meridian Books Inc, 1960.

Smith, F Kinchin & Melluish, T W. *Ancient Greek: A foundation course.* London: Hodder & Stoughton Educational, 1992.

Smith, Morton. *Jesus the Magician: Charlatan or Son of God?* Berkeley: Seastone, 1998.

Spence, Lewis. *The Mysteries of Egypt: Secret Rites and Traditions of the Nile.* Blauvelt: Rudolf Steiner Publications, 1972/

Stanley, Thomas (trans). *The Chaldean Oracles: As set down by Julianus.* New Jersey: Heptangle Books, 1989.

Stapleton, Michael. *A Dictionary of Greek and Roman Mythology.* New York: Bell Publishing Company, 1978.

Talbott, David N. *The Saturn Myth.* Garden City: Doubleday & Company Inc, 1980.

Taylor, Thomas. *Iamblichus On The Mysteries.* San Diego: Wizards Bookshelf, 1984.

Taylor, Thomas. *The Commentaries of Proclus on the Timaeus of Plato.* Hastings: Chthonios Books, 1988.

Taylor, Thomas. *The Hymns of Orpheus.* Los Angeles: The Philosophical Research Society Inc, 1981.

Temple, Richard. *Icons and the Mystical Origins of Christianity.* Dorset: Element Books Limited, 1990.

Thatcher, Oliver J (ed.). *The Library of Original Sources* Milwaukee: University Research Extension Co., 1907. [Scanned and modernized by Prof. J S Arkenberg for the Internet Ancient History Sourcebook, http://www.fordham.edu/halsall/ancient/cicero-republic6.html]

Thompson, R Campbell. *Semitic Magic: Its Origins and Development.* York Beach: Samuel Weiser, 2000.

Turner, Robert. *Ars Notoria: The Magical Art of Solomon, Showing the Cabalistical Key of Magical Operations.* Edmonds: Holmes Publishing Group, 1998.

Vernant, Jean-Pierre. *The Universe, The Gods, and Men: Ancient Greek Myths.* New York: Perennial, 2002.

Watterson, Barbara. *The Gods of Ancient Egypt.* London: B T Batsford Ltd, 1984.

Wright, Dudley. *The Eleusinian Mysteries & Rites.* Berwick: Ibis Press, 2003.

Wright, M R. *Cosmology in Antiquity.* New York: Routledge, 1996.

Index

A

B

C

D

E

F

G

H

I

J

K

L

M

N

O

P

Q

R

S

T

V

W

Y

Z

About the Author and the Prefacer

Tony Mierzwicki runs workshops and rituals in Australia and the United States which recreate ancient magickal practices, and include "The Magick of Alexandria" series. He is the author of "*Alien Magick: Exploring the UFO Phenomenon*" as well as numerous magazine articles and anthology contributions. Tony has completed three degrees at the University of Sydney – Master of Arts, Bachelor of Engineering and Bachelor of Science.

Donald Michael Kraig graduated from UCLA with a degree in philosophy. He has also studied public speaking and music (traditional and experimental) on the university level. After a decade of personal study and practice, he began ten years of teaching courses in the Southern California area on such topics as Kabalah, Tarot, Magic, Tantra, and Psychic Development. He has been a member of many spiritual and magical groups and is an initiated Tantric. Since that time he has been the editor of *New Times* and *FATE* magazine, and is now editor of *New Worlds*. His book, "*Modern Magick*," is the most popular, step-by-step introduction to real magick ever published. Other books by him include "*Tarot and Magic*," "*Modern Sex Magick*," and "*The Truth About Evocation of Spirits*." Don is currently studying for a doctorate in clinical hypnotherapy.

Notes

Tony Mierzwicki